Gum For Gracie

Laurel,
Gum fur Gracie is a
victory story for the survivor
in all of us.

Ona Marae 8/8/18

by:

Ona Marae

Flashpoint Publications

2018

Cover Design AcornGraphics

Edited by Nat Burns and Nann Dunne

ISBN: 978-1-949096-00-2

First Printing 2018

Published in the United States of America

Publisher's Note:

Additional Publishers Notes

This book contains scenes that some readers may find disturbing. Scenes will relate to the occurrence, affect and aftermath of a child raped by her father. Please take note of this before continuing to read this book.

Published by

Early Praise for *Gum For Gracie*

Caught in a crucible of guilt and recrimination, three women unite in mutual determination to heal gravely damaged ten-year-old Gracie in this unforgettable, deeply affecting, tangibly real story of love, courage, family, and redemption.

Katherine V. Forrest
Author of *Curious Wine* and the Kate Delafield mystery series

Acknowledgments

This novel took almost twelve years from start to publication. In that time, an army of Amazons helped me with the reading, critiquing, pushing onward, and staying focused. I had brain surgery recently and cannot remember all your names right now, but you are marked forever in my heart.

Renee Hoffman, Deej Garden, Laydin Michaels, Catherine Friend, Anna Furtado, Katherine V. Forrest, Michael, Tracy, Adrienne, Phil, Debbie, Alicia, Ingrid, Christine, and the many others, especially those whose names I have forgotten momentarily, who beta-read or workshopped this novel over the years.

Flashpoint Publications, Patty Schramm, Natty Burns, Nann Dunne, Ann McMann, and everyone who helped me get my feet off the ground.

Karen, my heartbeat.

Renee, Tory, and Dustin and all my besties, who kept me grounded through all the versions.

My class at the GCLS Writing Academy (2016) Tammy, Nancy, Cindy, Joy, TJ, Margot, and all the administrators and instructors.

All the teachers and mentors who believed in me and my ability to write.

Katherine V. Forrest, Lee Lynch, Dorothy Alison, Sandra Moran, and all the women upon whose shoulders I stand.

All the women in my WINGS group, the WINGS Art groups, the #MeToo folks and all the other survivors out there. You gave me hope to keep telling my story. You gave me courage to keep writing as I cried on the keyboard. You carry me forward. We know that healing is possible in life, despite our lack of control over certain things. If we hold on to friends and chosen family, we can survive anything.

Dedication

To every reader who ever picks up this book and breathes, "She gets me." I wrote this for you.

and

So that all of us might find a little grace inside and in the way in which we move through the world.

Chapter One

Wednesday, July 3rd, 1974

Something woke Bobbie that Wednesday morning. The sharp jangling shook her out of her dreams and disturbed the comfort of her soft bed. Was it the phone? She turned on her bedside lamp to check the clock. Its low light illuminated the clock radio. One in the morning. Dear God, was everything okay? She sat up, heart pounding, and grabbed the phone. "Hello?"

"I have a collect call for Bobbie Rossi. Will you accept the call?" a voice thick with amusement asked.

"Yes, operator."

"Bobbie?" A slurred female voice sounded over a shaky connection.

"Beth, is that you?" Bobbie gripped her pillow.

"Yeah."

Visions of a car accident, a house fire, a sudden fever in a child flooded Bobbie's imagination.

"Are you okay? Is everyone all right?" She tried to shake the confusion from her sleepy head.

"We're fine." Beth made a funny noise. "Oops, sorry."

"Are you drinking?" From three-hundred miles away, Bobbie sniffed in disbelief. In their twenty-eight years, she had never seen her twin sister drunk.

Beth giggled. "I drank two of Dan's beers. Well, two and a half. Won't he be pissed?"

Bobbie's first response was to smile at the infectious giggle. Her second response was much louder. "Oh, my God, what are you doing?"

"I couldn't sleep. It's probably ninety degrees in here, and I had to turn on a fan. I'm sweating, and my mind is spinning. And I don't have anybody to talk to...is it okay? You sound tired."

Bobbie grimaced and moved into a more comfortable position. "Yes, I'm tired because it's after one, but of course, it's okay to call. It's just a surprise. What's on your mind?"

"I don't know if I should tell you." A chair or something scraped in the background.

Bobbie sighed. "If you aren't going to tell me, why did you call?"

"I need to talk to somebody. But..."

Bobbie counted to ten. Quickly. Softening her tone, she asked, "If you needed to talk to me, why did you wait so late? I'm not criticizing you, just wondering. You know you can call me collect anytime."

"Oh no," Beth said. "Not when my girls are around. Cara still blabs everything to everyone, including her father. All I need is for him to find out I've been talking to you. Dan would kill me. God, he hates you. I don't know how he can hate you so much and—"

"Yes, newsflash, Dan hates me. You said you need to talk to somebody. So, talk." Bobbie didn't count this time.

"Now I need to pee."

Bobbie tipped her head back, her frustration draining away into amusement. Her fraternal twin sister might be a few minutes older than she was, but somehow, she had always seemed much younger. Bobbie couldn't stay mad at her. Beth was managing the best she could in a nightmare of a marriage. Silly goose. "Okay, you go pee, I'll get a glass of milk, and we'll meet in the middle when you're done. Can you walk okay? Those two beers seem to have hit the spot."

"I'm an adult. I can handle two beers." Beth hiccupped and dropped the phone on what sounded like the table. Bobbie could hear the long, curly cord drag it toward the wall. She rolled her eyes, laid her phone down gently, and went for a glass of milk.

Returning, she found Beth hadn't come back. She settled herself in as good a position as the cord would allow and played with the coil as she waited. Dan. What a loser. She hated that her sister was chained to the biggest jerk in Cottonwood Plains. Maybe in all of western Kansas. She hated the jerk. The jerk hated her. It was a mutual anti-admiration society of the fiercest nature. He had been calling her a dyke since she was sixteen-years old and had refused to let him cop a feel. Asshole.

Wait. She shook her head. This wasn't helpful. It would only piss her off and make it harder to listen to Beth. Apparently, Beth didn't really know why Dan hated Bobbie so much. Didn't drunks speak the truth? Beth had always said that, but Bobbie couldn't imagine that much innocence. No wonder she seemed so childlike and—

"Are you back? Hello?" Beth spoke so loudly, it hurt Bobbie's ear.

"I'm back."

"I don't want you to lecture me or yell at me. I just need to talk. Don't be mad at me, okay?" Beth's slurry voice got smaller as it trailed off.

Bobbie's heart melted again. "It's okay. Just tell me what's in your head."

Beth started, a few words at a time. "I was lying there, waiting for Dan to come home. My body gets all tight, and it takes forever before I can sleep. I guess I do understand how Gracie can lie under her tree and think for an hour. I do the same thing."

"What were you thinking about?" Bobbie crossed her fingers and hoped it would be about leaving Dan.

"Oh, the same thing I always think about. Dan. Our situation. I hate it. I hate him. I hate myself. I hate everything but my girls. I'll never hate or regret them."

Bobbie swallowed twice at Beth's candor and murmured soft encouragement.

"What would he do if I did take the girls and left like you want me to? Would he let me? Would he be happy? Be insulted? Make my life hell? He can be so cruel."

"Why don't I come for a visit? He's bound to have another twenty-four-hour shift at the fire station that I have free soon, and I'll just drive down. With this new fifty-five-miles-per-hour limit, it's about six hours. If I leave here early Friday, I can be there after he goes to his shift, spend the day, and leave the next morning before he gets home. It's all copacetic."

Bobbie could hear Beth sucking in air. "No, no, please, no. It's not copa-whatever. It's horrible when you leave. Even though Gracie rides a tight herd on them, Cara blabs all about the little goodies you bring them, and LeeAnn brags about your life within hearing distance of Dan. The girls fight so much that their father intervenes, and it's never pretty. Do you know what he did? I wasn't going to tell you and don't flip out, but he said if you come down again, he's going to take the girls and leave me."

"What?" Bobbie sat up hard and fast.

"When he said he would kick me out, I said that maybe it was a good idea. I would take the girls and move out. Oh, God, he got so mad. He said some really bad things. I freaked, so I tried to convince him it was a good thing. He would have his whole paycheck to himself, no paying for us, and he would have quiet for his TV and the baseball games. Please, you have to listen. He said he would take the girls and leave. He can do that. He can be a fireman anywhere. I'm a dime store clerk. I don't have credit. I don't have a bank account or my own car. He's got everything. He even told me—"

"I'll kill him," Bobbie growled.

"No, he said he would dump the girls in some orphanage, and I'll never see my babies again. Dammit." Beth stopped abruptly. When she started again, she whispered. "He won't do it if we just play along. He'll forget in time. Trust me. Things will go back to normal. He'll just complain about you and come to bed drunk when he's mad. At least he doesn't want to have sex anymore." She gave a giggle that sounded forced to Bobbie.

"What?" Bobbie asked.

Beth whispered, her lips loosened in a beer-can sounding hiss. "I like sex, don't get me wrong, but he gets rough or wants me to do things that I don't want to do. It's just better to go without."

Bobbie's eyes widened at this revelation, but Beth kept going. "Maybe he's getting it somewhere else. Maybe it's that girl Rita next door and her mother, the waitress down at the tavern. I know he looks. I don't care. If he doesn't give me a disease, I don't even care."

Beth paused a long moment. "I guess that's a surprise. I don't care... That can't be a good sign when a wife doesn't care if her husband sleeps around. I'm tired of being a wife. I'm tired of being his wife."

Bobbie collected herself before speaking up in a soft, sympathetic voice. "What else, sis, what else do you think about?"

"Well, if I left him, how would I support the girls? I mean, I've been a clerk at Woolworth's for four years. Yeah, right, that looks good on a job application. At least, I'm a loyal employee. I guess that part might look good. I don't know much about living in Lawrence, except that maybe it could be pretty cheap if you and I rented a house together. The girls are getting old enough that child care isn't such a big deal."

"Yes," Bobbie said. "You're right."

"I have a headache."

Bobbie didn't want to interrupt but didn't want a headache to end the conversation either. "Do you need to get an aspirin?"

"I don't think so. I only get headaches when I think. Maybe solving the problem would help. Fat chance of that happening. I've had this discussion with myself every night since May. I'm just going in circles..." The monologue trailed off into nothing.

Bobbie listened for a moment then pushed a little bit harder. "What about it, Beth, can you make a decision soon?"

"Before the school year starts would be best," Beth said, agreeing with her sister's unspoken argument. "I could pull them out of school, but that would be harder. Rent is paid for July. Can I make a decision in less than a month...or?" She paused. "On second thought, Dan pays the rent, so that's not money out of my pocket. Let him pay the rent and then move out on him." She laughed. "Oops. Shhh."

"You could move before school starts," Bobbie said. "I have plenty of time off in the summer to help you move and get settled in."

"Yeah, I know. It sounds better and better. I want my girls to have everything they need, and they aren't getting it here. I can stay and hope they get out like you did, Bobbie, or maybe I can even get out myself. That's something else you're right about. My life isn't over yet. I feel old but..."

Bobbie waited through another long pause. She was about to say something when Beth went on.

"You probably think I've made up my mind. Some nights I think I've made up my mind, too. But what holds me back? Fear. That's what it is. Fear of everything. Fear of not making it on my own. Fear of not being married. Fear of being alone forever. Fear of Dan. I'm even afraid of being afraid. Isn't that stupid?" Her final words of self-insult grated on Bobbie's ears.

Bobbie had noticed Beth's voice growing slower and slower for the past few minutes. If she didn't get her to bed, Beth was going to be sleeping this off in a kitchen chair. "Beth? Beth! Are you still awake?"

"Yes."

"You sound like you're relaxing a little. Do you want to go to bed now and talk later?"

"Okay, I'll go sleep. And Bobbie? I love you, I really do. You are the best sister in the world."

The best sister in the world laughed. "I doubt you'll agree with that when you're sober. But that's good to hear for now. You go to bed, and we'll talk soon, okay?"

"Good night. Thanks for listening." Beth's voice came over the phone line sweetly, once again the innocent farm girl of fifteen that Bobbie remembered, the memory she treasured of that year before Dan, the manipulating asshole, came into their lives. How one boy could make one girl hate him and one girl love him completely even after he proved again and again he was—

Bobbie cut off that line of thought.

She signed off and hung up the phone. Ten beats, several cleansing breaths, and a "Bobbie special" eye roll later, she pulled herself together. Anger would just get her into trouble. She put her junior-college-professor hat back on. Scooting to the edge of her bed, she smoothed the cotton bottom sheet and rearranged her pillow. She couldn't fix anything tonight, but she would fix it soon. She just had to figure out how. In the morning.

She checked the clock radio, and her brain registered two-fifteen. The neighbors in the apartment above started making a racket. It was as likely to be sex as an argument or possibly an argument and then makeup sex. All of it was disturbing. She turned on the radio, low, just to muffle the sound and shifted farther into the bed. There was no movement beside her. Good. Some people really could sleep through Armageddon and never even wake up. It always amazed her.

Leaning over, she kissed the freckles on the creamy shoulder beside her before sliding the sheet up and slipping into wakefulness disguised as an attempt at sleep. She snuggled up close and whispered along with the haunting song, "Billy, Don't Be A Hero," that was playing on the radio. But she stopped short of singing the admonition to not be a fool with his life.

She closed her eyes and wondered to whom the song was speaking.

Chapter Two

"And now Ray Stevens brings you 'The Streak.'"

Bobbie heard the familiar song as she felt Kathleen push the little transistor radio closer to her head. They were lying together in the shade along the bank of a creek.

"What are you doing?" Bobbie asked, jolted back to reality. The sun glancing through the shifting cottonwood leaves above her head made patterns of light like stained-glass windows in a cathedral. The smell of grass, mud, and baked earth swirled around her, and she had drifted off into memories from years before, lying on this exact spot after harvest had come and gone. The years—

"Bobbie? Earth to Bobbie. I was letting you have equal time with the streaking man and his dangling participles." Kathleen chuckled and moved a small stick out from under her back.

"I don't want that thing too close to my head because you never know what you'll hear." Bobbie paused as Ray Stevens finished singing and the disc jockey announced the next song.

"That was 'The Streak' and 'Jolene' is up next," the country station announcer said.

"No." Bobbie grabbed the radio. "I'm tired of her. Every time we've turned on the radio out here, it's been Dolly Parton."

"And you don't like her?" Kathleen stretched her lanky body out even longer so that more of her lower legs was in the water.

"I like her just fine when she's on occasionally, but every other song? She's in my face on every single country station."

"I'll get in your face." And suddenly Bobbie's view of the treetops was blocked by Kathleen's face, framed by reddish curls, above hers. Kathleen grinned down at her. "Are you cooled off from all that furniture loading? I thought we'd be carrying it down narrow stairs in some old farm house and was so glad to see it was in a barn. Then I realized how dusty a barn, and things stored in it, can be. But your nice cool stream took care of the overheating and could take care of the rest of the dust if you would like to join me in there."

Bobbie laughed. "It's so shallow you would stick out of the water from your calves up in most places, and your freckles would get sunburnt. Besides, what are you going to wear if you get your clothes wet and muddy? We only brought one change with us."

"I wasn't going to wear them in." Kathleen untucked her T-shirt.

"In that case, all of you will get sunburnt. I'm not going streaking, even though this is my land, and no one should be walking around on it. I'm not that trusting."

"Then perhaps you've gotten too cooled down, and I should heat you up again." Kathleen wiggled an eyebrow and smirked.

"I'm sorry, babe, but I can't right now. My mind's a million miles away. Or more like ten miles away."

"Okay. So, tell me what I can do to make you feel better." Kathleen rolled onto her side and lay with her head propped on one arm. With her free hand, she stroked Bobbie's hair, removing dried strands from her face and smoothing them back. She pulled sections of it out from under Bobbie's head and ran them through gentle fingers. Gentle fingers that suddenly tugged. "Hello. There you are. You disappeared. So, what are you thinking about? Bobbie, the wonder sister?"

Bobbie rolled her head and kissed Kathleen's fingers. "Just how close we are to Cottonwood Plains and my family but how far apart we are at the same time. I want to visit so badly, I can taste it."

"That's either dust or a mosquito caught in your mouth. You said your sister didn't want you to visit because Dan banned you from the house, right?"

"Right."

"And has that changed?"

"No." Bobbie's head rolled away from Kathleen's face. Those bright eyes were just too close for comfort. They saw too much and loved too deeply.

"Then how could you go? Not to mention that we have a truck loaded with a houseful of furniture, and we might be a tad conspicuous driving into a small town."

Bobbie willed herself not to clench her teeth when her lover spoke the truth. "Yes, but I live six hours away and—"

"And there must be a good reason Beth told you that. She wouldn't make things up."

Damn. Kathleen made too much sense. Bobbie had always wanted a partner who was smart, thoughtful, and gentle, but she wasn't always happy that she got what she wanted.

She sat up and kicked her feet a little. The water splashed up, and one drop made it as far as her face, narrowly missing her eye. She grumbled as she wiped it away.

"Then don't kick your feet like a petulant child. Talk to me, girlie. You know I'm listening, and if you want me to stop commenting, I'll even do that," Kathleen said.

"Could you be wrong more often, Kat? It's tiring to love an angel."

Kathleen roared with laughter, even falling over onto her back.

Bobbie thought about pouncing on her, but her heart still wasn't in it. When Kathleen finished laughing, she sat up and leaned toward Bobbie.

"You are priceless. Now stop fooling around and tell me more, so we can work this through and get you into a mood to take advantage of me in the wild. I've never been taken by a pioneer woman before, and I'm ready for it."

"Oh sure. After you try one of those old mattresses out, you'll decide to put your sleeping bag on the ground, and that isn't very comfortable."

"There was hay in the barn. It looked soft and inviting. Like a roll in the hay?"

Bobbie stared at the far bank of the creek "The hay in there will be moldy and musty. The straw might still be clean, but it'll be prickly and not soft at all. Take your pick. I'm sleeping on the ground outdoors where there might be a breeze. As for the rest, I'm thinking about dropping by to see Beth and the girls tomorrow morning. Just for a little bit. Just some hugs. That's all."

"You're serious? She said no visits. We planned this visit because Dan's working today and can't possibly catch us here. But that means he's off tomorrow, and we don't know if Beth will even be home then."

"He'll go to the lake fishing. He goes every weekend he's off, and he'll be gone all day. I'm not going to stay long." Bobbie didn't meet Kathleen's eyes. She picked at a long blade of grass and examined it minutely.

"Okay, so he gets off at the fire station at what, seven? And he goes home and runs off to the lake. What if he doesn't? What if he pulled a muscle at a fire and had to take it easy? Or gets nausea from bad cooking?" Kathleen's voice remained even and reasonable, which grated on Bobbie's nerves worse than a raised voice would have.

Bobbie drew herself up to her full sitting height, inches shorter than Kathleen but towering over her in attitude. "You apparently know nothing about firefighters. On a full shift, only the best cooks make the meals. And they aren't going to screw it up by making anyone sick."

She stood up and stalked off, mind swirling like the fallen debris in the muddy eddies of the creek. She batted at prickly bushes as she walked by and found release in the discomfort of small scratches. Yes, Beth said not to visit. Yes, it was on Dan's orders, but that was the crux of the issue. It was on Dan's orders. Not a mutual decision. Not even a compromise from an authoritarian, sexist a—

Deep breath. Another slow, deep breath. A third slow, deep, hissing breath. She'd be damned if Dan made the decisions for her.

Beth might let him, but not her. It wouldn't be for long, and nothing would happen. If she didn't go, Bobbie would hate herself for being ten minutes away from her only family and not stopping in for a hug.

Chapter Three

Gracie was reading a library book and minding her own business while she sat on the ground and enjoyed the sun. Then, someone big hit her from behind, knocked her over, and landed on top of her. Someone else jumped on top, screeching in laughter. It was a bad way to start a morning.

She yelled, "Doggone it, I told you if you trespassed on my half again I was going to tie you to the swing set. Get off me or I'm going to call Mom."

The two younger girls peeled themselves off her, giggling.

"You know where the line is. Do I have to draw it with a can of paint?" Gracie stood and dusted off her backside then checked her legs and arms for scratches and scrapes. Her mom said her little sisters were indestructible, but she wasn't. Not anymore. Maybe when you turned ten, you got grown-up skin? That could explain how a six-year-old and an eight-year-old could throw themselves on the ground and bounce back up without even feeling it.

Cara put her hands on her hips and jutted the right one out, just like Rita from next door did. "But you don't have a can of paint, ha-ha-ha!" She turned to flounce off, and Gracie grabbed her shirt by the tail.

"We can't see the line when we're spinning," LeeAnn explained.

"You're going to break your necks spinning, and then I get your Barbies," Gracie said. "And if you do it again, I'm going to break all your Barbies' legs, then I'm going to tell Dad."

The girls planted their feet. They squinted their eyes. They stuck out their tongues. But they stopped spinning, laughing, and bothering Gracie, much to her relief. They marched back to the big tree and sat, whispering, behind it. Gracie threw up her hands, so they would see she didn't care, and headed for the swing set.

When the younger girls were chasing one another around the big tree or any other silliness, Gracie would usually choose the swing instead of sitting on the ground. It was safer, and she could still look at the clouds. She searched to see if she could find a castle cloud. That was silly, too, but ever since she was six and first saw the castle cloud, looking for it had made her feel better. Searching right now, she jiggled her shoulders like the boxers did on TV. Some of the stiffness went away. She scanned the entire expanse of Kansas sky, finding a tree, an ice cream cone, and even a rabbit. Her stomach stopped jumping up and down, squishing out mean juice with every bounce.

It had been mean. Gracie knew it, but mentioning Dad was the only guaranteed way to get them to stop being mouthy and horrible to her. It was good for them. All it took was one mouthy thing around Dad, and the whole evening would be burnt up, including everybody's butts. LeeAnn was getting better about it and rarely did it on her own anymore. But when she was showing off for Cara, it was bad news. Both of them would have what amounted to a mouthy contest, and that made Dad worse than the wicked witch in Dorothy's tornado.

Gracie's stomach took one more good jump, and the mean juice went up into her throat, burning all the way. She was in charge. It was their fault if they were mouthy, but it was her fault, too, and she always got punished for it. Even if Dad didn't beat her butt right away, he would. Her throat burned that way every time the Royals lost. And every time Dad ran out of beer before the end of the week. And lots of other times. Doggone it. They knew it. He never changed. Gracie knew what Dad would do before he did it. It wasn't that hard anymore. The burning got worse, and a mosquito bit her left knee. She smashed him and scratched her knee so hard she left red lines. She looked up at the sky again. Oh my gosh, there was a convertible, a white convertible in the blue sky. Gracie laughed with delight. White convertible, blue sky...

Suddenly, Gracie Drew, Girl Detective, was driving down a windy highway next to the ocean and her best friend, George, was in the front seat with her. This was California, and they were going to Disneyland to solve the Case of the Haunted Rollercoaster, their toughest case yet. She might have to ride the rollercoaster to gather evidence, probably more than once. Maybe twenty times in a row, wondering if the mean juice would slosh around in her stomach and burn it up from going upside down. It looked like fun on TV. And if she was a little bit afraid, she could always say a ghost had surprised her. That was all. She laughed. Nothing went wrong when she and George were hot on the trail.

Something turned into their alley, and it sounded big. Looking up, she saw the Bobbsey Twins running to the back gate. A deep, exasperated sigh emptied her lungs.

She hurried to catch up with her sisters. She grabbed the backs of their shirts when she caught them hanging on the gate, trying to get a glimpse. A big white truck lumbered up the alley and groaned to a stop just past their fence. She pulled the shirts taut. LeeAnn and Cara started to pull away, until Gracie whispered to them. "You are going to want me holding on if it's men escaped from jail with big axes, come to chop mouthy little girls' Barbies into pieces." *And hopefully not the little girls, too.* Gracie crossed her fingers as best she could while holding on to the shirts. The doors opened. All three girls leaned over the fence to watch.

Aunt Bobbie jumped out of the passenger side of the truck. A bug flew into Gracie's open mouth, and she spit it out and shut her mouth. Goosebumps came out on her arms, and she let go of her sisters' shirts to rub them. Pushing up on her toes, she tried to see who was coming around the front of the truck. Kathleen. Gracie's favorite friend of her favorite aunt!

"Okay, my only aunt, but still my favorite," she had told the librarian once when she checked out her books. "Aunt Bobbie took us away on overnight trips with our mom twice. Once we went to the Oklahoma City Zoo."

That book about gorillas was overdue. She reminded herself to remember.

"Would you please stop screaming?" she begged the girls. "It's only eight and somebody might be trying to sleep in." It didn't work. Not only were LeeAnn and Cara screaming, but they were jumping up and down while they chanted "Aunt Bobbie! Aunt Bobbie!" between squeals.

Aunt Bobbie just grinned and held out her arms while she walked to the gate. Kathleen followed close behind, turning around to look ahead and behind them.

"Give me some hugs," Aunt Bobbie ordered when she came through the chain-link gate. The girls grabbed her and Kathleen, then her and Kathleen, back and forth.

"Good grief, Charlie Brown, would you let them walk?" Gracie pushed her way through her sisters. She grabbed Kathleen's hand and Aunt Bobbie's and pulled them toward the back door. "Mom is going to be really surprised."

The adults spoke at the same time. "We came to surprise you."

"And it worked," Aunt Bobbie said. "Let's get Mom and then give some more hugs."

"Oh yeah, it'll be a surprise all right." Kathleen almost dragged the others behind her as she walked. "Let's find your mom. Wait, is she here?"

"Yes, she's changing out sheets," Gracie said. "Otherwise she would have heard the hootenanny."

"You have quite the vocabulary," Kathleen said.

"My teacher told me I have the biggest vocabulary in the whole fourth grade and maybe the fifth grade, too. When school got out, our grade cards said I'm reading sixth-grade books, and the county librarian has to keep giving me older and older ones."

Warmth spread through Gracie's whole body. Beside her the little girls had moved in on Aunt Bobbie, taking her hands and chatting away. But Gracie didn't care.

Kathleen squeezed her hand. "I taught high school in Chicago for the past six years, and I bet you could read our ninth-grade books."

Gracie was about to answer when the back door slammed and her mother came outside.

Chapter Four

"Shhh. If you don't be quiet, I'll...I'll..." Gracie crouched as close to the crack in the door as she could get. Experience had taught her not to sit down while doing this. She might need to move quickly if her mother came back to let the three of them out of their bedroom. They weren't exactly grounded this time, but Mom had been so angry when she told them to go to their room that they weren't about to leave until she came and got them.

"What's happening?" LeeAnn asked. "Maybe my ears are better than yours, and I should listen, too."

Gracie shot her an "I don't think so" look, and LeeAnn turned back to Cara for support. Cara was playing with Barbies on the bed.

"Hey, that's my Barbie, and you didn't ask," LeeAnn said.

Cara shrugged.

LeeAnn grabbed the Barbie, but before Cara could open her mouth, Gracie whipped her own Barbie out of the top drawer of the dresser and stuffed it into her youngest sister's hands. Cara shot LeeAnn a triumphant look and turned her back. LeeAnn took her Barbie to the foot of the bed and created her own story. Gracie rubbed her forehead. Her head hurt, and she wished they would just stay quiet for a minute.

Through the door, Gracie heard her mother enter the front room.

"What are you trying to do to me, Roberta Ann Rossi? Are you trying to get me kicked out of my house without my girls? I told you what he said he would do."

"I'm telling you to stop a second and think rationally. He's at the lake, isn't he? And he's not coming back till Sunday evening, right? We're only going to stay a minute, and I don't have my car. Nobody knows this truck."

"Well, there's nothing like driving through town in a semi to hide your presence," her mom yelled.

Aunt Bobbie entered the front room, too. "It's not a semi, and I'll throw a damned parade next time I come. You could at least ask what I'm doing out here—we brought that truck to get Mom's furniture. Seemed appropriate that one mom with girls making a new start might use the furniture her mom used to make a new start with her girls. The truck's full so—"

"Would you stop talking and answer me? What are we going

to do if he comes back?" Her mom was really yelling then.

"We'll tie him up in the cellar and feed him bat guano," Aunt Bobbie told her.

There was silence then some muffled laughter. Gracie listened as hard as she could. If she only dared crack the door a little.

A minute or two later, she heard her mom again. She sounded farther away. "You are unbelievable, and I'm an idiot. I must be, too, but I need that hug."

Gracie's mouth gaped open.

Her mother continued, her voice stronger and clearer. "He got a late start, so he'll be out till tomorrow evening and not likely to come back. You know what? I. Don't. Care. I am their mother and have just as much right to their lives as he does. He's a jerk and an asshole, and I can't let him push me around." Her voice dropped and got a bit wobbly at the end. "I guess you can stay. But keep the noise down and be quick."

The conversation might have moved into the kitchen because all Gracie could hear was a muffled exchange for a few minutes. Just when she was getting lulled into relaxing, her mom came to the bedroom door. Gracie pretended she had been playing and not listening.

"Girls, I need to talk to you about something important," her mom said. "Your dad and I have been fighting. He doesn't like Aunt Bobbie, and he doesn't like us being with her. You've done so good not talking about things around him that I have another favor to ask. Can you keep one more secret?"

"Yes!" Cara shouted. LeeAnn nodded, and hope rose from Gracie's toes to her nose.

"Okay, no yelling. Your aunt came just to give us each a hug. But you must keep this a secret from Dad. Can you do that?"

All three girls nodded. Gracie saw flashes of anger in her sisters' eyes. This was like getting back at him. Even Cara, who was only six, understood getting back at somebody.

"Okay, she's in the kitchen with Kathleen. We have to be very quiet and not try to make her stay longer. Promise me, girls. Promise?" their mom said in a high-pitched voice. When they all nodded, her shoulders sagged, and Gracie remembered to breathe.

They swarmed into the kitchen, dancing like they hadn't hugged and kissed Aunt Bobbie in the backyard five minutes before. Cara pranced a bit as she waited for her hug. That usually meant that she was trying to keep her enthusiasm under control. Gracie was proud of her for not chanting or screaming. LeeAnn hung off Aunt Bobbie's arm, telling her about all the things she wanted to do with her. Her mom backed up against the wall and smiled at the girls, but it was a skinny smile. Gracie wished she wouldn't smile like that. It always made her nervous.

The noise of the girls talking at once kept Gracie from hearing the pickup truck out front. Without warning, the front door slammed open, and they all went silent.

"What the hell is that dyke bitch doing in my house! I told you, Beth, I told you!" Dad burst into the crowded kitchen like a moving disaster.

"Dan, she's here to say goodbye! She's leaving to teach in California." Gracie gave a little gasp of shock at her mother's words. "This is the last time."

"You're damned right this is the last time. I'll get my shotgun and put an end to this bullshit!"

"You aren't the only one with a gun. Do you want to play shotgun roulette?" Bobbie said without blinking.

"Okay, bitch, see what you think of this." He grabbed for Cara, but Gracie moved quicker and ran between her father and her youngest sister. He looked surprised but grabbed Gracie by the arm instead. "I don't care which little bitch it is, you'll never see her again." He dragged Gracie out of the house toward the truck. Gracie scratched at his arm and then his face. He slammed her against the side of the truck, stunning her and bloodying her lip. He threw her into the pickup across the seat.

Gracie could hear the commotion coming from inside the house. Cara's fearful wail meant she was trying to grab onto someone safe, and the adults yelled at her sisters to get out of the way.

"Daniel Walter Brown, you stop right now or I'll, I'll..." Gracie heard her mother.

"You'll do nothing, bitch, because there's nothing you can do," her father barked.

Aunt Bobbie screamed, "You chicken-shit failure of a man, you stop now, or you'll get what's coming to you!"

She pounded on the truck door and tried to open it, but Gracie's father just laughed.

Gracie managed to sit up as he threw the pickup into reverse and tore out of the driveway. She saw her mother, her aunt, and Kathleen following them out to the street and her two little sisters huddled by the doorway. Before she got too far away to see, she was just able to make out Aunt Bobbie and Kathleen running around to the back of the house.

Gracie hoped they were coming to get her. This was the scariest thing that had ever happened to her. She tried not to cry, but as she held onto the window frame and dashboard to keep from falling onto the floor, tears streamed down her face.

Chapter Five

Two hours later, Beth stood in her living room, a headache gripping her temples. It had started as a small ball behind her right eye, spread up and over the back of her head, and down to a point behind her nose. It throbbed with every beat of her heart, the blood pulsing through it, pounding against some unknown nerve.

"What's this you told my deputy about a kidnapping? That Dan took Gracie? That's craziness. He's her father," Sheriff Grimes said.

"He's drunk, and he threatened I'd never see her again—" Beth said.

"Now, Beth, Dan drinks a little—" He defended her well-loved husband.

"At ten a.m.?" Beth asked.

Her neighbor, Mrs. Northcutt, stood beside Beth and made "tsk, tsk" sounds.

"Mrs. Northcutt, go home," the sheriff said with a grimace. "You're in the way. Just walk yourself back over to your house and be a nice, quiet, good neighbor."

"I may not be blood, but I'm all the family she has in town, and I'll stay if I please." Mrs. Northcutt drew herself up as straight as her slightly bent frame would allow and glared.

"Can we get back to my daughter? My husband has her, and he's drinking and dangerous." Beth put her hands to her head.

"But I'm sure he'd never hurt his little girl. This must be a misunderstanding." Sheriff Grimes removed his hat to wipe sweat from his forehead.

You had to go there, didn't you? Beth's eyes narrowed. She grabbed the sheriff's over-sized forearm. "You don't understand. He threatened to kill my sister, too."

The crackle of the radio in the sheriff's car cut off his next sentence. "Now, what's that?" Grimes hustled out to the car window. He listened and yelled back at the house. "There's a fire out on County Road 92. I've got to go. I'll radio the guys to watch for Dan."

The volunteer fire station's whistle blew, and the sheriff tore out of the driveway.

Beth stood at the window and watched him drive off while Bobbie walked up the driveway. The room smelled like cigarette smoke, but the breeze out front was fresh.

Bobbie let the screen door slam and hurried into the front room. "What was that about?" she asked. She rubbed her eyes, and for the first time, Beth realized how dim the light was.

"There's a fire out on County Road 92 near your—" Mrs. Northcutt said.

"Farm," Bobbie said, catching Beth's eyes. Beth felt her sister grab her by the arm as her knees buckled, then Bobbie's strong hands were steadying her.

"Kathleen's getting gas. We'll leave as soon as she's back," Bobbie said. "Don't start falling down on me yet."

"I can't go. LeeAnn and Cara cried themselves to sleep, but they'll wake up soon..." Beth bit her lip and rocked from one foot to the other.

"Go, dear, just go. I'll watch the little ones," Mrs. Northcutt said, as a white truck pulled up into the driveway.

"Thank you," Beth said as Bobbie pushed her out the door.

****

"Where's the sheriff going?" Kathleen asked as Bobbie and Beth climbed into the passenger seat.

"We've got too many bags here," Bobbie said to Beth."You're going to have to sit on my lap or the.floor."

"I'll take your lap. Oh, Bobbie, I'm scared. Will he burn down the farm? What about Gracie?" Beth began hyperventilating.

"Slow breaths, Beth, or you'll pass out, and that won't help anyone. I'm angry I didn't think to look on the farm when we just now searched the county," Bobbie said. "Kathleen, we need to go back out to the farm. Do you remember how to get there?"

"Yeah." Kathleen drove out of town onto a country road.

The horizon flew past them, rarely interrupted by trees or buildings. Beth picked out the farms, naming them by name under her breath, trying desperately to keep from falling apart.

She said, "You were gone so long, more than two hours. Cara and LeeAnn just cried and cried and begged me to get their big sister back." The truck lurched as Kathleen hit a bump, but Beth didn't miss a beat. "Did you really think you could find him? He could be anywhere. Oh, my God, he could be anywhere, and he's had two hours' head start with her—"

"Of course, I would have found him, dammit. I won't stop until I do. Dammit, Beth, I said slow breaths. I want you able to stand up when we get there. The fire might not be at our place, but Dan could be." Bobbie gripped her sister's hand.

When they grew closer, however, Beth's hope dissipated as the smoke rose from the ruins of the pitched barn. Were they too late? Had he torched the farm and gone?

Beth fell off Bobbie's lap when she opened the truck door. Bobbie jumped out and helped her stand up. Paralyzed, Beth stared at the chaos. Bobbie dropped Beth's hands, and she and Kathleen raced toward the barn. "Gracie! Gracie! Gracie!"

Beth couldn't breathe. Gracie was her oldest and her little helper. She was a one-in-a-million child. Where was she? Was she okay? Beth ached to know. She looked down at her feet and got them shuffling through the dirt toward the other side of the road, but once there, she froze again. What if she isn't here? What if Dan threw her away on some country road? What if he hurt her? What if he beat her the way he threatens to beat me? What if he killed her? The "what ifs" paralyzed her, and the farm swam before her eyes. Slow breaths, slow breaths. She couldn't pass out now.

With a resolve born of love for her daughter, Beth took one step down the slope into the driveway. Then another. The smoke from the barn stung her eyes, and she cried for her lost Gracie, for her lost hope, even for her lost love. Her feet stopped again as she listened to the cacophony of sounds—the fire truck's engine, men calling out to one another, Bobbie screaming at her. Bobbie screaming at her? What was she saying?

"Come on, Beth. We have to find her. We must find Gracie. Take my hand. Now!" Bobbie dragged Beth, stumbling, toward the burnt-out barn.

A fireman intercepted them. He grabbed Bobbie's shoulders. "Who are you looking for?" he asked.

"A ten-year-old girl," Bobbie said between loud gasps for air.

"She's not in the barn. We searched it before it collapsed. We found a man but no child," the fireman said.

Beth sagged in relief.

"Bobbie," Kathleen yelled from the stand of trees behind the house, "I found her. Bring help."

Beth and Bobbie ran toward the trees between the house and barn. They almost stumbled over Kathleen, who knelt with Gracie's head in her lap. Beth nearly choked when she saw her daughter, lying on her back. She was pale, and a long strand of hair wrapped around her head and into her mouth.

Beth dropped to her knees beside them and bent to kiss Gracie on the cheek. Her baby's eyes were closed, and they didn't even flutter when she touched her. Beth's heart pounded against her ribs, drowning out the distant ruckus. She looked at her baby's swollen face and torn clothes and didn't even register questions about how they got that way. She just yearned for the chance to hold her and talk with her without all this dirt and commotion.

Someone tried to move Beth out of the way, but she wouldn't budge. It was a paramedic.

Bobbie said, "Come on, Beth. You have to get out of their

way. You can sit here and still reach her. He can't help her if you don't move." Bobbie moved Beth out of the way. She inched along, still holding Gracie's hand.

The paramedic worked to see if Gracie had any injuries. He lifted each eyelid and shone a small flashlight in her eyes and then gently felt along her torso, arms, and legs.

"She's in shock, but I don't see any signs of a head wound. We're going to take her to the hospital at Gerberville," the paramedic said.

"I'm coming with her. I'm her mother," Beth said.

"I'm sorry, ma'am, but we don't have room for you. You'll have to meet us there."

"I'm her mother. I am not leaving her side."

"I'm sorry, but you have to. Come to the desk in the emergency room, and they'll tell you where she is." The paramedic signaled his partner to get the stretcher.

Beth started crying. "You don't understand—"

Bobbie turned Beth to face her. "They're not going to change their minds. Come on. We'll get there before they do." She dragged Beth to her feet, through the trees, and toward the truck.

Kathleen got there first and helped the sisters into the truck. She climbed in and fired up the moving monster. "You won't believe this, but the paramedic asked me if I was able to drive. Me. Like I was fragile or something. I told them we would beat them there. Safely."

Once at the hospital, Beth and Bobbie rushed to the emergency room desk while Kathleen parked.

"My daughter, my ten-year-old daughter was just brought in. I have to see her," Beth told the receiving nurse. Her thoughts raged. Oh, my God, what have I let happen? What have I done?

"Yes, my niece, is she okay?" Bobbie asked.

"Fill out this form with your name and her name. What does she look like?" the nurse asked, looking from Bobbie's darker complexion and dark-brown hair to Beth's lighter, ash-brown pageboy and red, blotchy, tear-stained face.

Beth's knees wobbled, and her body swayed. Bobbie reached out to steady her. Bobbie said, practically dancing with anger, "She looks like her mother. She's probably the only ten-year-old you've had brought in during the past eight hours. At least tell us if she's okay."

The nurse took a half-step back. "You'll have to wait. The doctors are with her now. You'll be able to see her one at a time."

"I'm not sure that's a good idea, Nurse Warren," Kathleen said, squinting to read the nurse's name tag from where she had appeared behind the sisters. "Her mom's pretty fragile right now. Could one of us go in with her, just in the beginning?"

"I'll check with the doctor when the patient's cleared for visitors. Help yourself to a glass of water and tissues if you need them. And please fill out the rest of these forms." The nurse turned and walked away.

"Oh, my God. Why can't I see her?" New tears streaked down Beth's face, and her voice grew husky. "She's my baby. When can I see her? When can I see her? Why won't they let me...?"

Kathleen said, "Beth, I'm sure they're taking good care of Gracie. Why don't we sit down and fill out the forms, so you'll be ready to see her when the doctor comes out? Look, there are chairs right here where we can see both hallways." Kathleen directed Beth to an orange plastic chair and handed her the clipboard and pen she had dropped.

Bobbie stared at the door the nurse had gone through. "And you're not going anywhere yet," Kathleen told her. "Why don't you help Beth with the forms?"

Beth looked at the clipboard, and her vision blurred a bit. She reminded herself to breathe. That helped. Why couldn't she remember something that basic? How could she expect to help Gracie if she couldn't even remember to breathe? Once again, tears sprung forth and stained her cheeks. When would they ever dry up?

It seemed like an hour to her, but they had just finished the last form when the doctor came out the same door. "Mrs. Brown?"

Beth jumped up. "Can I see her now? Please?"

"Yes, you can all see her for a few minutes, then we need to talk. Please remember, it may look like Grace is asleep, but she's only lightly sedated, so she's awake and can hear you. Please be careful not to upset her with anything you say. Are you ready? Follow me."

The three women filed through the door after the doctor and into the first curtained room on the other side. Gracie lay in a hospital bed, too white and too still. Beth stuffed her fist in her mouth to stifle a sob. She pulled herself together and took Gracie's hand.

"Hey, baby, it's Mama. I'm here now, and it's going to be okay. We're all here, Aunt Bobbie and Kathleen and me, and some people who are going to take good care of you." Beth brushed her hand across the top of Gracie's cheek, arm, any skin she could touch. Anything to know her daughter was in there and alive.

Beth went on. "I love you, Gracie, and your sisters love you, too. They miss you and want you to come home. You're such a brave girl, and Mama is so glad to have you back. I can't tell you how happy I am to see you." She brushed the hair from Gracie's forehead as she spoke and kept a tight grip on her daughter's hand.

Bobbie sat on the other side of the bed, holding Gracie's other hand in hers and stroking her arm. She murmured soft echoes of

Beth's words while tears ran down her face unchecked. Kathleen stood at the end of the bed, cracking the knuckles on her right hand, and her left, then repeating.

After what felt like just seconds, the doctor returned. "Mrs. Brown, will you come with me, so we can discuss Gracie's care?"

"But I just got here."

"It's been five minutes, Mrs. Brown. I must talk to you. I need your permission about treatment for Gracie. Will you sign the forms?"

Beth grimaced. "Can't it wait?"

Kathleen went to Beth's side. "Come on, Beth. I'll go with you, and we'll get it done as fast as we can, so we can come back. Okay?"

"Do we have to do it now, Doctor? I just got her back. I don't want to leave her again so soon. What if she wakes up and is scared?"

"It's very important, Mrs. Brown."

Beth sighed and followed, with Kathleen close behind her. She stopped at the door. "Take care of her, Bobbie, I don't want anything happening while I'm gone."

Chapter Six

Bobbie's sister and lover disappeared out the door with the doctor, and the sudden silence of the room became oppressive. The peace she had longed to have with Gracie suddenly weighed her down like a pile of pig irons weighed down the back of a Chevy pickup. She scooted closer to the bed, tucked Gracie in tighter, and smoothed out the wrinkles in the bedsheet. She tapped her fingers and bounced her foot, all to no avail or any great distraction.

If she hadn't visited after Dan said no, and if she hadn't pushed his buttons while he was drunk, then he wouldn't have kidnapped her niece and they wouldn't have spent two hours scouring the Kansas countryside. She wouldn't have rushed to a burning barn or found an unconscious ten-year-old in a stand of trees. She wouldn't have raced an ambulance to an emergency room to sit beside a sterile hospital bed, holding the unresponsive Gracie's hand.

But she did, she had, and she was. And it sucked. It sucked bad. It was her fault. She had done this, and now she had to repair it. But how could she erase something this terrible? A kidnapping and other unknown trauma. Undoubtedly, Dan had yelled at Gracie, he might even have threatened her. Oh God, she hoped he hadn't hit her. She didn't see any bruises yet, but she didn't know how she would live with herself if bruises showed up tomorrow. She would just die. She created this disaster, and she had to fix it but didn't know how.

With every tick of the long minute hand on the institutional wall clock, Bobbie felt more guilt. All her decision making, or lack thereof, came back to haunt her. Why hadn't Kat stopped her? How could she let Bobbie do something that stupid? The tears threatened again, and she bit the inside of her cheek rather than cry anymore. She needed to be strong for Gracie, for the family.

She leaned forward and kissed Gracie on the cheek. "Aunt Bobbie is still here, babe, and I'll stay with you while your mom is with the doctor. Oh, honey, we were so worried about you, but everything's going to be okay now. We'll get you fixed up and get Cara and LeeAnn and then get some pizza. How does that sound? Pizza's your favorite, I know. Sausage just for you." She prattled on without much thought to the words, just needing to communicate with the silent child in front of her. "I don't have a pack of gum in my purse, but I'll send Kathleen out to get one for when you wake up. Maybe two, bubble gum and cinnamon. I know you have a hard time choosing."

She told Gracie how she would take the whole family on a trip to an amusement park in Kansas City before Gracie started school in the fall. She spoke to her nonstop, stroking her cheek and hand, until Kathleen came for her almost twenty minutes later.

"What on earth's going on?" Bobbie asked. "Where's Beth?"

Kathleen took one of Bobbie's hands and quickly kissed the palm before returning it to Gracie's hand on the wrinkle-free, white sheets. "She's still with the doctor, filling out forms, and asking and answering questions, but they wanted me to get you, so you could hear for yourself about Gracie's treatment plans. They're only a few doors away."

"But I don't want to leave Gracie alone." Bobbie gripped her niece's hand and then released it before hurting her. "Will you stay with her?"

"The nurse will come in when we leave. She needs to take her blood pressure again and check her temperature, and you know how they might have to do other things. We should let her do her job."

"I want to come back as soon as I can."

Kathleen blew out air and pushed back her round, black, eyeglass frames. She looked at Bobbie and ran a hand through her now rowdy curls. "You can stay in the hospital as long as you want to, I'm sure, just come with me and let the nurse do her thing."

"What's wrong?" Bobbie looked at Kathleen's narrowed eyes. "Talk to me, Kat."

"Bobbie, get out of here now, and let her take Gracie's blood pressure, will you?" Kathleen turned and left the room. Bobbie followed, after one last kiss on Gracie's cheek and a whispered guarantee that she was just down the hall.

She entered the door Kathleen held open. Beth sat at a desk. The doctor stood up and excused himself from the room. Bobbie looked at Beth, who had been crying for quite a while, judging from the pile of tissue in front of her.

"What's wrong?" Bobbie asked, quickly sitting down beside her.

Beth sounded no older than Gracie's age when she spoke. "They have to do surgery on Gracie to repair a tear. She's going to be okay, but she'll be in the hospital a couple of days. I don't know how long the surgery will take, but a nurse will take us to a surgical waiting room soon."

"Beth, what are you talking about? What happened? What surgery? What tear?" Bobbie's confusion and anger spilled out in rapid-fire questions.

"Dan is dead, but he raped Gracie!" Beth wailed.

Bobbie's heart stopped, her stomach rolled, and her guilt swallowed her.

Chapter Seven

The family planned their move to Lawrence, Kansas, for two weeks later, on August first. Kathleen had always considered herself a big-picture type of person and tried to think that way about this move.

Gracie remained in the hospital for three days. Beth hovered over her there most of the time, and Kathleen shuttled Bobbie back and forth while Mrs. Northcutt minded the younger girls during those short trips. Kathleen's experience growing up in a large family came in handy, as she remained the only adult available to deal with LeeAnn and Cara, girls who moved about the house like frightened ghosts. They didn't know what had happened to Gracie or their dad, but apparently the solemnity of the household and their fear of hospitals kept them from asking too many questions.

On the afternoon of the third day, Kathleen entertained the two younger girls. "Would you like to play hospital and doctor?" she asked.

The girls looked at one another, then to her without speaking, and nodded. They decided Kathleen would be the patient and LeeAnn would be the doctor while Cara played the nurse. Kathleen lay down on the couch. LeeAnn started by pretending to listen to her heart, then she stood still not knowing what to do.

"What does the nurse do?" Cara asked, leaning into the couch and Kathleen's hip.

"The nurse writes down what the doctor says and helps her do things," Kathleen said.

LeeAnn started to cry. "I don't know what to do. Is Gracie okay? What if she dies?"

Cara turned pale, and giant tears ran down her face. Kathleen sat up and pulled them both onto her lap, glad that the game had gotten them talking. "Gracie got hurt at the fire, and the doctors are making her better. She'll be able to come home soon. She might not want to play for a while. She might need to sleep a lot, but she'll be home and safe, and we'll all feel better."

"Did she get burned?" Cara asked.

"No, she didn't get burned." Kathleen didn't know what or how much to tell them. To her great relief, Cara didn't ask any more questions. "I think they'll bring her home tomorrow. I guess I should clean up the house before everyone gets here. Would you two show me how to do that and where the cleaning things are?"

They "helped" her clean all afternoon, and by the time it was done, the house looked as shiny as a dilapidated old house could look. That evening, while the girls were running through their baths, Kathleen realized that no one had told them about Dan's death, and they hadn't asked.

All three girls shared a full bed in a tiny bedroom. When Cara and LeeAnn were tucked into it, Kathleen sat on the side of the bed to tell them a story. She still felt a little awkward about the issue of Dan's death, so she decided to feel them out. "Is there anything else you want to know?"

LeeAnn shook her head.

"No!" Cara said.

"Wow, you sound angry, Cara," Kathleen said.

"I'm mad that Daddy took Gracie away, and she got hurt. I hope he never comes home." Cara spoke the words, but Kathleen could see a flash of agreement in LeeAnn's eyes.

"He'll never come home, and he'll never hurt any of you girls again. Your mom can tell you more about that tomorrow," Kathleen said.

LeeAnn spoke without emotion. "He's a mean dad. He spanks us for no reason, and he yells at Mom and at us, too. I don't want him for my dad. Mom didn't have a dad when she grew up. She told us we're lucky, but I think she's the lucky one."

Oh God, she wasn't touching that one. "Well, we'll all have to talk about this more when your mom and aunt are here, okay? Bed now."

****

Gracie came home the next day, faded out and muted, like the burdensome gray clouds that hung low over the driveway in front of the house. Bobbie drove the gold, 1968 Impala and Beth sat in back with Gracie. Kathleen and the younger girls watched at the front door. Beth helped Gracie out of the car and guided her toward the house.

LeeAnn looked up at Kathleen. "Are you sure she's okay?"

"She's okay. She's just on strong medicine and very tired. She's going to sleep in your mom's bed with her. Guess what? You and Cara get to camp out in front of the TV in sleeping bags. Aunt Bobbie and I will squeeze into your bed."

"All right," Cara said. "TV party!"

Kathleen pulled the girls back by their shoulders. "Now remember, don't be too loud, but let her know you love her and are glad she's home." Bobbie opened the screen for Beth, who led Gracie in and past her sisters, without stopping, back to her bedroom.

Kathleen held the girls by the shoulders again. "Okay, she must not feel good now. You can tell her later. Do you want to play quietly in the house or the backyard?"

Both girls headed for the back door. Kathleen sighed. She wondered if Gracie was truly still in this bad of shape. Or were her mother and aunt the ones in bad shape? She walked down the short hall to Beth's bedroom. The twins already had Gracie in a nightgown and lying under a sheet, staring at the ceiling with fluttering eyelids.

"Hi, Gracie," she said. "I'm glad you're home."

Beth pushed Kathleen out of the room. "She needs to sleep. If you want to be helpful, you could bring a glass of water for her next set of pills in an hour."

All righty then. Kathleen knew when to move on. Maybe she should focus on dinner. She was looking at the nearly bare kitchen cabinets, wondering how creative she could be with hotdogs and creamed corn when Bobbie stepped up behind her, scaring her into the middle of next week.

"Make a noise, would you?" Kathleen asked. "Where's Beth? Is Gracie sleeping?"

"She's asleep. Beth's watching her and holding her hand in case she wakes up and needs something."

"Isn't that a little extreme?" Kathleen asked.

"I'm going to take the next shift when Beth needs to put LeeAnn and Cara to bed."

Kathleen's mouth fell open. "Are you seriously going to keep someone with her twenty-four hours a day? For how long? What are you thinking? She'll never get better if she's smothered. Give her a spoon and a pot to bang on if she needs anything and help me with the house and the younger two."

Bobbie stood and turned to leave. Kathleen caught her by the arm, turned her back around, and wrapped her arms around Bobbie's shoulders. "I'm sorry, babe, I didn't mean to get angry." She stroked Bobbie's hair. "I'm tired and scared for Gracie, for you, and for Beth. You're all pale and silent as death. We don't need any more death in this house. We need some life. LeeAnn and Cara deserve to have their lives keep going. They've been on hold for days, and being in limbo is no fun. I'll be glad when we can get out of here, move everyone up to our new house."

She tipped Bobbie's face up to meet hers. "You and I can start teaching, the girls can start school, and maybe Beth will even start school. A new life. Can't you just see it? Smell it? Taste it?"

Bobbie pulled away. "Remember, Beth and the girls don't know about us, so we have to be careful."

Kathleen let go, and Bobbie left the room. Kathleen looked at the ceiling and back down at the creamed corn.

****

Kathleen pulled Beth away from the pile of papers on the kitchen table. "Give it up for a while, sister. It'll all be there in the morning, but you'll be better rested. Besides, Cara wants to use your bubble bath and we don't have any idea where you hide it. Can you help her with her bath?" Beth's shoulders relaxed, and she went down the hallway.

"You lie," Bobbie said from the sofa. "It's under the nightstand. LeeAnn said Gracie showed her last May."

"She needed the break, and she has a mule-headed streak like her sister. Besides, LeeAnn and Cara need some one-on-one time with her." Kathleen stacked Beth's individual piles of papers into one organized pyramid. "Did Beth tell you what she asked me to do today?"

Bobbie shook her head no.

Kathleen sat down beside her on the old sofa. "I had to call Dan's parents in Wichita with the news. His father was cold, even before I told him how Dan died and what he had done. Mr. Brown said they wouldn't come back for the service. Beth was relieved. Did you know that after the parents left Cottonwood Plains, they never even sent cards or gifts for holidays or the girls' birthdays? Cold people."

Kathleen stretched and went on. "Oh, and the other big phone call today was from Beth's boss. He told her how sorry he was, to take all the time she needed, and did she know how long that would be? She seemed thrilled when she told him, 'Forever.' I suppose this means the town knows. Since we asked Dan's captain at the fire station to handle the service and the burial, I thought it wouldn't take long. But no one else has said anything except the neighbor, Mrs. Northcutt, who keeps bringing those groovy cookies every day. Thank goodness for her."

****

The next night, the three adults collapsed at the kitchen table before going to bed.

"Staying with Gracie all day is more tiring than you think. What did you do today, Kathleen?" Bobbie asked.

"I brought home Dan's stuff from the fire station, so Beth could sort through it. I'll box it up with all his stuff from here and his fishing gear and take it back to the station where his buddies agreed to take care of it. I paid his tab off at the tavern, and Mrs. Northcutt drove me out to the farm to get the pickup. I put the boxes Beth has packed into the white truck. Oh, and I got Dan's last paycheck from the station," Kathleen said, not making eye contact with Bobbie.

"Thank you so much, Kathleen." Beth put her head in her hands. "I don't know what I would do without you. Every day ten more details pop up. All those bills are coming in now. Ambulance, hospital, doctors, everywhere, even the plot. His last paycheck won't cover them."

Bobbie said, "We'll write notes saying they'll be paid in time, and you can sign them. You can do a change of address, so the coroner can send the death certificate to the right place and do the other details there." She apparently had little sympathy for long, drawn-out processes.

"Right now," Beth said, "I just want to get the hell out of Cottonwood Plains, to somewhere I can relax and cry for a week."

That thought hung in the air by itself for a long, long time.

Chapter Eight

Bobbie pulled her nightshirt lower on her legs as she rocked on the rusty swing set, her trailing feet unused to the parched grass. Even at two in the morning, the hot metal chains stung her hands. They were sharp, as well. The seat, too, left its imprint on her bare legs, still hotter than plastic had any right to be five hours after the sun stopped shining directly on it. Her gaze shifted, and she looked up at the stars. How long had it been since she pushed herself on that childhood swing set? Since she'd run barefoot on the dry prairie with calloused feet? Not long enough.

Someone coughed and shifted in the front room, catching her attention. One of the little girls in sleeping bags probably rolled over but didn't get up. The two of them slept with one low lamp on; at least they'd done so since all of this happened. The light helped her sneak through the front room when the oppressive heat drove her out of the full bed she shared with Kathleen, through the kitchen, and into the backyard, seeking some reprieve. She hadn't found any. All she had found was stale, left-over, baked-earth warmth and self-recrimination. Her hands ached.

She rubbed her gritty, dry eyes. The chains cutting her hands seemed a petty punishment for her crime—destroying a family, a child's life, and her sister's...her sister's what? God, she couldn't even think at this hour, but she couldn't sleep either. She just lay there and thought about it over and over again. Her family's pain and brokenness. The scene played out in her mind a hundred different ways, but it always ended the same. Always the same. Her fault.

The back of her throat hurt, and she tried to swallow but couldn't. She tried repeatedly. Just like Gracie must have tried to get away repeatedly—damn, this was going nowhere and doing Gracie, Beth, and none of them any good. If she couldn't change it, she would have to fix it.

But how on earth did she plan to do that?

Deep breath. Do the tangible things first. Move them out of this town. In progress. Get them into a house with proven adult support, that was Kathleen and her. Check. Get Beth into school again. Still on the drawing board. Find doctors for Gracie's body. Still on the drawing board. Find doctors for her mind. Maybe Beth's too. Another damned drawing board.

But those were the easy things. Other things couldn't be

checked off a list. Much more difficult things. Today, when Beth walked with Gracie to the restroom, and they passed Bobbie in the hallway, Bobbie found herself reaching out to tousle Gracie's hair like she always did. Then she pulled her hand away. What was that about? Was she afraid to touch her niece? Afraid she wasn't worthy? Afraid to feel her niece's condemnation? Or her sister's?

"You've done enough damage, don't you think? Haven't you hurt me enough for one lifetime?" The words she had not yet heard burned a place in her heart just as surely as if they had been spoken a million times.

Fixing it, back to fixing it. She was going to fix it; that was the only solution. There was no other option. She could do this. Whatever drove her to earn her B.A. and Ph.D. in ten years without financial support from home would drive her to make this right again. If she could succeed in school, a woman from the sticks, alone in the academy, she could make the ones she loved better. She had to. There was no other choice. She tried to swallow again. Her throat hurt, and her mouth tasted sour. Damn, she was a baby. If Gracie could survive... No. No, No. Bobbie closed her eyes and tried to empty her mind. Thinking about it was too overwhelming. If she could just get a moment's peace, a clear thought—

The cloud that had stolen over her mood had moved slowly between her and the moon as well, darkening the night. Or at least, Bobbie thought it had until the shadow of it reached out and touched her on the arm. She nearly fell off the swing set but was caught in Kathleen's strong, heated hands.

"Oh," Bobbie said, her smile so faint it might not have been at all. "Thanks."

"You're welcome." Kathleen grinned and released her shoulders. "Are you busy out here?"

"Nope."

"Oh, my hot, monosyllabic mama, give me the chills with your concise soliloquy." Kathleen grinned again and wiped the back of her neck with her hand. "Although in this moonlight I can see how pale you are because of the dark circles under your eyes. No, I'm not criticizing your looks, but I'm worried about how much you aren't sleeping."

Bobbie looked at the moon. "How can you sleep under a moon as bright as a harvest sun?"

Kathleen laughed, "That deserved a Pulitzer prize for waxing poetic on the job. Yes, it's bright, but between the roof and my closed eyelids, they usually do the job. C'mon, what's the story, morning glory?"

Bobbie swung the seat away from Kathleen, once again clinging to the chains until they dug into her palms. Her shoulders shook with bottled-up sobs, emotion that was quickly becoming less and less repressed.

"It's all my fault," she said with a moan. "It's my fault. There's no way around that. I made the decision, and there's no undoing it. If I can fix it...no, *when* I fix it. Yes, even when I fix it, will Beth be able to forgive me? Will Gracie? Even if Gracie, if Gracie—damn, it must be when Gracie gets better—will she be able to forgive me for causing the whole damn thing? And my sister, will she ever forgive me not only for causing the whole damn rape but for dragging them away from...oh, hell...never mind..."

"Girlie, look up. No, look up. It's not your fault. Dan was a loose cannon and an alcoholic. He could have blown anytime, and most likely it would have been when you weren't down here to help. You heard the doctor say that the scar tissue suggests he had been molesting her for a long time, so that wasn't anything even related to you—"

Bobbie whimpered. Kathleen pulled her close and continued to speak. "As far as fixing it... What are you talking about? I have no idea how you fix this. But I do know that the middle of the night, when you're still grieving, is not the time to come up with a plan to fix anything but breakfast. And in terms of forgiving you? If there's anything to forgive, you'll just have to see in time, but I know how much they love you and I think that will win out over everything else. It does, my love, it does."

"Oh God, I can't think about it anymore for tonight. It keeps running through my mind, over and over, what I could have done different, or better, or not at all. What I need to do now, or in the future, or never again. I've got to stop thinking for a few hours. It will all be there in the morning when I wake up and see them."

"Do you want to take a walk?" Kathleen asked. "It's got to still be ninety degrees in that house."

"What, and get shot?" Bobbie answered.

"Here? In your hometown?"

"In my almost hometown. Number one, I was a farm girl. Number two, I'm a stranger now. I've been gone ten years, and yes, they recognize every silhouette walking down the street, or, at least, everyone that *should* be walking down the street, in their opinion."

Kathleen made a big act of strapping on a six-shooter. She took a bow-legged pose. "I'll mow 'em down faster than you can say 'feminist ethics and Shakespearean insults meet the untamed frontier,' so there."

Bobbie almost smiled. "Well, number three, that's not very fast. And number four, I might get away with it, but if someone turned on a porch lamp and saw short, bright-red hair on top of skin so white it reflects the light, well, you would definitely be a wild card, and... On. Your. Own." At those words, she finally smiled just the tiniest of smiles.

Kathleen grinned. "Do you think I would be mistaken for a man?"

"Hmm, it's likely, I guess. You're quite a few inches taller than I am and not nearly as feminine in the way you walk."

"Hey," Kathleen said. "You aren't all that feminine yourself, Donna Reed."

Bobbie laughed quietly. "Yes, I am, but I can see I've made your evening, dear one."

"Sharing a bed legally with a certain curvaceous professor from the Wild West makes this McClintock's day, and you know it always will. Especially when we're in the lion's den."

"Well, okay, lion tamer, why don't you rub my neck for a while, so I might be able to sleep?" The love in Bobbie's heart was so filling, it spilled out directly toward Kathleen, sending an unspoken message. It must have worked.

"Okay." Kat moved behind Bobbie's swing.

Bobbie let her head drop forward so Kathleen could rub out the knots that held her neck into a many-beaded cord. Kathleen worked out knot after knot without comment, except for Bobbie's occasional grunt or Kathleen's sympathetic clucking.

"Thanks," Bobbie said many minutes later. "You've gotten the worst of them, and I think we've gotten the best of the breeze. Shall we go back inside?"

"Am I needed inside?"

"I need you inside."

Kathleen stood taller, smiled broader, and shook her head. "I'll follow you."

Bobbie struggled a bit getting up, and Kathleen offered her a hand, pulling her up to her feet. "What time is it?" Bobbie asked.

"Three forty-five."

"Ugh, I came out here almost two hours ago."

"Did you find what you were looking for?" Kathleen asked.

"More questions than answers and more heat than breezes. But then you came out with my answers. Unfortunately, you also fanned the flames, so it was six of one, half-dozen of another."

Kathleen smiled. "Good to know. Always good to know."

Chapter Nine

"Damn, I'm hot." Bobbie crammed one more bag into the trunk of her Impala. Unexpected sounds of small shoes on the porch behind her preceded the slamming screen door.

"Aunt Bobbie said damn," Cara announced to the house, the elderly neighbor walking across the lawn, and probably the rest of the block.

"Aunt Bobbie," Mrs. Northcutt said, with a grin. "I guess I'm glad I came over at seven, before the morning and the language got more heated."

"I'm sure the morning will," Bobbie said then grunted. "At least, it's not supposed to be ninety-four degrees like yesterday, more like the low eighties. That will make driving a whole lot easier. But it's still hot and sticky, and I've been lugging bags and—"

"Would you like a cookie, dear? I brought three bags for your trip. One for Beth and Cara, one for Kathleen and LeeAnn, and a special one for you and Gracie in the boat. I mean the Impala."

Bobbie grimaced. "Another detractor for my lovely golden chariot. Come on in and hand out your cookies. We've got to get on the road by eight if we want to meet the landlord in time to get help with all the furniture."

"Will you have enough beds? I mean for all of you? Beth and Dan had such a tiny place..." Mrs. Northcutt was always gracious.

"I have my apartment's worth of furniture, and Kathleen has her bedroom furniture and desk in storage. We'll have plenty of furniture—"

"Who is Kathleen, if I may ask? She seems like a sweet young woman, but I've never heard your sister mention her before." Mrs. Northcutt fidgeted with a bag, her fingers showing the first hints of arthritis as she tried to untie the secretive bulges.

"She's my best friend from college. She's from Chicago and has been teaching high school math there but got a job at my junior college. We were going to get a place as roommates, but luckily, we hadn't signed a lease, then this place came available for Beth, the girls, and us. It's a big house. It's got four bedrooms and a   double garage on a double lot, with a front yard for playing in and a backyard for a big old garden."

Mrs. Northcutt moved in close to Bobbie. "I am so glad those girls won't be sleeping three to a bed anymore. They're getting so big now."

Bobbie nodded, searching the windows for little faces. "Beth did the best she could, but you're right—they each deserve their own bed and they'll have it in Lawrence."

The front door flew open, and the two younger girls ran out to greet Mrs. Northcutt and her bags of goodies. Bobbie took advantage of the opportunity to finish packing the backseat and then waited for her sister and Kathleen to join her outside. That had lasted all of thirty seconds before curiosity got the best of her and she went inside to see how Gracie was doing instead.

Gracie was sitting on the floral bark-cloth couch that the family had decided to leave behind, staring at her shoes. Bobbie stopped at the door, unsure for once of what to say. This could be a long ride.

"Hey, kiddo, where's your mom? Or Kathleen? Are we ready to load up yet?" Bobbie asked. Gracie looked up but didn't answer.

Kathleen's voice came from the next room. "Kathleen and Beth are in the kitchen. They're packing the cooler with the last few lunch things in the refrigerator. Here's Kathleen now, carrying said cooler into the living room. Hi, Bobbie."

"Okay, smart alec." Bobbie shook her head. "Just put the cooler in the back of my car and let's get on the road. Mrs. Northcutt brought cookies for each vehicle, and I'm sure another round of hugs awaits us since clearly last night's hugs weren't enough."

She smiled. The sweet, older woman might miss the girls, and it had been nice to get fresh baked goods every day, but Bobbie was in a hurry to get on the road and this was taking up time.

Perhaps everyone else was as eager as she was because by seven thirty, the caravan was on the road, well ahead of her scheduled take-off time. Maybe they would get there before Jimmy, the landlord, was expecting them. She could call him from a pay phone, or maybe he would answer the citizen's band radio. Since there was one in his truck, he might have one in his car or home and that would be more convenient and cheaper than stopping for a pay phone. Handy things. Who needed a pay phone if they had a CB to call ahead a little way and let someone know they were coming? And for long drives, it was awfully fun to listen to truckers talk in their made-up language. Ten-four, good buddy, that's a go. But for now, it was put the pedal to the metal time.

Three hours later, including one restroom break, Bobbie's stomach grumbled and her back was aching. Was Gracie as ready for lunch as she was? Gracie stared out the windshield as she had for the past hour, maybe without seeing anything, certainly without saying anything. Bobbie was sure she had been the best choice for driving Gracie to her new home. Gracie hadn't said more than three words the entire time. Anyone else might have missed the significance of this and just chattered away. It wasn't that she hadn't talked to Gracie. She talked, sang, and even asked questions. She also let Gracie sleep. Kathleen would have cared about her, too. But Kathleen didn't know her as well as she did and wouldn't have the depth of connection she and Gracie shared before the horrific attack. Beth cared of course, but by now, Beth would probably have been in tears and begging Gracie to talk. That or she would have sung Gracie to sleep and kept her asleep the entire time, and that wasn't healthy either. Yes, she was the best one for the job.

The CB squawked, and Kathleen asked if they should take the next picnic stop in sixteen miles. It was technically a little early, but she was hungry, and I-70 had limited rest stops, so why not? She didn't hear Beth's response. Maybe Cara was talking her ear off, and Beth had missed Kathleen's question and Bobbie's agreement. Wait. There. Now everyone was on the same page. This was going to be a challenge, this living as a family again. Kathleen was as independent as she was, but Beth... Well, with a husband like Dan, one would assume that Beth could watch out for herself. Maybe not. Tidbits of conversations floated to mind. To be honest, she had never heard any arguments between Dan and Beth but only because Beth never argued back. Certainly not a good healthy quarrel the way Bobbie never hesitated to jump into if Dan gave her crap. It was never an intellectual challenge, but it was always a rhetorical good time—how long would it take her to trap Dan in his own argument? Never very long. He wasn't stupid, but he was overly impressed with his perceived importance. Men like that were easy to trick into saying things they'd have to defend at their own cost. She remembered one time when—

"Damn!" she said. She passed the exit and had to radio the others to meet at the next one. So much for deep thinking and driving. Damn that Dan. Even after death, he still gave her fits.

****

Pulling into their new neighborhood, Bobbie smiled at her wristwatch. It wasn't even close to rush hour. It had to be ninety degrees, but luckily, she found a tree to park under. She woke Gracie and they stood under the tree to await the others. Kathleen pulled up next, adjusting the moving truck so it could be unloaded into the driveway while LeeAnn loudly chattered a mile a minute, asking questions Kathleen couldn't possibly answer. After parking, Kathleen and LeeAnn joined them on the sidewalk in the shade and waited while Beth parked the pickup behind the moving truck. Cara jumped down from the pickup, fell onto the grass, popped up, and began bouncing around her new yard. Bobbie sighed and smiled.

So, this is the way it was going to be.

After getting everyone's attention, Bobbie gave the girls and Beth the outside tour of the house. She proudly displayed it all, from the spacious front yard that had many flower bushes and bulbs planted, to the little yard between the house and the garage where Jimmy had promised to place a swing set, and finally, to a garden area behind the garage. It was back in that area that LeeAnn wandered into a caged enclosure with a cement floor that ran six feet wide and the length of the garage.

"What is this?" LeeAnn pressed her face against the wire fence.

"That's a dog run," Bobbie said. "The garage helps block the wind, and the fence keeps the dog from getting away when kids aren't outside playing with it. There's usually a house in there, too, but I guess the last renters didn't have a dog or took their doghouse with them."

Immediately the two little girls began dancing around their mother. "Can we have a dog? Can we? Can we? Can we?" they sang. Beth looked at Bobbie with a blank face. In all their discussions of moving up to Lawrence, pets had never come up. Dan had never let the girls have a pet. Bobbie wanted to give them this gift but didn't want to clean up after a dog on hot, humid days. Kathleen spoke up and temporarily saved Beth and Bobbie.

"Jimmy's here with the keys. Who wants to see their new bedroom and pick out where their new twin bed is going to go?" Kathleen had just the right tone of excitement in her voice because the little girls forgot their clamoring and ran for the back door.

"You owe me one," Kathleen said to the twins as she sauntered after the girls.

Bobbie closed her eyes and took a moment to be grateful that LeeAnn and Cara were still excited to see new bedrooms and even to pester their mom about a dog. These were the most normal kid things that had happened in their childhood in more than two weeks. Had it only been two weeks? The move was masterminded before Dan's attack, so that was part of what made it happen so quickly, but nonetheless, it was mindboggling how fast it had all happened. And yet, here were Gracie's little sisters just running around being normal little girls. How long would it take Gracie to get back to talking and thinking about anything normal again? What would normal even mean for her?

Bobbie heard her name called, and she turned to the house to join the girls' first tour. She beckoned Gracie to join them and waited for her. Bobbie longed to hold Gracie close and comb her fingers through the ash-brown hair that fell into her niece's eyes. How long would she be waiting for Gracie?

Chapter Ten

If moving was controlled chaos, then pandemonium was the word for unpacking and sorting through three households. Thursday, after the long drive, the landlord and a few of his friends had helped them unload the moving truck and position furniture throughout the house. Friday morning, Bobbie's friends from the junior college helped them pack and move the items from her old apartment, followed by Kathleen's stored furniture and boxes on Saturday. Getting everything into the house and garage, however, took a giant shoehorn. Unpacking to the final box was another thing.

Badgered and beaten up, but unbent and unyielding, Bobbie pushed onward. She decided she would have a working household before school began, and she recruited students to help. She tried to supervise, but she also realized it might take months to find some things.

Sunday afternoon, Sabrina, one of Bobbie's favorite students, stood by to assist as LeeAnn and Cara "helped" unpack their single box of clothing and a few toys in their large new bedroom. The girls gave her many hugs when she left.

"Can Sabrina come over to play someday?" Cara asked.

Bobbie laughed. "Maybe she could be your babysitter if we ever need one."

"Where did our beds come from?" LeeAnn asked her aunt, catching her off-guard.

"And the drawers?" Cara asked.

"The chest of drawers and twin beds belonged to your mother and me when we were your ages. That's why they match. Kathleen and I packed them up out of the barn into the moving truck before...well, before everything happened," Bobbie said.

LeeAnn drew a circle on the bed with her stuffed bear. "Is that why you and Kathleen drove the big white truck to our house and not your boat car?"

Bobbie took a deep breath. She knew this was coming. "Yes, we came down to Grandma's farm to get the furniture out of the barn so we could use it in this big house. Kathleen and I were going to be roommates here, and we wanted you, your mom, Gracie, and Cara to come live with us. But we didn't have enough beds."

"Oh," LeeAnn said.

"We don't have anything in the drawers. Well, most of them," Cara said.

"Then you can both have one for make-believe clothes. Don't

worry about it right now. What do you think about having your own bed?" Bobbie asked.

LeeAnn shouted, "I like it!"

"I want to sleep with LeeAnn, but she wouldn't let me last night." Cara bemoaned this fact with flailing arms and a theatrical sigh.

"What did you do?" Bobbie asked.

"I slept as close to the wall as I could. I guess it was okay."

Bobbie grinned. "Well, you know what's on the other side of that wall?"

Cara's eyes grew big, and she shook her head.

"My bed," Bobbie said. "And I heard you banging and kicking against the wall all night, so I know you slept some!"

LeeAnn laughed and put her hands in front of her face to hide it. "She used to do that next to me in the big bed. I would get bruises sometimes from sleeping beside her. She's noisy, I bet, huh, Aunt Bobbie?"

Cara crossed her arms, whirled around, and pouted.

"Oh, sweetie, I just wanted you to know that I'm right over there, and there's nothing to be scared of," Bobbie said. "Besides, if you stomp loud, your mom will hear you downstairs. Did you know that? Your room is right above the living room. So, if you go to bed and don't go to sleep, you'd better not get up and play, or we'll hear you, and then you'll be in trouble."

"Bobbie, can I talk to you?" Beth's voice came from the hallway.

Bobbie joined her in the den. Really a wide hallway, it was big enough for two desks, and the educators had claimed it for their offices. The other large bedroom was across the top of the stairs from this office. It had been broken up by some former renter into two smaller rooms separated by a half-wall. Beth had taken the back half of the room, and Gracie had been given the front. Beth had her double bed and Gracie won the furniture lottery. The ever-thoughtful landlord offered the new renters a log bunk bed that just perfectly fit that half of the room, in his opinion.

"It has a bed on top, but instead of a bottom bunk, there's a built-in kid's desk. When the last family left, it was too much trouble to move it out. And they didn't need it anymore. That makes you the lucky ones. Will the girl in this room use it?" Jimmy had asked.

"You bet," Bobbie told him. "She's a letter writer of biblical proportions. I'll even make sure she finds it all set up with stamps and a package of stationery, just waiting for her."

So far, much to their disappointment, Gracie hadn't opened stamps, the stationery, or the packages of gum the family had left. However, Beth seemed to take great comfort in walking into her room frequently when Gracie was there, checking up on her, Bobbie supposed. Given the layout of the house, it was the most privacy they could give the ten-year-old. And yet, it gave the adults some sense of security, false or not. Gracie had nightmares and cried out every night. She didn't want to be touched or held, just left alone after being awakened. At least one of them could hear and respond quickly, especially her mother.

"Are you listening to me?" Beth said in a voice that suggested it wasn't the first time she had said it.

Damn, woolgathering again and caught at it. "What do you want? I was spending some quality time with my nieces," Bobbie said.

"I said, don't do that—tell them we'll hear them, and they'll get in trouble and then make me the bad guy. If you want to threaten them that you'll be listening, you go right ahead, but don't make them scared of me. They were plenty scared of Dan, and I don't want that, now that I'm their only parent."

"Oh, come on now, Beth, we just had one parent, and we were scared of her plenty of times, and it didn't do us any harm. In fact, Mom put the fear of Mom in us pretty good, and it looks like we turned out just fine."

"When we were scared of Mom, it was because she was strict, not because she was going to beat us. That's what my girls were scared of, and I don't want them to be scared of me. What if they are afraid of that deep down?" Beth asked.

"You're overreacting. Like I said, we turned out just fine, and your girls are old enough to know the difference between you and that asshole you married."

Beth blushed a deep crimson. "Maybe you turned out 'just fine' but it looks like I didn't, and I don't want that for my girls." She left the den and walked quietly down the stairs.

If it had been up to Bobbie, she would have argued more or at least stomped down the stairs. They were wood and creaked. She had noticed and wondered about that in regards to how she and Kathleen were going to manage to have any intimate relationship without waking the household. Kathleen. Now that they were in the house, she could give some thought to Kathleen again. But first, she better figure out things with Beth. Otherwise, it could be a long evening of pouting.

****

"So, how do you like your new bedroom?" Bobbie said to Kathleen after dinner. "You're pretty special, you know, with the only bedroom on the ground floor and a bathroom to yourself. The five of us have to share the same toilet in the morning."

"Yes, but I have to traipse all the way upstairs to your tiny shower if I want anything other than a bath. And everyone who comes into this house, which is the entire town of Lawrence I swear, gets to see the color of my toothbrush if I forget to take it back to my room." Kathleen appeared to be in a good mood, even though they were unpacking books. Again.

Bobbie lowered her voice. "The other cool thing about your room is that it's the same as mine. Same walls, windows, and doors. Not much creativity in architecture here. And I noticed that we have located our beds in the same place, which means when you lay in bed at night looking up, you're staring at me, you pervert."

Kathleen laughed. "You're the pervert. I simply look up at night and wish you a good night's sleep, considering how busy your mind must be, what with all your thoughts of how you will organize this and manage that and plan something else. You're the Eleanor Roosevelt of the block, you know?" Kathleen managed to make that sound suggestive.

"I'm not sure what I think of that comparison. You could be saying I'm a feminist hero or a dead, rich woman with her fingers in many, many pies. Either way, I'll take it under advisement." Bobbie laughed, and Kathleen joined her. Bobbie stopped laughing and just looked at her lover.

"What now?" Kathleen asked.

"I can't believe we're here."

"Unpacking the last six boxes?" Kathleen dusted her hands off, tossed an empty box aside, and used her box cutter to open another.

"No, silly." Bobbie felt like her face was melting. "We're finally back in Lawrence, settling down in one house, ready to start a school year and help Gracie heal from all the horrible things that monster did to her. Sometimes, especially when we were sitting in the hospital, or right after we got her back to their house, I wondered if this day would ever come."

"Do we need to move this conversation to a room with a closed door?" Kathleen asked. "I lost track of where everyone got to after dinner."

"No. Beth got excited again when Cara asked, 'Mom, where's our new school?' and they walked up there to swing and maybe use the slide if it's cooled down enough."

Kathleen tipped her head to the side. The sunset through the window shone on her glasses, obscuring her eyes from Bobbie. "Gracie, too?"

"Yeah, they dragged her along with them. Which is good for her. She needs to be up and out in the sun a little. The heat of the day is over, but it's still light enough to swing. Or sit there, whatever. But back to us..."

Kathleen smiled and wiped her hands. She got up off the milk crate she'd been sitting on, knelt, and took Bobbie's face in her hands. She kissed her gently. "I've thought for many years about playing house with you. I've even thought about us having a family, but I expected dogs, not three kids and a sister-in-law. Three adults and three children in a four-bedroom house, even if it is two stories, are a lot of people in a tight space. Make two of those women lesbians, and when do we get to play our own little game of 'Lavender Jane Loves Women' without endangering them or us?" Her face was so earnest, it made Bobbie's eyes tear up.

Kathleen misunderstood. "Oh, Bobbie, no! I don't mean anything bad. I'm so glad they're here and safe. I want them here with us. I was just teasing about something serious. I'm in love with you, and I want to love on you, but I don't know how or when to do it without having one of the little girls see something. For example, what if LeeAnn mentioned it at school, and got all of us in trouble? We could lose our jobs, then they wouldn't have a place to live, and we would be removed from teaching. I mean..." She turned her head away before going on. "Would it be safer if I moved out and just came to visit, and then you could visit me in an apartment?"

"Don't you even dare think that!" Bobbie's voice rang in the still room. "Don't you know you're family to these little girls already? Who cared for them when Beth and I lived at the hospital for three days? Who takes care of Beth when I hurt her feelings? Who takes care of me when—" Her voice caught. "When the guilt catches up with me, and I remember that Dan was angry at me when he kidnapped Gracie, not at her? That it was my fault the whole thing happened? What would I do without you to hold me together when all my parts start to spin off into space?"

What had started as fear in her voice ended as a breathy pain in her side. It hurt. It hurt so deep in her side and in her chest, but she wouldn't take her eyes off Kathleen.

Kathleen turned back to her, met her eyes, and searched them, then she took Bobbie into her arms. "I won't, babe. I promise I won't. You'll never have to figure that out, and I'll always be here to hold you together. I'm not sure how this will work, but we'll make it work." She rested her cheek on Bobbie's and tugged on her hair. "No matter what happens, grief or pain or fear will not get the best of us. You aren't alone, neither is Beth, and neither is Gracie. I love you, Bobbie Rossi."

Bobbie leaned her head back to make eye contact. "I love you, Kathleen McCormick, and I have a lifetime worth of more things to tell you, but it's a good thing we're young because I hear Cara shrieking all the way down the block." She laughed. "So, kiss me and hand me a box of books before they charge up here to go to bed."

Kathleen winked at Bobbie. "You're the best officemate I

could ever want to have. And the sexiest, if I may say so."

"You may say so." Bobbie curled her hair around her finger and batted her eyelashes. "Now, why did we have to have a heart-to-heart when we could have been making whoopee?"

"Because you obviously don't know, or you would have mentioned it, the one difference between our identical bedrooms. Mine has a latch inside the door. I found it in some hardware in a coffee can in the garage and put it on while Jimmy was banging on the bathroom door. No one even knows but you. So, if you're nice, or even better if you're naughty, perhaps sometimes you'll get invited downstairs for a late-night, partial-night sleepover, my dear. How does that sound?" Kathleen waggled her eyebrows and wiggled a Groucho Marx imaginary cigar.

"Positively delicious," Bobbie said as the back door slammed. She pressed one last kiss to Kathleen's lips, then they broke apart and returned to filling the built-in bookshelves that wrapped around the top of the staircase, freeing up space for their little office love nest. She smiled as she thought of it that way and told herself she should tell Kathleen that's what they should call it, their office love nest.

Chapter Eleven

Bobbie's daydream jolted away when Kathleen tramped through the back door and dumped an armload of books on the dining room table. It took Bobbie a minute to reconnect to what she'd been doing with the papers spread out on the large table, and she blushed a little. But her red-headed lover didn't notice.

Kathleen slumped into a chair. "I've been teaching for six years and never had this much preparation, ever," she announced.

"Welcome to Lawrence County Junior College life," Bobbie said with a sweep of her arm above the spread-out papers and files she stood over. "There's a policy, manual, memo, and something else on every issue and subject possible. And that's before you start looking at curriculum."

"The curriculum may be the easiest part. That I can teach. Give me something simple like calculus any day." Kathleen rolled her shoulders and cracked her knuckles.

"I'm glad I have last year's things to build off, especially now," Bobbie said.

Kathleen looked around and listened. "Where is everyone?"

"Beth took Cara and LeeAnn walking up to their new school for the seven-thousandth time. They're incredibly excited. Gracie's sleeping."

"How's Beth doing today?"

Bobbie paused before answering. "I think those two keep her busy, and that's a good thing. She blames herself, which I understand, but she's crying, yelling, and getting it all out, which is pretty impressive considering they haven't even lived here a week yet. I guess we make her feel comfortable."

"What about Gracie?" They both hesitated at that question. They had to prompt Gracie to get up, to dress, to eat, to move into the living room.

"I don't know. The doctor said she would be in shock for a while, but this seems like a long time," Bobbie said. "I know she needs to talk with a professional. I've called the principal at the school, and the guidance counselor will be getting back to me. I also called the psychology department at the University of Kansas but haven't connected with a good person yet."

"And how are you?"

Bobbie began straightening the piles of books and pushing in chairs.

"Bobbie, how are you?" Kathleen asked again.

Bobbie held perfectly still, then she turned into the taller woman's arms. She couldn't keep the muscles in her face from knotting up, and she cried into the collar of Kathleen's shirt. Kathleen rocked her. When Bobbie's tears slowed, Kathleen grabbed a tissue from the box she had strategically located in every room. She directed Bobbie into the living room, toward the couch. They sat.

"I don't know. I still blame myself." Bobbie blew her nose. "He didn't want to rape Gracie. He wanted to rape me. What if I hadn't goaded him into it by showing up?" *Or just by existing?*

"You mean what if it had been postponed till you weren't there to help?"

"What if it would never have happened?" Bobbie asked.

"You know from what the doctor said—" Kathleen began to say.

"Molesting her maybe, I don't know, but that's not the same as rape. He raped Gracie." Bobbie crumpled into Kathleen's arms, fighting back sobs this time. Kathleen held her and rocked her again.

They stayed that way for a long time. Finally, Bobbie pulled back and wiped at her eyes. Kathleen grabbed another tissue.

"I think I might need to talk to somebody, too. This falling apart, this weakness, it's not helping Gracie."

Kathleen smiled. "Good girl. I know something else that will help you."

"What?" asked Bobbie.

"You're sleeping downstairs tonight."

"I can't." Her face grew hot as she looked to see if her sister or nieces were anywhere near home yet. It simply wouldn't do to be caught having this conversation.

"Yes, you can. I have a very quiet alarm. You can get up early and go back upstairs. Beth's still taking those sleeping pills, and the little girls will play in their room like they do every morning. I'm not pressuring you to do anything at the wrong time. I just want to hold you, and you can let it all go for one night's sleep." Kathleen could be quite persuasive.

Bobbie played with the end of one curl while she thought about it for a moment. "That would be so nice. Do you think we could pull it off?"

"Hey, babe, I've been casing the joint. It'll work," Kathleen said in her best gangster voice, rolling up imaginary sleeves.

"Your impersonations have always been terrible." Bobbie rolled her eyes but grinned.

"Yeah, but you love me."

"I do. I love you more than you'll ever know."

For a little while, they just looked at one another.

"And how are you?" Bobbie asked. "You've run the entire show without a day off since...since the beginning."

"I'm okay. I'm tired and I'm grieving for Gracie, but I'm getting by. I'm worried about you, Beth, and Gracie, and want you all talking to a professional this week."

Kathleen reached into her back pocket and pulled out a folded piece of paper. "I used the college phones and got a list of numbers that we, meaning you, are going to call now. Appointments all around are the soup of the day."

"Thanks. I hope we haven't asked too much of you."

"They're part of you, Bobbie, and I love you, and I love them, and we're all going to get through this together, right?"

"Right. Okay, phone calls it is. If Gracie's still asleep, I'll make them in the office."

"Why don't you make them in the office anyway? If she hears you, you can tell her you all need to talk with someone to help you. She needs to know help is coming," Kathleen said.

"Good point." Bobbie took a deep breath and swallowed hard. She was looking forward to a phone call for the first time in a long while, at least since before this July.

She jumped. Kathleen had said something, but she missed it. Kathleen hadn't noticed and was going on. "Besides, I'm going to make a mess out of the kitchen. It's been too long since I made anything hot, so it's sloppy joes and homemade French fries for dinner."

"You spoil us, Kathleen Marie."

"You're worth it, Roberta Ann."

"Okay, on my way. Back soon," Bobbie said.

"Good, I'm hungry."

****

At dinner, Bobbie made an announcement. "I have some good news. I've found a lady doctor who will see us all this Friday morning."

Gracie looked up, her eyes narrowing and looking a bit suspicious of the word "doctor." Bobbie and Beth had taken her to a couple of those since moving to Lawrence and many more before that.

"She's going to talk to us all as a family, and then we'll make appointments to talk to her individually." Bobbie watched the entire family for their responses. It wouldn't do to have anyone left out or resisting when what they all needed was help. Surely everyone would welcome a professional's opinion, wouldn't they?

"Will I get a shot?" Cara asked, her hands clenched on her

shoulders and her body upright and rigid. LeeAnn's eyebrows shot up at the suggestion.

"No, this is a talking doctor. But I thought you two could go with Kathleen to the flea market that day and look for some things we still need. I have a whole shopping list for you."

Kathleen gave a melodramatic groan and slumped forward, but the girls loved the idea.

"What can we buy? Can we have some money? Will it be ours to share or will it belong to the whole house?" They asked above one another.

"Your mom, Gracie, and I will talk to this doctor for a while and then meet you at home to see what you bought. Okay?" Bobbie asked.

Everyone agreed except for Beth, who looked embarrassed, and Gracie, who looked down at her sloppy joe.

"Okay, that's a plan then." Bobbie couldn't wait for everyone to get excited about the idea. Hell, she was scared, too, but if it helped, it was worth it.

Chapter Twelve

Gracie didn't listen when Mom and Aunt Bobbie told her about Dr. Langston and the family therapy. Her mom helped her dress, and her Aunt Bobbie took her hand until they got to the outer office door, where she balked. "No."

"You have to go," Beth said.

"Oh, honey," Bobbie said. "This doctor is going to help all of us feel better—"

"How?" Gracie asked.

"By talking with us, answering questions, and helping us handle our emotions, I guess," Bobbie said.

Gracie stared at them and refused to go through the door.

"Sorry, but you're going. It's not a choice." Beth pushed her into the waiting room.

Gracie didn't sit down and stood with her arms crossed in front of her, not moving until it was time for their appointment. A slim woman with a brown bob and a pleasant face opened the inner office door and followed an older woman to the hallway entrance. "I'll see you next week."

She turned to them. "You must be the Brown family. Please, come in."

Beth and Bobbie stood and walked toward the office, but Gracie didn't. Beth gave her a slight push to get her moving. It took less of a shove to get her into the inner office than it had into the waiting room. She scowled and doubled up her efforts to appear uninterested. Once in the office, she walked to a large window overlooking shorter buildings and a park with trees and sidewalks. She studied the park carefully.

"Gracie, turn around and sit down," Beth said.

Gracie didn't say anything or move.

"Gracie—"

The doctor interrupted her mom. "Excuse me, but why don't we let Gracie look out the window?" she said. "I'm sure she's listening, and if we get something wrong, she'll help correct us. What I'd like to do today is get to know you a little bit better. I spoke with Ms. Rossi on the phone. May I call you Bobbie?"

"Yes, and this is my sister, Beth Brown."

"My name is Dr. Langston. I'd like to get some more information from you, Bobbie, and from you, Beth, and from you, Gracie, if you would like to share today. Let's start with

why you're here in Lawrence, since I understand you recently
moved, and here in my office."

Gracie leaned against the window. Everything reflected in its
heavy glass. Dr. Langston sat waiting. Bobbie and Beth looked at
one another. The wall clock ticked louder than Gracie's breathing,
which already rasped as loud as a rusty box fan.

Beth sat up straighter and took a deep breath. Knotting her
fingers on her lap, she said, "We're here—"

Gracie whirled, glaring at her mom with fury and venom. Beth
cringed. When Beth stopped talking, Gracie's shoulders gradually
dropped, and she turned back to the window.

Rigid and silent, she threw daggers at the reflection. Bobbie
sat without any words. Beth didn't make a sound. After forever,
Dr. Langston spoke.

"Well, that was an intense moment. It looks like your daughter
doesn't want you to talk about why you're here. But, Gracie, you
don't appear willing to explain it to me either. So, let's set the
question of why you're here aside for the moment and talk about
what happened just now. Is that okay?"

Beth and Bobbie nodded but Gracie didn't move. "Beth, does
Gracie often try to control or limit what you say?"

"No. That was the first time ever," her mom said.

"That says to me that this is a very important subject to Gracie,
one that feels like it isn't safe to discuss. Is that true? Is that why
you're here, in Lawrence and in my office? Because it's so scary
that it feels unsafe to talk about, especially to a stranger?"

Gracie waited until her bones felt as though they were going to
jump out of her skin before she spoke, her voice strained with
anger and fear. "None of your business," she said, still facing the
window.

"In some ways, you're right," Dr. Langston said. "How do you
know if you can trust me? Tell me, Gracie, what could I do so you
would trust me enough to let your mother and aunt tell me why
they're here? Not your part of the story, but theirs."

Gracie dropped her arms as she whipped around to face the
doctor. "I'll never trust anyone again." Her voice rose, and she
tried to push it down into her throat and stomach. "If I don't trust
you, you can't hurt me, right?" She shifted from one foot to the
other, wanting to run out the door and down to the park to hide.

"Oh, kiddo," Dr. Langston said. "I'm sorry, but in life, you get
hurt whether you trust or not. Getting hurt is part of life. What we
do is learn how to get hurt as little as possible, how to take good
care of ourselves when we do get hurt, and how to get help to heal
those hurts. The only way not to get hurt is to stay in bed the rest of
your life."

"I will."

"I'm sorry, Gracie. I shouldn't have used that example because you can't really do that. You could do it for a day now and then, but not forever. But I shouldn't be doing the talking. Our session is about you, and what you think and feel. What does trusting feel like to you?"

Gracie stared at her.

"Okay," Dr. Langston said. "Can you tell me how your body feels right now?"

Gracie's shoulders and jaw hurt. She had a headache and a terrible stomachache. Her legs hurt even worse in that restless kind of way, wanting to run. Her chest burned from holding her breath.

"No!" she shouted and ran for the door.

Dr. Langston was faster than Gracie expected. She and Bobbie hit the door first. "I can tell it doesn't feel safe talking," the doctor said. "There's a beanbag chair in the space beneath my desk. You could still hear us talk, but it would be like your own little room. Would that space feel safer to you now?"

Gracie's hair fell into her eyes as she nodded.

Dr. Langston pointed the way without touching Gracie. "There. You can listen from here until we finish. It won't be long."

Gracie crawled onto the cold, vinyl beanbag beneath the desk and faced away from the light. She heard the doctor and her Aunt Bobbie return to their seats. She only caught snippets of the rest of the conversation, names and ages of her sisters, safe things like that. She closed her eyes and drifted away.

In no time at all, her mom was touching her legs. "Gracie, it's time to go home. Are you ready?"

She bumped her head on the desk getting out. It had been safer than the room, but she was ready to get in her own safest bed.

"I'll see you next week, Gracie," Dr. Langston said.

Gracie didn't respond but they wouldn't see one another if she had anything to say about it.

Chapter Thirteen

Bobbie sat in the Pinto for a few moments to think after Beth and Gracie got out at home. The family therapy had not gone well, but she guessed it could have been worse. It turned out okay. Gracie was far more tuned in than she thought. She saw the boat pulling up in her rearview mirror, so she went to help Kathleen, LeeAnn, and Cara unload the floor-to-ceiling bags in the backseat.

"I didn't give you that much money," Bobbie said to Kathleen.

"It's a flea market," Kathleen said. "I got all of this in exchange for a finger painting and the promise of a batch of cookies. Besides, Nixon's resignation today was the talk of the adults and I thought I should distract the girls until I found out what Beth wants to tell them about it. I know what I'd say."

"I'm sure you do, Kat. Let's go see what you got," Bobbie said. Kat smirked and bumped her hip against Bobbie's as she passed on the way toward the back porch.

When the adults finally sat down at the dining room table, Kathleen whispered to Cara and LeeAnn. They ran off and brought back bags from the piles.

"Gracie," Kathleen said, "your sisters got you a couple of posters for your room and a comforter. Why don't you all go up and put them in good places? There's tape on my desk."

Gracie followed the stampede to her room. They disappeared, and when the adults could hear the discussion begin about where to put the pony and dolphin posters, Kathleen queried the other two. "So, how did it go?"

Beth surprised Bobbie by speaking first. "Wow. It was intense. Gracie tried to scare-stare me into not talking. She was terrified, furious, and tried to run out the door, but Dr. Langston and Bobbie caught her. She ended the session under Dr. Langston's desk. Which reminds me, could you sit in the waiting room while we're in there for a few weeks? I know it would be a boring, probably useless hour for you, but it might give her a safe place in case she needs to run. But back to your question, I think she's cool."

"I'd be glad to be your kiddo's safety valve for a while," Kathleen said.

Bobbie followed. "She seems to be a good doctor. I hope she's right for adults and kids. I don't think I'll see her except as a group."

"Yes, you will." Kathleen was blunt.

"Excuse me?" Bobbie asked.

Kathleen repeated herself. "Yes, you will. Is this your fault?"

"Yes, but—" Bobbie said.

"But nothing. If you still feel it's your fault, you'll see her."

Bobbie and Beth gave her the eye. "Look, we want everyone to heal. Please, Bobbie?"

Bobbie grumbled, then glared, then acquiesced.

"What about Gracie?" Kathleen continued.

"Dr. Langston's very sweet," Beth said, "and I think she'll be good. She has some children's books and a few dolls in one corner of her office. I saw Gracie look at them."

"I'm glad to hear that. You all go on Fridays?" Kathleen asked.

"For now," Bobbie said. "Until we work through a few months, and then we'll see what needs to happen. I want Gracie to see her as long as she needs to, no matter what."

"I've been thinking about that," Beth said, picking at her cuticles. "You know, there's no way I can start school this fall. My mind just isn't there." She met Bobbie's eyes. "I thought I'd look for a job during school. That way I could watch the girls and pay our bills at the same time."

"Beth, you—" Bobbie was cut off by her sister.

"Don't 'Beth, you,' me, Bobbie. I need to do this. I need to feel more stable before I start another 'something big and new.' And I need to pull my weight."

"Shouldn't the girls get some survivor's benefits?" Kathleen asked.

"We should consider that. I'm sure there's a pile of paperwork to do," Bobbie said. "The county fire department will be sending all the stuff up here for you to fill out for Dan's life insurance policy. That will cover the bills, or I will."

Beth shook her head. "Not this time. I'm the head of the house, and I will. Besides, that money needs to go in the bank just in case something happens that I can't cover with work. I can get a job at the school, I bet, and have the same hours the girls do."

Bobbie opened her mouth to respond, but Kathleen cut off her response. "I think that's a good plan."

Bobbie glared at Kathleen.

Kathleen shook her head at Bobbie, then continued. "Beth, could you cook dinner? Would you mind? I have questions for Dr. Rossi about my employment paperwork, which to my great dismay still is not complete, despite the piles and piles I've turned in."

"Sure. I'll call up to you when it's done," Beth said.

Bobbie followed Kathleen, stomping on the creakiest steps. "What was that about, agreeing with her?" She crossed her arms and stood with her feet planted where she could tower over the taller woman who was seated at her desk.

Kathleen looked up at Bobbie. The reflection on her glasses hid her eyes and any signs she wasn't taking Bobbie's feelings seriously. "You heard her. She said she doesn't want to start school now. That means she's planning to start school at some point. You've been waiting for her to make that decision. You have to let her time it. She's an adult, and she's right, you can't pay for everything. It's not good for you or her. She's a single mom now and will be for the foreseeable future. Let her do her thing."

Bobbie stuck out her lower lip and frowned but didn't say anything while she considered how wise her lover was and how much it ticked her off sometimes. Like now.

"Come on, pouter, you know I'm right. Besides, if you let her make her own decisions, I'll let you fill out my papers. Deal?" Kathleen grinned.

Bobbie smiled just a tiny bit, took out a pen, and sat down.

Chapter Fourteen

Life goes on. Bobbie doodled philosophical-sounding phrases as she peered out the second-story window beside her desk. And each of us struggles in our own way. But there were some moments of triumph. A clean, pre-semester, post-syllabi-writing desk was one. Footsteps on cement made her look out the window again. Beth was running up the walk. Bobbie headed downstairs to hear the news.

The porch door slammed, and Beth ran into the kitchen. "I got it! I got it!"

"Got what?" Kathleen asked from the front room.

"I got the job in the cafeteria. It means I'll be on the same schedule as the girls, so when they're out, I'm out. No child care." Beth went into the dining room.

"That's great," Bobbie said.

"How wonderful." Kathleen gave her a high five.

"I don't know what I'll do over the summer, but I'll figure something out," Beth said.

"Probably sweat like the rest of us," Bobbie said.

"Yeah, you're a funny one. But seriously, I told them I'll be walking the girls to school, so I'll be in a little late and just stay later to help with all the cleanup and prep for the next day. It's the best job ever," Beth said.

"Does that mean you have to wear a hairnet?" Kathleen asked, wide-eyed and innocent.

"Even if I shave my head, silly," Beth said.

"Eww, don't do that." Kathleen shivered.

"This is coming from the woman with the shortest hair," Bobbie said.

"Shorter but not shaved," Kathleen answered.

They sat and listened while Beth gave more details about her job.

"But don't plan on walking the girls to school in the dead of winter," Bobbie told her sister. "Winters here can be brutal."

"They can't be that much worse than winters in Cottonwood Plains," Beth said and gave her sister one of Bobbie's own patented eye rolls.

"You still don't want to walk both ways," Bobbie said.

"Well, the pickup won't take four of us." Beth smoothed her hand along the edge of the table.

"Just listen for once. I can drive the pickup to work, and you can drive the boat," Bobbie said.

Kathleen interrupted their argument. "I've been wondering about something. It's a little off the subject but not all the way."

Bobbie and Beth listened, but not until sticking their tongues out at one another.

"What are you going to do with the farm?"

The twins looked at one another. Bobbie got the impression that Beth hadn't thought about it either.

"Why do you still have it?" Kathleen asked.

"Well," Beth said, "there was always a possibility that Dan and I could move out there, but he wanted to stay in town, even though the farm would be free. And maybe Bobbie would want to come back."

Bobbie coughed twice, glad no one could read her mind. "There's not a lot of land left, just enough money from the renters of it to cover the property taxes. And then there's the site with the house and outbuildings." Beth frowned.

Kathleen said, "I know nothing about farms and farmland, but it's got to be worth something, and you don't want to keep it, do you?"

"No!" the twins cried, almost as one.

"I guess we can sell it," Beth said.

"Maybe you and Bobbie could get new cars and still have some left for savings, or retirement, or the girls' education, or whatever you want," Kathleen said.

"Great idea, but what's wrong with my car?" Bobbie asked.

"It's a boat," the other two said, grinning at one another.

"It's old, it will need repairs, it sucks gas, it's expensive, and need I go on?" Kathleen added.

Bobbie pouted. "I've had that car since forever."

"I know. That's part of the problem," Kathleen said. "But you can always name the new one 'boat two' if that would make it better."

Beth laughed then grew quiet. "I never want to go back there."

Silence fell, heavy like a falling tree by the creek or hay bale from the loft, an almost deadly silence. Bobbie's throat constricted.

"Why don't you wait until spring," Kathleen said, faint traces of her Chicago Irish heritage showing in her voice and cadence. "Unless that's a bad time to sell a farm site. Or let a real estate agent handle it for you."

"An agent now might be a better idea," Beth said. "If someone wants the land, they may want to plant milo in the spring. It's too late to sell it for some things, but who knows what someone will want to do with it?"

"I'll call the neighbors and get the names of some local

agents," Bobbie said. "We'll get rid of the damned thing as soon as possible." She walked upstairs, her mind whirling. As she climbed the steps, she heard Beth talking.

"This cafeteria lady will get some practice by making dinner. Any requests?"

Kathleen soon followed Bobbie and took a seat at her desk facing her love. The phone cord was stretched from the telephone table between their desks to Bobbie's chair, where she sat facing the wall, tapping a pencil.

She placed the phone less than gently on the cradle on her desk. "No one inside. It's too early. I'll call again tonight."

"You know the number off the top of your head?" Kathleen asked.

"It's been their number since I was a child, so yes."

"Hey, I just asked."

"Hey, I just answered. No, wait, I'm sorry. Your question about the farm. It's got me...pissed off." Bobbie turned back toward the wall and began tapping again.

Kathleen came around and sat on the end of Bobbie's desk. She leaned over and spoke very softly, her breath ruffling Bobbie's hair. "It's okay. It's a pretty pissy subject to begin with. But feel whatever you feel. We didn't leave anyone behind on the farm before, and we won't leave you there this time either, girlie." She kissed Bobbie on top of her head. Then she went back downstairs to help with dinner.

Chapter Fifteen

Bobbie was the first one home on Tuesday and took advantage of the quiet house to start some business calls. Her first call was to the bank in Cottonwood Plains.

"May I speak with Mr. Moore?" she asked the secretary, hoping he still worked there.

"Bob Moore speaking." A gruff voice answered the transferred call. It softened when she explained who she was. "Little Bobbie Rossi. Fancy you calling me from the big city. I heard you were here this summer, but what with the tragedy and all, I wasn't surprised that we never ran into one another. Is your sister doing all right now? She moved, and I hope she's moved up near you."

"Yes, we're roommates, as a matter of fact. And I'm calling about selling the farm. Since the tragedy, neither one of us has the desire to go back there. But I don't know the best way to go about doing that, and you're the businessman I know best and trust most in town, so I figured you would have some options. What are your suggestions?"

"Well, I would hate to lose your business. I helped you set up your first savings account when you were what, eight? I suppose the best advice I can give you is to talk to a real estate agent. What you're selling isn't a farm anymore. It's what people around here call a house with an acreage. You don't need a farm expert. You need a real estate man."

"Do you have one for me?" Bobbie asked, drumming her fingertips on her desk calendar.

"That I do. A new guy in town. Not exactly new, I guess. He's been here two years, but he knows rural and city selling. You may need those dual talents."

"What do you mean?" Bobbie asked, biting back her impatience. "You lost me there."

"The Chuvarsky place sold last winter in a deal like yours, but it sold to a family from Denver who wanted a summer home and a place to come for hunting season or holidays. Dustin handled that for them."

"Then Dustin sounds like my man. Do you have his number?"

"I can do better than that. I can hand the phone to him. He's sitting in my office with me, talking high school football. Here he is."

A soft-spoken man came on the line. "Well, Miss Rossi, what

can I do for you?"

Bobbie ran over the highlights of the farm and asked his opinion.

"I can list it both ways, as a farm house with limited acreage for locals who want out of town and as a getaway or retirement home for city folk. You know farm values are skyrocketing, and this is a great time to sell. May Mr. Moore have permission to take me out and show me around the place if he's been there before? He's nodding his head, yes. He's been there before. If so, I can fax you the information I'll need from you and my information for you to keep. We can set up the deal long distance with faxed signatures, but to close on a deal the owners or one of the owners, carrying the other's proxy, will need to come out here. Is that doable?"

"That, sir, would be wonderful." Bobbie wondered if he could hear the smile in her voice. "Do you have any idea how fast the farm, I mean house, might sell?"

"Depends on how much you want for it, who's looking, and how you hold your tongue when the wind's blowing from the north. But it might be quick." Dustin sounded confident and competent.

Bobbie concluded her business and copied down the numbers in a more orderly fashion to show Beth and Kathleen after dinner. She bet this post-meal announcement would create the most excitement they'd shared in quite a while.

Chapter Sixteen

Gracie's Top-Secret Journal Entry

Today was my first day of private therapy
with Dr. Langston. I was supposed to have an
hour with her by myself, but I wouldn't go.
So, I just went back to her office with Aunt
Bobbie for a few minutes after Mom got done
talking with her privately. I didn't want to
say anything. Dr. Langston said that was okay
and she wanted to tell me about what would
happen in therapy.

I've never been to a therapist before, so
I didn't know what to expect. She said we'd
mostly talk, but we could also write or draw
or play with her dolls. Her dolls aren't like
Barbies. They're more like real little kids
with all the real body parts. When I saw that
one of the girl dolls had boobies and kind of
looked like me I put it down and went to the
other side of the office. She asked me if
there was a reason and I shook my head.
Instead of talking about it more, she just
pointed out the park you can see from her
window and told me what it's called, but I
forgot. It has a lot of sidewalks, and her
office is pretty high up, so you can see most
of it.

The only really good part of the session,
which is what the hour is called, is that she
gave me this journal. Mom promised to buy me a
diary back in Cottonwood Plains. She said
since I'm getting so grown up and like to
write so much she'd get me one at the
Woolworth's where she worked. It would have a
little lock and two little keys, one you'd
hide and one you'd wear around your neck all
the time, so your little sisters couldn't read
it. This one is even cooler. It is taller and
thicker, and it has a lock, but it is a dial
and it has all the letters in a circle, and
only a secret code will open the journal, and
I doubt my little sisters could guess it.

I can write in it anytime, EVEN DURING
SCHOOL if I'm upset. But I don't think I want
to take it to school, what if I lost it? So, I
can write on notebook paper and copy it into

the journal. Dr. Langston wants me to bring it
to therapy. She says I don't have to show her
what I write, but she'd like for me to read
some of it to her or I could let her read it
if that is easier. She says sometimes that's
easier than talking. And we can talk about the
things that bug me, or make me sad or angry,
or whatever is in my journal. I don't know
about this doctor. She seems okay, but I'm not
going back to therapy, so that's just too bad.
What I do know is that this is a cool journal.

Chapter Seventeen

Beth went to her room the next Friday night and checked on Gracie as she always did. Gracie either slept or faked it quite well, with slow and steady breaths. Beth breathed easier, too. At least some. She reached out and knocked on the wooden nightstand. She hoped this would be a night without a nightmare, without the fast, shallow breathing, and mumbling or even crying out that kept Beth aware that Gracie remembered and always would.

Beth sat down on her bed, unable to do anything else but brood and grieve. She was a monster. Something went on for who knows how long, and she never knew it. What kind of mother was she, her child abused and her not knowing? If Bobbie had lived with them, she would have noticed something funny. Her eyes landed on her last school photos of the girls, sitting on the nightstand. That photo was burned into her retina as the last professional documentation of Gracie's childhood. She had seen that photo in her mind once before that day, as she spoke with Dr. Langston.

****

"Beth, did you sexually abuse Gracie?" the doctor had asked.

"No!" Beth's hand flew to her chest and she shrank back, before she could catch herself.

"Then it's not your fault."

"But it is. I never saw it. Even with her not sleeping well, I still never saw it."

"Well, then, maybe part of it is your responsibility," Dr. Langston said.

This time she sat stunned, tears blurring her vision.

"Beth," Dr. Langston spoke gently, "you married Dan and made a life with him. You did your best to raise a family with him. If you'd been gifted with magic vision, you might have seen what he was doing. But you didn't see it. And that's something you'll have to live with as long as you choose to blame yourself. You've told me several times how you see yourself as a monster. Tell me again why."

Beth focused on the photograph on the wall above the doctor's head. It was of two young children holding hands. She saw Gracie's face on the girl, and her heart ached. She took a shaky breath. "I'm a monster because I didn't protect my daughter. If I had, this never would have happened. I'm as much an animal as Dan was, maybe more. He had to be crazy to do what he did, but I'm sane, at least, I think I am, and I let him hurt my Gracie. I'm a terrible mother." She broke down in sobs and couldn't speak anymore.

Dr. Langston let her cry until the tears eased up. "I want you to look at me and listen carefully. Dan was a man who made horrific, perhaps even evil, choices. You were a sane woman caught in an insane situation. You can choose to believe it was your fault, or you can choose to put the blame on the man who took the actions. As far as being Gracie's mother, the mother of an abused and raped child, you're correct, you are. And you will always be. The question is, does seeing yourself as a monster help Gracie and her sisters? Or does it distance you from them? You'll have to learn to live with what happened. The question is where to go from that point."

Beth nodded and wiped her eyes.

"Does that make sense? Tell me what you heard me say."

"That it was Dan who decided to attack Gracie, and that I'm deciding to see myself as a monster, and that doesn't help my girls," Beth said.

"And it doesn't help you, either. You're not just a mom, you're a woman with a future and feelings, too. You're going to have to learn to live with some of these feelings and how to let some of them go, or you'll drive yourself sick with guilt and shame, and then you won't be useful to yourself or your family."

"So, I have to see myself not as a monster," Beth said, tears starting again.

"But not as a victim either. You're making a new life for yourself and your girls. You took them out of that town with bad memories and associations, and you brought them to a new, healthier place. You're helping them get what they need to move on, new schools, and a new family. You're resilient, Beth. You and Gracie are both fighters. You did survive. That's a strength you need to hold on to. You're not a monster, but no one can convince you of that but yourself. Can you let go of that picture of yourself?"

"It'll be hard. I feel so much guilt at not protecting her." Beth looked down at her lap. Her throat constricted around every word.

"Then you'll have to learn to live without it disabling your relationship with your girls. It can be done, and it's also possible to learn to let that guilt go away and place it on the person who deserves it. That takes time and effort. Will you give it both? For your daughters' sakes and your own?"

"I'll try," Beth said. *Damn those tears.*

"Good, that's the first step. Why don't you do some writing

this week? Some journaling, especially if you have those feelings again. Tell me how you felt and why. Remember our conversation and write about how the two are related. Bring the pages in next week. We'll look at them together and get a little insight."

"Okay."

"Beth, I promise you, if you do the work, you won't always feel this horrible. Okay?"

"Okay."

****

Beth found herself still sitting on the bed, her hands shaking. She was torn between seeking some much-needed oblivion and writing about how she felt. She decided she better get out the journal that Dr. Langston insisted on and make the effort. She picked it up, opened it on her lap, and began.

> I. Am. A. Monster. What sort of mother lets her ten-year-old daughter be raped by her father? I am a horrible mom. I should have seen it or sensed it or something. Why couldn't she tell me? Why didn't I know? Her life is ruined and it's my fault. I hate myself, I really hate myself.

Beth's fingers hurt from gripping the pen so tightly, and she shook out her hand to let the words flow. Tears ran down her face, blurred her vision, and wet the page. But she kept writing.

> Dr. Langston says it wasn't my fault. But I don't believe her. I know Dan did the abusing, but I let it happen somehow, in my house, down the hall from my bed. I look in the mirror, and I see a horrible person staring back at me—a weak, spineless, useless woman who couldn't even protect her baby. I want to die.

She couldn't continue writing. It couldn't be what Dr. Langston wanted, but it didn't matter. That was what was in her heart. It was all she could think, over and over. She couldn't die. She had three daughters to raise, three girls who needed her, including one whose life would never be the same. She couldn't just quit, though she longed to. She still felt furious, she realized, as she laid the journal aside to wipe her eyes. But the tears came faster and harder as her heart poured out its woundedness. She began to sob and stuffed her hand in her mouth to stifle the sound. Gracie was in the next room and would hear her. She tried to cry in silence but couldn't hide the moans that leaked out from her broken spirit. She fell over toward the head of the bed and lost it.

She didn't hear Gracie climb down from the bunk bed in the other room. She didn't hear anyone enter her half of the bedroom. But someone laid the quilt from the bottom of Beth's mattress up over her shoulders. Through puffy eyes, she looked up and saw Gracie staring at her from the foot of the bed, her expression unreadable. Beth watched her daughter turn and leave the room. She hadn't said a word, but there was no question an angel had visited.

Chapter Eighteen

Bobbie took a seat but huddled on the edge of the couch. She rubbed her fingers over her perch, so smooth she could hardly find a place to hold on. Lately, she felt as though she barely scratched a toehold on life.

Dr. Langston's voice broke her reverie. "Bobbie, You look like a bird in a storm. Do you have something specific to talk about?"

"Yes," Bobbie said. "I've been thinking about it a lot lately, and I feel so guilty, I have to tell someone. It's a long story. Can I tell you?"

"Please, tell me." The therapist nodded her head, and her brown bob swung in agreement.

"I used to be the girls' favorite, I guess only, but still favorite, aunt. Maybe special is a better word. I would show up with surprises like books, candy, and a trip for Gracie to sleepover camp, or even weekend sleep-away trips for all of us to the Wichita River Festival or the Oklahoma City Zoo. The sorts of things I thought they would love, but you see, I did them without thinking of the ramifications for the girls or Beth. Last year was my first year as an instructor at Lawrence County Junior College, but I lived like I was still a Ph.D. student, so I had money to treat them a little."

She drew up her knees even closer to her chest. "I pushed Dan's buttons with these trips over the summer. And I just kept pushing. I knew he hated me from back as long ago as high school, and I knew that my success, my getting out of our little town in the middle of nowhere and being in a city...anyway, my success made him furious. I hurt his pride in high school, and here I was having what he wanted and couldn't have. And I flaunted it this summer..." She tuned out for a moment.

"Bobbie? I asked you, what did he do?" Dr. Langston asked. "How did he respond?"

"He banned me from visiting. And we weren't visiting this time. Kathleen and I went down to my mother's farm, our farm now, Beth's and mine, to get some furniture for the big house we were going to rent so Beth could move the girls and come up here to live with us. We just happened to stop in town. Okay, I knew Dan usually went to the lake on his two days off, and we dropped by just for a hug..." Her voice trailed off into the air, as lost as her vision.

Dr. Langston waited a few seconds. "And then?"

"That's when he caught me, kidnapped Gracie, and burnt down the barn after raping her." She blew out a deep breath and rubbed her hands on her knees.

"I'm not sure I understand. Can you tell me—"

"What's important is that it's my fault, Doctor. I knew he was dangerous. I was trying to get Beth to leave him because he was so mean to the girls and abusive to her. Why couldn't I pay attention and put the two together, that my actions would have results for the ones stuck living there? It was like my fall from grace, to use an unrelated metaphor, and I am guilty, guilty, guilty." She put her head in her hands, and tears fell between her fingers.

Bobbie felt a tissue box against her leg. She took it and Dr. Langston waited. When only the occasional gasp shook her, and she looked up, the doctor spoke to her.

"You're right about the metaphor 'fall from grace,' if not for the unfortunate use of the word grace. I think the more theological use of the words sounds like a very apt title for how you feel right now. You told me a great deal of what you did. Can you tell me more about how you feel?"

"I feel horrible. Wouldn't you? It's all my fault. If I hadn't done those things, this never would have happened, and Gracie would either be living with me anyhow or still living in Cottonwood Plains—"

"Still being abused," Dr. Langston said. "I'm sorry to interrupt you, Bobbie, but you're telling me what you did, not how you feel. There's a big difference. How you feel now is what I'm interested in."

"I told you I feel horrible."

"Can you describe horrible a little more? I know you're an English professor, so give me some adjectives and adverbs or similes or metaphors. Describe it in your body."

Bobbie looked at her like she was a five-legged calf. "I feel...I feel cold and clammy." She paused. "I feel lightheaded. I feel like I need to throw up."

"That's good. That's very descriptive." Dr. Langston clasped her hands before her.

"No, I honestly need to throw up..." Bobbie grabbed her bag and hurried from the room.

She dashed through the waiting room, tossed her purse to Beth, who sat waiting for family therapy with Gracie, and ran down the hall to the restroom where she lost her lunch.

But none of the horrible feelings.

Chapter Nineteen

Bobbie stomped up the stairs, feeling as dark and cloudy as the summer thunderheads that often hung above the Kansas prairies. She took perverse delight in hitting every creaky board on the way. She might be too old to yell, too mature to cuss, and too angry to cry, but dammit, if that didn't feel just a tiny bit good.

"I thought you were all three of the girls coming back from the playground with Beth," Kathleen said from the desk. "You do know how to make an entrance."

Bobbie stopped on the top stair when she heard her voice. Dammit. So much for some alone time. She swung around the corner into the office, slammed her journal down on top of her desk, and dug in the top drawer for a new pen.

Kathleen, her usual unflappable self, watched as Bobbie grew more and more frustrated in her search. "May I loan you one of my pens?"

"No."

"May I give you one?" She held out a pen, easily in Bobbie's reach.

"No."

"What's wrong?"

"Everything. Nothing. You wouldn't understand. Does it matter?" Bobbie slammed the drawer.

"All righty then, you're pissed. Want to talk?"

"No." Bobbie walked to her bedroom and sat down on the bed.

Kathleen followed her. "Let me rephrase that. Let's talk. May I come in?"

Bobbie glared at her but didn't say no. Maybe she did want someone to listen to her and to lean on.

Kathleen came in, closed the door, and sat on the chair beside the dresser. "Sometimes life sucks."

"No shit, Sherlock."

"So, what sucks the worst?"

"Having a nosy lover," Bobbie said.

"If that's the worst, then things aren't so bad." Kathleen leaned forward. She looked so earnest. Bobbie couldn't take it.

"It's not funny. Life sucks right now. Classes start in less than a week. I'm nowhere near ready. Half my book list hasn't come in yet. And Gracie still isn't speaking at therapy." Bobbie turned her face away from Kathleen.

"I bet it's the last one that has you the most upset," Kathleen said.

Bobbie glanced back and glared at her, afraid of having the scab pulled off the great wound in her heart.

"It's not?" Kathleen asked.

"No. Now why don't you leave me alone? I have work to do, lots of work, and I won't be down for dinner." She decided that Kathleen was too annoying in her willingness to listen.

"You skipped lunch, too."

"Would you stop watching me?" Bobbie asked. "Every time I turn around you're there watching me with those big old eyes, looking like you know what's happening, like you understand everything. Well, you don't. You don't understand shit."

"Good thing we don't have a dog. Would you like to kick me instead?" Kathleen asked.

"Dammit, Kat. I'm serious. I can't focus with you being so damned solicitous. Could you be wrong for once? Could you just stay out of my hair on one thing?" Bobbie stood up and stalked over to the wall, balancing a hand on the headboard of the bed.

"Which one thing?" Kathleen asked.

"I'm counting to ten. Get out," Bobbie said through her teeth.

"No, I'm serious, too. Which one thing do you want me to stay out of your hair about?" Kathleen asked again.

Bobbie's shoulders sagged as her anger suddenly dissipated. "I just want everybody out of my head for a while."

"It's not just me?" Kathleen asked.

Bobbie almost got whiplash on her way to shoot a dagger of a glare at Kat.

"Now don't get mad all over again. I'm just trying to figure out what's going on with you. You're miserable, disorganized, and you avoid everyone. Spill it, Bobbie. What is it you want from us?"

"It's not you. It's her." Just saying that made Bobbie's stomach acid churn up in her throat, and she could taste it there waiting to burn a hole in her heart.

"Beth? Gracie?"

"God, no. Dr. Langston, if you must know," Bobbie said, refusing to make eye contact.

"So, she's gotten into your head. That's probably a good thing for a shrink."

"Well, she doesn't just listen, she gives advice, and I'm sick of it." Bobbie retreated to face the wall again. She peeled a blue paint chip off the old wallpaper seam. It was all coming apart.

"What advice this time?"

"I just said I'm sick of it, so drop it," Bobbie said with an exasperated stomp of her foot.

"No. If I'm getting yelled at for it, I deserve to know what it is."

Bobbie looked up at the ceiling. Kathleen waited.

"Okay. We've been talking about what happened, obviously. Mostly about whose fault it is."

Kathleen waited some more.

Bobbie heaved a huge sigh. "She said that the choice to go into town was mine, and the choice to rape Gracie was Dan's. And that's it."

"That's it?" Kathleen asked.

"Isn't that enough?" Bobbie turned on her heel to face her.

"What do you mean?"

"Don't play stupid. It means she thinks it's my fault," Bobbie said.

"That's not what I heard at all."

"Well, it's what she means."

Kathleen thought for a moment then spoke. "If I threw this chair at you, and you had a loaded gun on the bedside table, would you have to take it and shoot me?"

"That's a little bit of overkill."

"Would I make you shoot me?" Kathleen was persistent.

Bobbie just stared at her.

"No. Your reaction, from yelling to ducking to shooting me, is your choice. Not mine. I pissed you off, but it's you who chooses how to respond."

"Great, now you're in my head, too."

Kathleen's face didn't change. Her voice didn't rise. But somehow, she grew in stature and authority in Bobbie's eyes before her mouth even opened. "It's all nice and good to feel like it's your fault. Be the martyr. It won't change what happened to Gracie. It won't help her get better. She needs her aunt well-adjusted and involved with the family, not hiding out up here. Isn't getting her better the point? Deal with your guilt about making him angry, but be angry at him for his choice. Live with yours."

Tears ran down Bobbie's face at these last words. "What if I can't?"

"Then kill yourself or run away."

Bobbie sank to the bed. "That's harsh, Kat."

"That's life, Bobbie."

Both women sat in silence for a long time. Kathleen was apparently going to wait Bobbie out, and Kathleen was more patient and better with silence than Bobbie was.

Bobbie sniffed. "Okay, I get it. What do I owe you?"

"How about letting me have my soulmate back? I'm tired of the woman who's living here in her place. She locks everyone out and locks herself in through the process."

"Okay," Bobbie whispered, her eyes filling with tears.

Tenderness colored Kathleen's voice. "What now, girlie?"

"I'm afraid that if I don't love me, why would anyone else love me?"

Kathleen moved to the bed, beside where Bobbie was sitting. "I love you, and nothing changes that. Not a choice, not a guilt complex, not a houseful of people who don't know or understand. It's me, and I'm not going anywhere."

Bobbie turned into Kathleen's arms. Kathleen's shoulder muffled her voice. "Why are you always the one comforting me?"

"Because you need it right now. And because I haven't had to grade my first midterms yet."

Bobbie sniffed again and laughed a bit. "Gotcha. My turn later."

"To be announced. Now, what about dinner?"

"Okay. But may I ask a favor first?" Bobbie pulled away from Kathleen's shoulder.

"What?"

"A kiss?" Bobbie asked.

"You're always welcome to that."

Chapter Twenty

Bobbie sat down at the dining room table opposite Kathleen. "Tonight's a lot quieter than last Thursday was." In the window, her reflection stared back from the night. Her jaw was clenched, and her shoulders hunched up ridiculously close to her ears. She dropped them, but they relaxed just a fraction of what they needed.

"That's just because it's their second week of school. Tomorrow night will be wild again." Kathleen laughed. "I'm glad their school started a week before ours. I like their earlier bedtime on weeknights. Makes it easier to work. Getting started has been so crazy for me, I don't even remember if Beth had her meeting with the principal yet."

"They met before the kids started school and had a long talk about where Gracie is. She reads on an eighth-grade level and writes on a sixth-grade level, according to last year's grade card. Emotionally, well, you know."

"How was it?"

"She said he was very understanding, and he assigned Gracie to an experienced teacher. He's supposed to speak with the gym teacher in case some of the activities are more than Gracie can handle. Beth was almost in tears when she told me."

Bobbie and Kathleen grew quiet. School seemed to help Gracie, even after such a short time. Beth had shown Bobbie the teacher's note about how the first two weeks were going. Gracie would occasionally answer questions if she was talking one on one with the teacher. She did her papers and got decent grades, if not as high as she had earned in Cottonwood Plains. She didn't do any creative writing, though, or any letter writing. She was still locked down. She would speak if spoken to at home, in response to direct questions—one or two words at a time. That morning at breakfast, Bobbie had asked her if she wanted cereal or eggs and was caught off-guard when Gracie answered her.

"I said, Bobbie! Earth to Bobbie! Come in, Bobbie!"

"What?" Bobbie jumped. Beth was sitting on her right side, peering at her pile of papers to see what she was working on. When had she joined them?

Kathleen's teasing tones mocked her. "You were woolgathering again. If I had a nickel for every time Beth or I caught you—"

Sometimes Kathleen's unflappable nature got on Bobbie's nerves, but it wouldn't tonight. "If you had a nickel for every time, your math students would have enough word problems to last all four semesters at junior college."

Kathleen's face fell. "And some of my students would be sent to you for remedial English to learn how to spell nickel."

Bobbie's guilt shot through the roof. She had made Kathleen feel bad about her students. Wait. This was too convenient. Kathleen was too levelheaded for this sort of reaction. What sort of game was she into and should Bobbie play along? Just in case? "The new students on campus are already saying how wonderful you are. And it must be tough. I'm sure they have quite a range of ability."

"Oh, yeah, I've got students ready for calculus and students that can't have possibly taken a high school math course. Or at least, passed it," Kathleen said. "I was worried the junior college wouldn't take me since I only have a bachelor's degree, but that's what they wanted for the remedial courses and tutoring position. And they wanted good experience in teaching high school. That I certainly have, and a lot of experience in one-on-one tutoring..."

Beth yawned, excused herself, and headed upstairs.

Kathleen watched until she went up the stairs. "I guess she wasn't captivated by the 'How Kathleen Got Her Job' speech." She grinned wickedly, scooted over to the chair beside Bobbie, and began to rub Bobbie's neck.

"I was, but I guess we talk school, and we bore her. Tell me more. For one thing, I don't know when your graduate classes start." Bobbie smiled lovingly at Kathleen during a rare moment of privacy.

"In another week," Kathleen answered. "This first semester, as a part-time student, I'll just be taking a few seminars over weekends and writing up an independent study of what I want to focus on and what I want to bring away from the experience."

"Didn't you have to do that to apply?"

"Yes, but this will be in greater detail and with the resources of the faculty here. It was a lot harder to do that when I was corresponding from Chicago. They want to see what I hope to take, if it's comprehensive enough, or if I need to be redirected. They also want to find out what I already know. I guess they weed students out early, which makes sense."

"What will you be writing about?" Bobbie laid down her pen.

"I'll be writing about the Stonewall riots of 1969." Kathleen's eye's flashed fire, but ice shot through Bobbie's veins.

"Stonewall riots?" Bobbie asked. "You mean that bar in Greenwich Village, with the cops and all? That was only four years ago. Is it safe? I mean, will you lose your career over it?"

"Better to work at Woolworth's than to work in an academy that denies not only the rights but the very existence of some of its members," Kathleen said.

"But to write about riots? Surely there's some other way. What about the Daughters of Bilitis? Could you write about them? They've done, or did, substantial work for ten? Fifteen years?"

"I'm sure there are already term papers about Kent State and the war on Vietnam. And wouldn't writing about a lesbian civil and political rights group be just as obvious?" Kathleen pointed out coolly.

"But homosexual riots?" Bobbie asked.

"You don't have to stress about it. I'm writing it, not you." Kathleen flipped her head back and stopped rubbing Bobbie's neck.

"But I live with you, carpool some days, work at the same school... Don't you think it's a narrow bridge to cross from one to the other?" Bobbie furrowed her brow. Was that too reactionary?

"If you don't want to be out, don't be out. I'm not out at the junior college because you work there. And I don't advertise I work there when I'm at KU, because of you. But I won't hide in the closet in grad school. The revolution is now, even in Kansas." Kathleen's voice got softer when she got more serious, and Bobbie could barely hear her.

Bobbie blew out a deep breath of air. "Okay. Let me think. I could never ask you to change who you are for me, because I love everything about you. All of you. I guess I'll just ask that if you're going to do a presentation or something where you might be outing yourself that you warn me? Or if it just comes up, could you let me know afterward so I'm prepared if there's fallout at our place of employment? Otherwise, just rock 'n' roll and do your thing." *Holy shit, what am I giving her permission to do to me?* "Be the you I love and admire so much."

Kathleen's eyes often flashed green when she was shifting gears. "Would you be willing to let Beth use your boat to go to the flea market?" She began to rub Bobbie's neck again, but with an entirely different rhythm this time.

"Sure. But why didn't she ask me?" Bobbie's voice was still a little wobbly.

"She hasn't asked yet."

"Huh?" Bobbie's eyebrows went up again.

"I'm going to hint until she does ask. I want to try out that new latch on the inside of my bedroom door."

Bobbie smiled. Finally, she relaxed enough that certain body parts tightened in a much more enjoyable way. "You, my dear, are a letch."

"You are correct, my dear, and one with a terrible hunger. And you're an English professor who can be more descriptive than that."

"Okay, lascivious?"

"That'll work." Kathleen stretched an arm out around Bobbie's shoulders. "I'll be Paul Anka and you be Odia Coates." She sang to her. "Having my baby." She hummed the rest of the first two lines.

Bobbie stifled a laugh. "I'm not sure I'm even having your puppy. We have enough children in this house already, don't you think? Besides, the biology doesn't work."

"Some separatists claim that parthenogenesis really can happen."

"If two women can create a baby on their own, I suggest we be more careful."

Kathleen gave her a wicked grin, reached over, and closed Bobbie's books.

Bobbie didn't return to her bed for three more hours or to sleep for six.

Chapter Twenty-One

Bobbie surprised me yesterday. She brought me a journal from Dr. Langston. She said everyone in the family, except Cara and LeeAnn, has a journal to help them get through this hard time, and Dr. Langston wanted me to have one, too. I told Bobbie thanks and asked what I was supposed to write.

"Anything and everything. Write about me, if you don't know what else to write about. It's private. I won't read it, but I'll feel good knowing you're writing about me. If you write good things."

I laughed. "Of course, I will, babe." And I gave her a kiss.

So here I sit with my new journal. I guess it's supposed to be my sounding board when everything's crazy or aggravating, and maybe when things are good. I'm not sure what to write about, so I'll just start with our first nights.

Last Thursday night was the first night Bobbie joined me in MY bed to make love. Until my brother brought my furniture down from Chicago, we slept in her bed. At least until we moved into the house. And who's had time since we moved? But we set an alarm, so she could sneak back upstairs. Was I thirsty for her in my bed! And no, it didn't slake my thirst. A year could not slake my thirst for her. She's the love of my life. Ever since meeting her in college ten, almost eleven, years ago, I haven't looked at another woman. I hadn't planned on coming out to her this summer or declaring my love to her either, but the moment came up, and it happened.

I remember the whole experience word for word and nuance for nuance. Beth hadn't moved up yet, Gracie hadn't been raped yet, and Bobbie and I were house hunting in the paper since her little one-bedroom apartment wouldn't even do for us as roommates, let alone with her sister and the girls. She had folded the paper and was telling me about my new job at the junior college and what it would involve when her mouth dropped open, and no sound came out.

I was sitting on one end of the sofa.

"What? Come over here and tell me why you stopped talking."

She joined me on the couch. "Your graduate program. You haven't told me how long it is, or how long you'll be here. I've been making plans for us without even asking."

I looked at her. The evening had grown late, and the light was fading. Bobbie leaned against me as she reached around me for the lamp pull. I closed my eyes until she was finished.

"I like you making plans for us," I said. "I've been making plans for us, too, in my head."

"Like what?"

"Like spending more time together than just a summer. About being roommates and sharing."

"Well, we'll certainly be sharing."

"Not exactly what I meant." I was squirming on the inside, but I tried to look composed. "I was so scared when I got to college in sixty-four. I'd never been away from my family before, and I felt lost on campus. Even with the other out-of-state students, I felt out of place. But you and I clicked right away, and I had one place that felt like home."

"I felt that, too," she said.

She was so beautiful sitting there that it made my mouth dry. It was hard to go on, but I forged on for some glorious reason.

"I had so much fun being roommates with you. And when we shared education classes, it was even more fun. I was so glad we were both going to be teachers. I knew we would have time off during the same months. I was glad to go back to Chicago after graduation, but I missed you more than I can tell you. My teaching was the best part of the school year. Visiting one another was the best part of the whole year."

I paused. But she was used to my silences and waited.

"I never wanted to have a child, but that doesn't mean I don't want a family. I just never found anyone I wanted to have it with. Except you."

Her face was unreadable. I licked my lips and swallowed before I continued. "My mother loves you. My father loved you before he died. And I love you."

"I love you," she whispered.

"No, Bobbie, that's not what I meant. I mean I love you and want to be with you forever. We're soul mates, and I could never be with anyone else. I want you to be my family. And my lover," I said. It sounded louder than it needed to in the complete silence of the room.

"I love you, too, Kat—"

"Wait. Don't say anything else. I can't hear that you love me like a sister. Just don't say it. I'm not saying I'll leave if you don't return my feelings. I'll stay in the house with you, Beth, and the girls, until Beth gets through school, and I finish my grad program. But my feelings are strong, and they won't change, and you have to know how I feel."

"Kat, shut up."

I looked at her, so confused. My palms were sticky, and that wasn't the only place.

"I love you, too. I know it must have been tricky for you to bring it up in the middle of this mess with Beth. But I feel the same way, and I want the same thing, and my heart danced when you said you were moving here. If I couldn't have you as a lover, I could, at least, have more of you than a one-month visit a year."

I'm sure I looked stunned. "Now what?"

"Now you kiss me, silly."

My heart almost exploded. I took her hand in mine, lifted it to my lips, and kissed her palm. And then I kissed her.

We sat back, beaming and forgetting to breathe.

"Being a lesbian is hard enough when you live together in a two-bedroom apartment with an old-maid roommate. How are we going to do this in a house with four other people?" I wondered aloud,

She stood up and took my hand. "Carefully, very carefully."

★★★★

The morning after our first kiss, she woke up, slow like she always does, on her side, away from the light of the window. She yawned and rolled over to greet the sunshine. I was next to her, propped up on one arm.

"What are you doing?" Her smile was a little soft and maybe unsure, but her eyes shone with love.

"Watching you sleep, Roberta Ann Rossi," I said happily.

"And how long have you been watching me sleep?" she asked.

"Since I got to college."

"I meant this morning."

"About six hours I would say." I grinned.

Her eyes widened. She couldn't stay up late, let alone all night. "Did you get any sleep?"

"Who needs sleep?" Now I was serious, and I just wanted to take the entire moment in, to make it last forever.

"I'm sorry," she said.

"I'm not." I leaned over and kissed her again.

The pen trailed down the page. Sorry for the big blob I'm now writing around. I was lost thinking about that first night and morning. I wouldn't say it hasn't been as special since—each time has been special, just different. It felt good last Thursday night to be in my bed. I don't know. It just did somehow. It's too hard to explain. I'm so glad I decided to tell her I love her, even in the middle of the little mess before the big mess. Just meeting Beth and the girls and hearing how they were living and what they were going through with Dan, well, that was a disaster. Listening to Bobbie try to convince Beth to leave him and move up here and renting this big house before we knew if she would or not, that was risky enough without me telling Bobbie I love her. But maybe it helped. Maybe it helped to have me as an anchor before that bastard raped Gracie. Bobbie hasn't been the same since. Without me, she would probably be even more lost. I like to think I'm helping in some way. I want to—I love her so much—she's the center of my world.

Watching her suffer like this almost tears me apart. But I won't let it. She needs me in one piece. I need me in one piece. The family needs me in one piece. And maybe she'll grow from this. She wasn't perfect before, and she won't be perfect afterward. I just hope she's wiser and not as broken. If she isn't as broken, I'll be happy.

Chapter Twenty-Two

One more journal entry. This makes two days in a row. I'm sitting outside a women's bookstore and coffee shop in Kansas City, and I'm six hours early. I can't go in yet. So, I'll tell you the story of how I got here. Last Saturday afternoon, when Beth took the girls to the flea market, Bobbie and I had some much-needed privacy. It's so rare that we get to be alone. Four hours of privacy was unbelievably important to me. But that Saturday seemed to be a harbinger of bad times. Bobbie got grumpier and hasn't communicated with me since Beth and the girls returned.

Cara and LeeAnn have taken on a decidedly nasty outlook and fight with one another constantly. Sunday morning, they had a twenty-minute fight over who would sit at the head of the table for breakfast. The table's round. They came to blows and hair pulling. They fuss at their mother, their aunt, and me for what seems to be no reason. Bobbie's spoiling them silly, but even that doesn't sweeten their dispositions. Beth ignores them, for the most part. Or she puts on a show of fussing, but the girls know nothing will be done to back it up. They know they have control over Bobbie and Beth and are taking advantage of it.

I'm confused by it all. I've tried giving them time to work it out on their own, but even my patience gets tested. I have no one to talk to. I need someone to share it with and to ask questions of, but who?

So, this weekend, I announced I was going to Kansas City, and that I would be back Sunday evening. Beth nodded, and Bobbie kept trying to get Gracie to eat something. Their response, or lack thereof, made me angry. I fumed as I packed my overnight bag. I do everything around the house. No one would eat, sleep, or work without my prompting. I manage the schedule, the finances, everything. Fine. We'll just see how well they do without me for two days.

The drive to Kansas City didn't take long. It took me longer to locate the address of the

```
out-of-the-way bookstore and coffee house
where I've been directed. Five-and-a-half
hours early for the meeting. Oh well, there's
nothing else to do now because I've been
writing till this very moment. I'll sign off
and at least go inside and make sure I'm in
the right place.
```

Kathleen finished her journal entry and took a deep breath. She double-checked to make sure her Pinto was in park and took another deep breath before she went inside. The store didn't look like any other coffee shop she'd ever visited. Books were stacked on shelves around the room, there was a small stage on one end, and the only patrons were women.

She approached the woman behind the counter and introduced herself by her first name only.

"Seems to me I spoke to a Kathleen on the phone two days ago," the woman said. "I'm Megan, and would you be that Kathleen?"

"Yes, I am. You invited me to come up and meet some women."

"Yes, and it looks like you made it. But how did you hear about us?"

"From another student in a graduate women's studies course I'm taking. We had lunch together, and her, um, the woman she lives with met us there. I also have a special woman I live with, so we have that in common, as well. I asked her if there were any local places or groups where I could go to talk. She said not really, but then she gave me your number. I called you, and here I am."

Megan smiled. "One Saturday night a month, I close early, and we have a womyn's circle. This happens to be that lucky weekend. I'm glad you could come up. You've got a few hours before we start. May I suggest a book to read until it's time?"

"A book will do me fine. I must say I'm a bit nervous. I've never been with a group of lesbians before."

"Dykes are what we call ourselves in this circle. Does the term bother you?"

"Oh no, and I'm glad you corrected me."

"Maybe I'll call my lover, Pat, and see if she could cover the store for a while. You look like you want to talk."

"I do, I really do," Kathleen said. "Would that be an imposition?"

"Oh no, my dear." Megan laughed. "That's what this store's about, a place in the storm for those of us who don't belong anywhere else."

＊＊＊＊

Pat came to watch over the store, and Kathleen followed Megan to their upstairs apartment. The two of them talked all afternoon. Kathleen spoke about taking a lover and almost losing her to a family disaster.

"We were best friends until early this summer. I don't want to sound selfish, but after all these years we can finally be together as more than best friends, and now, her mind is somewhere else. And the worst part is, I get so angry sometimes. I don't know what to do. I don't know how to fix it. I do the best I can, I do as much as I can, but it's never enough."

Megan studied Kathleen a moment before speaking. "Maybe you ought to stop trying."

Kathleen's mouth fell open.

"You aren't Bobbie's mother or her sister's or the children's. You can't fix it, so why not be honest with yourself? Either time will fix it and they'll pull it together, or it won't happen."

Kathleen was still speechless. But now her chest was heavy, her breathing labored, and her palms clammy.

"Are you the oldest child in your family, dear?" Megan asked.

"Yes."

"And you helped raise the others and fix things for them?"

"Yes."

"And you're still trying to do that, except this time you can't fix it and you can't make them fix it either. No wonder you're angry and frustrated."

"I don't think—"

"Stop for a few minutes. Don't say anything until I've made us a cup of tea."

While the water boiled and the tea steeped, Kathleen thought about the past few months. She was resentful. Her help hadn't resolved the problems and, frequently, hadn't even been acknowledged. She was still deep in thought when Megan brought two cups of tea. Kathleen accepted hers and found herself telling Megan how she felt almost useless.

"Do you ride a bike?" Megan asked.

"Yes," Kathleen said, thrown by the change in topic.

"And how did you learn? Did the person teaching you hold on to the bike for the first year?"

"No, my father taught me, and he let it go after a couple of days. I fell several times before I got the hang of it."

"Then stop holding onto everyone's bikes. Maybe they're so used to you rescuing them, they've stopped noticing. Now they depend on it and expect it."

Kathleen tucked that away to consider later. She and Megan talked the rest of the afternoon. They were deep in conversation when Pat appeared and said the women were arriving.

"Oh dear, I've talked your ear off, and now your afternoon is gone. I'm so sorry. Was there something you needed to do that I can help you catch up on?" Kathleen asked

"Don't worry about it. I was also a first child and a fixer. It took me years to figure things out. I thought maybe I could share some of it with you while you're still young." Megan touched her arm and smiled. "But it's up to you to figure out how it works in your life. Now it's time for the potluck. We'll have several hours of music and discussion. Somebody always cries, and we laugh a lot. Let's go down."

Megan introduced Kathleen to the others, and she was warmly welcomed and soundly hugged. She participated a bit but listened and watched more. It felt good to be around other lesbians—dykes, she reminded herself. These were mostly educated, some not, all politically active women, not unlike her friends in the women's studies program. It was a good fit. She would be back. She couldn't wait to get home and tell Bobbie what she had learned. She decided to go straight home instead of staying in a motel.

The next morning, Kathleen tried and saw there was no way she could talk to Bobbie. It would have to wait for a better time. Bobbie was fixing breakfast and begging everyone to eat. Kathleen started to take over. When she realized what she was doing, she stopped. She finished eating, rinsed her plate, and returned to her room.

When Bobbie sat down at her desk in the afternoon, Kathleen tried to talk with her but was rebuffed. Later that night, Kathleen spied Bobbie relaxing in the front room. She checked to see where Gracie was and found her in her room. Seeing that Beth had taken the younger girls for a walk, she tried again to talk with Bobbie but to no avail. She was disappointed and angry that Bobbie wouldn't listen to her, but that was Bobbie's problem, not hers. She would give her time.

Chapter Twenty-Three

Gracie's Top-Secret Journal Entry

> I had that bad dream again last night, the one where Dad caught the curtains on fire and beat my butt for it. Mom came and woke me up because I was screaming, but she didn't ask me why. I guess she thinks she knows what it's about and is afraid to ask. Maybe I'll talk to Dr. Langston about it today. Maybe that will make it go away. She says that sometimes talking about dreams does that, but she doesn't make me tell her about them until I'm ready. I like that about her. She gives me time to decide if I want to talk or not. She treats me like a grown-up.

* * * *

Gracie wasn't eager to go to this individual therapy session but found she wasn't reluctant to go either. Dr. Langston greeted her.

"How was your week? Did anything special happen?" Dr. Langston asked, as she always did.

"I want to talk about a bad dream I had last night."

Dr. Langston's eyebrows went up a bit. "Sure."

"Here's my journal entry. But I'm going to have to think how I can tell you about it exactly."

Dr. Langston read Gracie's journal entry. "I see you got your butt beat because your Dad caught some curtains on fire. Did he blame you?"

"Yes."

"That had to be pretty scary. Take as much time as you need and then tell me what happened. After that we can talk about your mom not asking about your nightmares, okay?"

"Okay." Gracie sat with her hands on her lap, playing with her fingers as she thought about the story. Now that it was time, she was a little scared to tell the doctor what had happened. *Oh, stop it. Just tell the story. He's dead now and you're safe if you tell.*

"That week was really crappy. It was after Aunt Bobbie had taken mom and us girls to Wichita for the River Festival. Dad was pretty grumpy about that. Mom's boss swapped her closing shift from Thursday to Friday. That sucked because Dad worked

Thursday, and Mom wouldn't be home when Dad was home on Friday. My sisters and I would be stuck with all of his mean moods.

"By Friday night, Dad was already broke and that pissed him off, too. He sat in his brown recliner listening to the baseball game on the radio. I put my sisters to bed early and got in my place. I usually crouched inside the kitchen door and watched so I could keep a fresh beer in his hands all the time.

"'Crappy game. Crappy, cheap beer.' Dad was still mad about Aunt Bobbie's visit, and he mumbled things under his breath. He went through the beers quicker than usual. Because of that, he went through his list of moods faster, as well—irritated, loving, and relaxed, and then the dreaded mean.

"My legs would get tired from crouching and sometimes I stretched them by walking around the kitchen table, then back to my spot. The ashtray on Dad's round table always overflowed with ashes, but he kept adding to it with his nonstop smoking. I went to check on him after one of my walks around the table and the curtain beside the table was on fire.

"Daddy!" I screamed.

"He tried to fan them out, but the curtains were already on fire halfway up. He jumped to his feet and pulled down the entire curtain. He stomped the fire out, cussing at the curtain, the fire, and then at me.

"'What the hell were you doing? I know you watch from the kitchen. Were you trying to burn down the house? You probably lit the fire, you little bitch. What did you do, toss one of my butts over and wait for it to light before waking me? I knew you were useless, but, hell, you're dangerous, too. I should beat your ass.'

"I got so scared I ran behind the sofa.

"'Get out here, bitch. Don't you hide from me.'

"I slowly came from behind the sofa.

"'What in the hell are you wearing?'

"I had on one of his old stained T-shirts for a nightgown. 'Is that my T-shirt? It's awfully short on you. What kind of slut are you turning out to be? Just like your aunt. I knew she was a bad influence on you. Talk to me. Explain yourself, you little shit.'

"I was crying, but I tried to explain that my nightgown was dirty, and I was just wearing this until Mom did laundry. But he wouldn't wait for me to stop crying. His face got redder and he got hotter.

"'Get over here, you little shit. I'm gonna beat your ass and teach you a lesson.' He pulled his belt off.

"I crept over to him, I was sobbing and not able to breathe. He grabbed me by the shoulder. He hauled me across his lap, pulled down my panties, and beat me. He hit me on every word as he screamed at me. 'You'll never do that again, or I'll beat you till you can't walk.'

"I was howling and pulling away from him.

"'You little shit, you lie still and take it. Damned kid, ruined my life. Got me stuck in this stupid town, kept me from getting away to some real city.' He shoved me on the floor. I curled up in a ball. My backside was burning like nothing I had ever felt. I was terrified to make a sound, but I couldn't stop crying and gasping for air.

"Then he sounded like a dog as he barked at me. 'You're pathetic. At your age, I could take a whipping with no whining. Get your nose into that corner until you can act your age.'

"I crawled to the corner where he pointed. My legs shook so bad I could barely stand, even with the wall to hold me up. I didn't make a sound, except for the gasps that snuck out when I tried to breathe. My mind was screaming, but nothing made sense. I slid my hand down my leg to see if I was bleeding. Instead, there were welts, which only scared me more.

"I was afraid he was going to kill me. I fought to get back in control before he decided to beat me again. I braced myself against the wall, closed my eyes, and locked my jaw tight.

"I don't know how long I stood there. Ten minutes? An hour? Finally, his voice busted through my screaming mind.

"'Gracie! You better jump when I call you. Get me a beer and get your ass into bed, you hear me? And no telling your mother about this when she gets in. One word and I'll beat your ass again, you hear me, dammit?'

"Nodding, I stumbled to the kitchen and got the beer. It took me several tries to get it opened. When I got back to the front room, Daddy had bundled the destroyed curtain into a big, black lump.

"'Get this out back to the trash can and get your ass in bed. And no waking your sisters.'

"I took the bundle out to the alley. Pebbles and stickers poked my bare feet, but I barely felt them. Back inside, I went to bed as quietly I could. I didn't even wipe off my feet before I slid under the sheet beside LeeAnn. Tears made my body shake. I could hear my mind screaming in panic and terror. But I held as still as I could until I stopped jerking, the same way I did when I had those horrible nightmares. Then I turned over and cried myself to sleep."

"Oh wow, Gracie, that is some story. How do you feel now that you've told me?" Dr. Langston asked.

Gracie opened her eyes, surprised that she had told the story at the same time she remembered it. "I don't know. Kind of embarrassed because I told you what, well, you know..."

"Oh, honey, your father was drunk when that happened. It was all his fault. He chose to drink. He chose to drink enough to be drunk, and he chose to beat you. Nothing that occurred was your fault. I am so, so sorry that it happened. How did you feel when you saw the fire and then he beat you?"

"I felt bad, like I was a terrible kid. If I hadn't stretched my legs, I would have, well, I still couldn't have seen the curtain catch fire because the recliner was in the way, but I could have done something else about it, sooner."

Dr. Langston shook her head, a gentle look on her face. "I don't think you could have, Gracie. I know you tried very hard to take care of your little sisters and to help your mom, but you're a child. It's the grown-ups' job to take care of the children, not the other way around. You weren't a terrible kid. You aren't a terrible kid. You're a very good ten-year-old who did the best she could in a terrible situation."

Dr. Langston sat there for a few minutes while Gracie thought about things. That was another thing Gracie liked about her. She understood thinking time and that talking got in the way of it.

Gracie lifted her head after a while, dried tears on her cheeks.

"May I ask if those are 'I'm terrible' tears or 'I'm glad someone knows I'm not terrible' tears?" Dr. Langston asked.

Gracie smiled. "They're 'I'm glad someone knows I'm not terrible tears.' And I know you're going to ask how I feel now. I'm Gracie, Girl Detective, and I'm on to you, Dr. Langston. I feel a little better. I still feel shaky in my stomach, but I can make a joke. And maybe I won't have that dream again."

"I'm glad. Now I have a question for you. Can I tell your mother about this? I get the feeling she doesn't know what happened that night. The two of you should talk about it. Would you rather tell her yourself, or with me? Or do you want me to talk about it in my private session with her?"

Gracie looked at Dr. Langston for a long minute. "Why do you want to tell her alone? Before you always made us talk about things in the family session."

"Because there wasn't a story like this one before. If I do talk to her about it, it might come up in the family session. Is that okay? Did you bring homework to do in the waiting room?"

"No, I don't have any homework. I get to start a new Nancy Drew book," Gracie said.

"I'm sure that will keep you busy. So, what do you think about me telling your mom?"

"I think you better. I bet she's going to feel really bad, and you know how she cries when she feels guilty." Gracie smiled a sad smile and gave a little shrug.

"Yes, I do. But let's leave that up to her, how she chooses to react. Why don't you go out there, give her a big hug, and send her in here, okay?"

"Thanks, Dr. Langston. You made it easier than I thought it would be."

"Thank you for trusting me enough to share, Gracie. Bye for an hour."

"'Bye." Gracie left the inner office and went into the waiting room.

"How did it go, babe?" her aunt asked.

"Good," Gracie answered and gave her aunt and her mom a hug before her mother disappeared into the office with Dr. Langston.

"Do you want to tell me about it?" Aunt Bobbie asked.

"No. I mean, I told her about a bad dream I had. We'll probably talk about it in family session. I want to read my book right now if that's okay."

"Okay, then," Aunt Bobbie said. "Let's both read for an hour."

Chapter Twenty-Four

It took Aunt Bobbie twenty minutes to get Gracie out of bed and dressed. When the entire family was at the breakfast table, Aunt Bobbie made an announcement. "We didn't get you girls back-to-school haircuts, but I'm taking Gracie this morning. LeeAnn and Cara, your mom will take you this afternoon."

"Okay," Gracie said. She was very happy to lose, or try to lose, the reminders of her femininity.

It was one more way not to get hurt.

The chatter around the table stopped and everyone stared. Gracie rarely spoke this early without being asked a question.

"Let's go after breakfast," Aunt Bobbie said.

"I'm done." Gracie pushed her plate back and stood up.

"Any rules for haircuts, Mom?" Aunt Bobbie asked.

"Just cute and easy to take care of," Beth said.

Gracie stood by the back door, waiting.

****

A woman approached them at the beauty shop. "My name is Clara and whose hair am I cutting today?"

When Bobbie pointed to Gracie, Clara led her to the chair and draped her with a long, blue cape. "What kind of haircut do you want today, honey?" she asked, looking at Bobbie in the big mirror.

"Short." Gracie fidgeted beneath the drape.

"Oh, Gracie, you girls have never worn it short," Aunt Bobbie said.

"There's a very popular haircut for young girls right now called the pixie," the beautician said. "It's short around the neck and longer on top." She picked a magazine up off the counter and handed it to Gracie. "Here's a picture of it. What do you think?"

"It's awfully short," Aunt Bobbie said. "But it's kind of cute."

Gracie looked at it and nodded.

"I suppose we can try it," Aunt Bobbie said.

"If you don't like the pixie, I'll give you a free cut next month. How's that?"

"Do it," Gracie said.

"If she doesn't like it, she'll have to wait several months." Aunt Bobbie shrugged her shoulders and sat down.

"It was all the rage for young girls going away to camp this summer needing something easy to care for," the beautician said as she took Gracie to wash her hair.

The water flowed through Gracie's hair as a flood of memories came back.

****

It had quickly become her favorite birthday card.

"Dear Gracie...early birthday present...week of sleepover at Girl Scout Camp...Love, Aunt Bobbie."

Two months later, as everyone sat around the campfire, watching sparks shoot and bugs fly, the counselors took out guitars and sang. Gracie had never felt so good. Every night, full of the day's activities and wrapped tight in her new sleeping bag, Gracie drifted off to sleep feeling safe and secure. She didn't even think about the nightmares that plagued her at home until the fifth night.

That night, as she snuggled into her sleeping bag, something bothered her and kept her awake. She hadn't had any nightmares since coming to camp. She'd forgotten about them and now LeeAnn was sleeping on the edge of the bed. What if the nightmares got her? What if they were already getting her?

Gracie sat up on her cot. She couldn't find the zipper on her sleeping bag with her shaking hands, so she crawled out the top. She stumbled out of her tent and to the counselors' tent in the partial moonlight.

She stopped at the knock-knock tree and called out to the counselors.

"Knock-knock, Angel, Bug, somebody wake up, hurry!" She danced in place while she waited. She kept calling knock-knock, until Angel came to the door of the tent, her afro flat on the side she'd been sleeping on.

Angel grabbed a lantern and stepped outside. She sat down on a rock and hugged Gracie. "You're crying. What's wrong?"

"I have to go home tonight. I have to go to my sister."

"Did you have a bad dream about her?"

"No, but she—I've got to go, or they'll get her, too." Gracie cried harder.

Angel pulled Gracie onto her lap, held her, and swayed a bit. "You're going to have to tell me more. I don't understand." Her compassionate eyes shone.

"I can't. I've just got to go. I have to go now."

"You can't go now. I think you had a really scary dream and your sister's okay at home. She's probably sleeping, too." Angel tried to soothe her.

"I have to get to her!"

"Shhh, Gracie. It's okay. What's your sister's name?"

"LeeAnn."

"LeeAnn's probably asleep right now, and maybe she's even having a dream about you."

Gracie's eyes enlarged to the size of pop-bottle bottoms. She fought at Angel's arms, trying to get out, to get home, to get somewhere. Angel called another counselor to come help. It wasn't but a moment before Bug was kneeling in front of Gracie.

"It's okay, honey, it's okay. What's wrong?" Bug asked, rubbing Gracie's arm.

Gracie spit out words between sobs. "The nightmares. LeeAnn. Going to get her."

"What nightmares, Gracie? Did you have a nightmare?"

"No! The ones at home. The ones on the edge of the bed. I have to go home. Protect her from them."

Bug stroked Gracie's head while Angel kept a tight hold on her. "Honey, you can't go home tonight. It's the middle of the night already. But if you're still upset in the morning, we can call your mom and see if your sister's okay."

Gracie clung to Angel and cried and cried, afraid to tell them about the nightmares, afraid to call her mom, afraid that LeeAnn was already getting hurt. Through her sobs, Gracie heard Angel whispering, "I have no idea how to handle this."

"Let's carry her up to the unit house where we can turn the light on and she won't wake anyone else. Maybe the light will make her feel safer," Bug suggested.

They carried Gracie through the silent camp to the unit house. Gracie buried her face in Angel's shoulder when the lights came on. Angel tried to set Gracie down, but Gracie clung to her. Angel tipped Gracie's chin up, so she could see her face. "I promise you're safe. Bug and I are here, and nothing can hurt you, but I need you to tell me what's wrong. Tell me about the nightmares, Gracie."

Gracie whispered the nightmare into Angel's ear, then looked at her, afraid of Angel's reaction. Angel's eyes grew wide at the mixed-up content of Gracie's nightmare. She looked at Bug with an ashen face but couldn't find words about the nightmare.

"Can you get us a blanket?" Angel whispered to Bug. A few minutes later, Bug returned with two blankets and two pillows. She spread one on the floor for Angel and Gracie to sit on.

Angel wrapped herself and Gracie in the other blanket. She told Bug to go back to their tent, that she would talk to her in the morning. Angel rocked Gracie and sang to her in whispers. When daybreak came, Gracie was silent and stiff. They washed away their tears and went to dress for breakfast.

****

Clara held up a mirror and nudged again. "Are you in there? The back, hon, look at the back."

Gracie pulled herself back to the present and looked in the mirror. The back of her hair was short but not like a boy's. Clara spun her around so that Gracie could see what the front looked like. She looked different, but she liked it.

"Will it do, hon?" Clara asked.

"It'll do."

Aunt Bobbie stood up and walked in a circle around Gracie. "It's cuter than I imagined it would be."

"Can we go now?" Gracie asked. She stood up and pulled off the drape before the woman could do so, scattering hair everywhere.

"It's not a race," Aunt Bobbie said. "We have plenty of time."

But Gracie was already at the door. She could hear Aunt Bobbie hurriedly paying and coming after her. Aunt Bobbie caught up with Gracie at the curb and grabbed Gracie's wrist. "Hey, hey, slow down and look at me. Are you okay?"

Gracie looked at her and, in silence, pulled her toward the car.

"Guess not. Okay, the errands can wait. Home it is. Can you tell me what's wrong, Gracie? Did the haircut upset you?"

"No, let's just go home, please?" Gracie's voice was high and had a pitch of urgency.

"Okay, home now it is. Lock your door, Gracie, if that will make you feel better."

At home, Gracie went straight to her room, climbed into bed, and pulled the covers over her head.

One more way not to get hurt.

****

Someone shook Gracie. "Gracie? Gracie, babe. Wake up. You're having a nightmare." It was Aunt Bobbie.

When she heard the word nightmare, Gracie sat up and rubbed her eyes.

"You kept calling out for angels. Were you dreaming about angels?" Aunt Bobbie asked.

"My camp counselor was Angel. She helped me with a really bad nightmare," Gracie mumbled, still half asleep.

"Do you have nightmares?"

"Only in Cottonwood Plains, on the edge of the bed."

"But what about now?" Aunt Bobbie pressed on.

"Only about Dad." Gracie was wide awake now. She rolled

away from Aunt Bobbie, determined not to answer any more. One more way not to get hurt.

Chapter Twenty-Five

The parent-teacher conference Bobbie attended with Beth made her wish she smoked. That night would have been a good cigarette night. Gracie managed to establish passing marks in everything but math. Barely passing fifth grade couldn't be good. Junior high was one year ahead, and high school was two short years after that, and college— Wait, she's a fifth grader. She's going to be eleven in a few months. Her grades now won't ruin her college prospects. Just chill, Bobbie McFreak.

Math. Gracie had always hated math, but now she refused to have anything to do with it. The teacher suggested a truce. Instead of math continuing to be a standoff, she would let Gracie do some other type of class work. Gracie could draw, write, or read. She could choose her activity as long as she didn't disturb the rest of the class.

Bobbie let out a breath.

Beth rubbed her palm along the back of her neck. "That's a good idea. Thank you for understanding. Gracie used to be a great story writer. She drew pictures to go along with them."

"Good," Mrs. Hartfield said. "I'll talk to her about it tomorrow. I'll make sure she has some supplies, and we'll see what happens. Creativity may be helpful for her healing."

Bobbie thought the idea was great, but something tickled at the back of her head later that night. She was unable to focus on grading papers while she tried to figure out what about the idea was bothering her. Creativity. Stories. Pictures. Oh, God. Gracie once showed her a picture of a nightmare she had. Gracie wrote a story to go with the picture that bothered Bobbie. Bobbie couldn't remember when Gracie showed her the picture and story, but it must have been early in the summer.

****

"I think the key is her nightmares," Bobbie said, as she joined Beth and Kathleen in the kitchen after she tucked the girls in bed. "She said her life is a nightmare. We have to find out what those nightmares were about."

Kathleen looked up. "What on earth are you talking about?"

"Last week in therapy, Gracie said that her life is a nightmare."

"How do we talk her into telling us what her nightmares are about?" Beth asked,

"She told one person, a camp counselor," Bobbie said.

"One of the counselors at Girl Scout Camp months ago? What did she have to say?" Kathleen asked.

"That the counselor helped her with a nightmare."

"How do you know it's the same nightmare? Besides, how do we find this counselor?" Kathleen asked.

"I'll call the local Girl Scout office. They should have the number for the camp. And hopefully, they'll have records of the staff."

"Do you remember her name?" Kathleen asked.

"No," Bobbie said. "But they should know which two counselors were in Gracie's unit. It has to be one of them."

"Are these full-time Girl Scout staff?"

"Well, no. They looked like college students on a summer job."

"So, you expect"—Kathleen held up a finger—"one, to find out the name of an eighteen-year-old seasonal employee, and two"—a second finger—"you expect this girl to remember the dream of one child out of a summer of girls?"

"Dammit, Kathleen, it's the only thing I have."

"Do what you want, Bobbie. Just don't hound the girl and don't take your anger out on her if she can't help you."

"I have to try."

"I understand that. I want you to understand the chance of success is very slim. Maybe we should be thinking of other things."

"You do that, Kathleen McCormick. And I'll do what I have to do." Bobbie turned on her heel and went upstairs.

At her desk, she grabbed a legal pad and wrote out the facts she had as she knew them:

1. In therapy last week, Gracie said her life is a nightmare.
2. This summer, she showed me a picture and story of a nightmare.
3. She mentioned a counselor who helped with her nightmare

Hmmm. Number one happened only a week ago, so it was fresh in Gracie's memory, but the other two were from early summer, maybe six months ago. Bobbie's memory felt spotty, so she thought she might have to write a bit to see if she could refresh the details in her mind. That would work. Dr. L's journal was always available for late-night sessions.

****

This summer when I went down to Cottonwood Plains to take all of us to Oklahoma City and the zoo, Beth encouraged the girls to draw pictures and write stories for me. Before we left on the trip, I took a little time with each girl to go over her art and praise it. When I saw Gracie's drawing, I wanted to talk with her alone. I asked Beth if she could take the other girls across the street to the gas station to buy sodas for the trip. As soon as they were gone, I asked Gracie to tell me about it. It was drawn in grays, browns, and blacks, and didn't depict anything I recognized. She said she had written a story about it and pushed her paper toward me while looking out the window. The story was a portrayal of the picture. It didn't give any details, just sensory implications, and it was frightening in its starkness. We heard the others coming up the driveway, so I asked her if we could talk about it later. She said maybe, but we never got back to it.

Going home in the Impala from Oklahoma City, the girls slept in the back while Beth and I chatted. "Does Gracie have nightmares?" I asked.

"I don't think so. At least, she doesn't complain of them. Why do you ask?"

"She showed me a picture and story about a nightmare. They were quite haunting, and I wondered if they were typical for her."

"She does wake up some mornings with a red face and puffy eyes but has never mentioned bad dreams. Should I ask her?"

"No, leave it for now. I'll get back to her later about it," I said as the girls began to stir.

At the end of June, Gracie went to her first sleep-away camp—an early birthday gift from me. When I picked her up at the end of the week, the parents were meeting the counselors. I asked her if she wanted me to meet her counselor and she said yes. When we got to the front of the line, she walked up to a young black woman and slipped her hand into the counselor's hand. The counselor knelt and pushed a strand of Gracie's hair behind her ear. Without speaking, they hugged.

"Was that your counselor?" I asked her when she returned with her sleeping bag and suitcase.

"Yes. Her name is Angel, and I love her. She helped me with a nightmare. Can I come back next year?" I was surprised at Gracie's declaration. Gracie, my little reserved niece.

****

Bobbie had hoped the search would only take a couple of days, not a week. When she wasn't working on finding the counselor, she was complaining about how hard it was to find her.

"Would you get off the phone already? It's getting late, and you'll wake people up," Kathleen told her one night.

Bobbie slammed the phone down mid-dial. She knew Kathleen was right, but she just couldn't let it go. She dropped the thick phone book and yellow legal pad on the floor beside her desk and pushed away from the desk so hard she hit the wall.

"You need to blow off some steam," Kathleen said, sitting down to face her. "Why don't you tell me about it?"

"The local council here is no help. The council where the camp is located is practically no help. That council's records about their summer staff are spotty. I can't locate phone numbers for half of the eighteen names they gave me."

"Wow, you've narrowed it down to eighteen names. That's much better than I would have been able to do." Kathleen smiled.

"Well, it's not working. The council wants me to wait until their staff calls each of the girls' families to get permission to let me have their college or work numbers. I wouldn't have these names and hometowns except for a clerical error on some temp's part."

"Why not wait for them to make the calls, so you don't have to play Nancy Drew yourself?"

Invoking the name of Gracie's hero just made Bobbie angrier. "Because they'll get to it when they get to it. I'm not a high priority and, stop it—I see the words coming out of your mouth before you speak them. This is a high priority, and I want the information now. Who knows how helpful it could be?"

"And who knows how useless it could be? What are you doing anyway, calling people this late at night?" Kathleen refused to get angry.

"I'm trying to locate that counselor. But first, I must call everyone with the same last name in her hometown to find her family. Then, I have to sweet talk the family into giving me her school phone number, which they will barely cough up. They make it sound like I'm some crazy stalker."

"Well, calling at nine thirty at night to someone you don't know, looking for a girl the family may not know, makes you sound like a crazy stalker." Kathleen grinned.

No response.

Kathleen took a more serious approach. "What about this? Why don't you wait for the office to make official calls, do your legwork for you, while you write up the questions and let them get back to you?"

"And throw Gracie's eighteenth birthday party while I wait? Don't tell me what to do about Gracie or what to do about some rotten system that can't keep track of their employees." Bobbie stared at Kathleen, daring her to disagree.

Kathleen stood up and headed down the stairs.

"I'm right. You shouldn't be telling me what to do," Bobbie said.

Kathleen came back. "You're right. I shouldn't boss you around, but I won't take verbal abuse when I'm wrong. And I won't take your anger spilling out on me about a poor Girl Scout employee."

"What do you mean by that?"

"You're angry on Gracie's behalf. I get that. You want to follow up on a clue that might help her somehow. I get that. But you're rude about it, and you're taking your anger out on me. And if that college girl can't help you, I can picture you taking your anger out on her, too."

"I'm not taking anything out on anybody." Bobbie tossed her hair over her shoulder. "You don't see how helpful this could be."

"This isn't even about being helpful anymore. This is about Bobbie not getting what Bobbie wants when Bobbie wants it. You're not the center of the world, and just because you think something is a priority doesn't make it a priority for everyone else—"

"But it should be—"

"But it's not and don't cut me off. See? You're doing it again. You and your needs are so central that you can do what you want, including cutting me off when I'm talking. Bobbie, I love you like life itself, but even I don't think the earth revolves around you. You've got to get over yourself, or you'll push away all the people who can help you, including the people closest to you."

"Well, if that's the way you see it, don't let the door catch you on the way out."

Kathleen turned and went down the stairs again.

"Wait," Bobbie called. Kathleen didn't stop.

"Fine." Bobbie didn't follow her down the stairs. She picked up her legal pad and began her work again, muttering to herself.

Later that night, Bobbie slipped down the stairs, trying not to wake the rest of the family. Once downstairs, she knocked gently on Kathleen's door. Kathleen didn't answer. Bobbie knocked again and then tried the doorknob. The door caught. She had the nerve to lock her out. How dare she lock her out? She seethed as she went back upstairs.

Bobbie couldn't sleep as she thought about what Kathleen had said. Did she really think this was about her? How could she not understand how important this was for Gracie? Even if she didn't understand, Bobbie should never have told her not to let the door hit her on the way out. That was stupid and tacky. But locking her out, that was big. Maybe this was their first big fight. So much had happened since they got together, there hadn't been time to fight. Maybe they could talk tomorrow, and she wouldn't be such an ass and would listen to Kathleen. Bobbie loved her so much. Life would be so empty without her. She couldn't even imagine it. She made up her mind. She would make it better tomorrow, no matter what she had to do. She couldn't lose Kathleen *or* Gracie.

Chapter Twenty-Six

Bobbie stretched and stepped out of her room the next morning just in time to be run down by the Cara-LeeAnne runaway train, barreling out of their room and toward the stairs at top speed. She stepped back into her room, grazed by their passing, and listened to their footfalls down the hall and the stairs. She was glad she wasn't on breakfast and driving detail today. It had been another long, restless, noisy night. She changed her mind and decided to stay upstairs until Kathleen fed and took the three girls to school, before going on to work herself. Thursdays and Fridays were Beth's early mornings in the school cafeteria, and she was long gone already. So, when Kathleen and the girls left, Bobbie could have a peaceful cup of coffee alone in this big house, an event she loved.

As soon as all four doors on Kathleen's Pinto had slammed shut, Bobbie got her purse together. As she came out of her room, she slammed her door. It made her feel better. She slammed the younger girls' door for good measure. She slammed the bathroom door as she walked by it and into the office where she gathered her book bag and checked her calendar one last time. She headed downstairs and as she walked by Gracie and Beth's room, she reached in, took their doorknob and gave it a good slam as well. The door vibrated splendidly, and in her grumpy mood, she enjoyed the sound. She took the doorknob, opened the door again, and as she went to slam it—

Something grabbed it and yanked it back open. Not something, someone. A fuming, distressed-looking Beth stood there in her nightgown with the doorknob grasped firmly in her shaking hand.

"If you touch this or any other door again, I will kick you from here to St. Louis myself," a pale, squint-eyed Beth croaked at Bobbie. "I have a migraine, and you're killing me."

"Well, you scared the crap out of me. How was I to know?" Bobbie placed her hand over her pounding heart. "I need to sit down."

"You need to sit down? You need to be quiet. I need to rest, not listen to doors slam. I need some more pain medicine. What time is it?"

"It's only eight."

"Damn, it's too soon, I'll throw up, and that'll make it worse." Beth leaned against the door jamb and shielded her eyes with her hand.

"Come downstairs and have some coffee. I used to get stress

migraines when I was writing my dissertation and caffeine helped get rid of them."

Beth stared at her then turned and went into her bedroom. After a two count, she emerged again. "May I take a moment of your precious time?" she asked.

"Yes?" The way Beth asked took a wrecking ball to the lining of Bobbie's stomach.

"Come into my room where it's darker and cooler, and I can sit down before I fall down."

Bobbie followed Beth into her room and stood at the end of the bed. "What's with the precious time comment?"

She got stared at again for her efforts. "Did you ever think of offering to bring me up a cup of coffee so I could stay lying down in the dark? No, come down to the bright-yellow kitchen with a migraine, Beth, and have a cup of something that will wake you up with no guarantee of curing your splitting headache." Beth's voice was low, but curt, and had spikes on it. She went on. "Did you think to offer to go out of your way for someone else? Your self-centeredness is getting old already, as a sister and more as a roommate."

The spikes hit dead center in Bobbie's heart. For a moment, they clashed on the iron shell and sparked an angry response, but the pathetic look of her sister on this bed broke the shell open, and the spikes dug in. "I'm so sorry. You're right, it's thoughtless of me. I'll get the coffee. And maybe my ice pack if I can find it or, at least, a cold, wet washcloth. Have you had enough water? I could bring up a big glass of water, too. I'm so sorry I made it worse. I'll call the pharmacy and see what I can do to fix it—"

"Stop it. Stop it, Bobbie, and I don't mean just right now. I mean stop all of it. I'm sick and tired of the Bobbie show. First, it's your self-centeredness. It's all about you, and you're not thinking about how things are going to affect other people."

Bobbie lifted a hand but didn't even break her sister's verbal stride.

"No, don't interrupt me. That's what I'm talking about, see? I was in bed last night and heard your fight with Kathleen. I didn't understand it all, but jeez, you can be such an ass. And second, if you aren't walking on other people, you're feeling guilty and trying to fix things. You can't fix things for other people. Hasn't our therapist told you that yet?"

Bobbie couldn't stand by and listen any longer. She talked right over the top of her sister's last sentence. "Beth, you aren't well, and things must feel out of proportion. I'll get you some water or juice, and you rest. We can talk again when your head is better."

"There you go. Telling me what and how I'm feeling and

doing. You have no idea what I'm feeling or doing. Don't tell me who I am or what I know. I can't take it anymore, and I don't have to. You can't do this. It's not good for you, and it's not good for the girls or me." She turned her head away from Bobbie and bit her nails.

Bobbie's empty stomach rolled over and fell a foot. She swallowed twice, and tears welled up in her eyes. "I'm sorry. I didn't realize I was treating you so horribly. But I can do better. I can work with Dr. Langston. Just give me a couple of sessions, and then we can meet with her together and talk it through. I know you'll feel differently then. Just give me some time, please? I'm so sorry." She swallowed again and wiped her eyes on her arm.

"There you go, fixing me again. Falling all over me isn't going to fix how angry I am. And while I'm on the subject of falling all over people, the falling all over Gracie has to end, too. It's not helping her. It's making things worse, and it's going to mess up the other girls in the process." Beth's tight voice had slowed and lowered, and her shoulders sagged.

"I don't know what..." Bobbie started to say and ran out of words.

"Maybe..." Beth took a deep breath and looked up at Bobbie with old eyes. "Maybe it would be best if I took the girls and went to Wichita. I could ask Dan's parents or brother if we could stay with them until I figured out what to do."

The Cara-LeeAnn runaway train of earlier became a race car in which Bobbie's mind and heart were helpless passengers. It hurtled down an unlit road and slammed into an unseen wall. She waited to see if they would crawl out of the wreckage, unable to tell what damage had been done yet.

"Wichita?" she asked in a quavering voice.

"Yeah. It's only been a month of therapy, but I'm learning what healthy is, and this isn't healthy."

Bobbie couldn't swallow this time. "I need a day to come up with an appropriate answer. Would you give me a day? Promise me you won't make up your mind or go in a day?"

"Okay, a day. Do you want to talk with Dr. Langston tomorrow about it? We could even talk Saturday since tomorrow is a work and therapy day and I don't feel like derailing what could be the last family therapy session Gracie might have."

Bobbie took a deep breath and cut into her palms with her nails to keep the room from spinning. "Shit. Tomorrow I'm going to Cottonwood Plains for the closing on the farm if you're still in agreement on that. I have your power of attorney, but if you've changed your mind and want to go back, I guess I could call the bank and tell them—"

"No. I could never take the girls back to live on that farm. I can't believe you would suggest that." Beth's face grew red.

Bobbie remained silent. She didn't know what to say. She couldn't believe Beth would even play with the idea of leaving Lawrence at all, let alone returning to Cottonwood Plains. If she was going to leave, who was to say a free house wouldn't cross her mind? She decided she had to say something.

"Anyhow, I need to know whether or not I'm authorized to sell the farm. I guess it would give you a nest egg," Bobbie said, hesitantly. "But back to the question. I need some time to come up with good, workable answers, and I would like to talk with Dr. Langston. Maybe I can call her on the phone today and arrange something. I don't know, it's up to her. But we do need to talk again. Can we talk on Sunday or even next week?" Bobbie felt her heart beating so fast she feared it might explode.

"Yes, but don't take too long. I'm serious."

Bobbie sucked in a deep breath. "I'm taking you completely seriously. I'll think about how I am and how I can change and get back to you as soon as I can, I promise."

"Okay, I need to lie back down and rest this headache. I'm going to pass on the coffee. I'll take some more aspirin in an hour and pick up the girls after school."

"See you later then." Bobbie stood on shaky knees.

Beth just grunted as she lay back and pulled the sheet up over her head.

Bobbie headed for the phone to call the English department and ask for someone to cover her afternoon class. Today was going to be a thinking day.

Chapter Twenty-Seven

Bobbie's Personal Log, Stardate 9.19.1974. 23:00 Hours. Crap, there I go making jokes when I'm going to be writing about something very serious. But I'm scared, and I guess I'm avoiding it. I can't. I had a fight with Kathleen on Wednesday and another with Beth today, and I guess you could say a personal revelation tonight, via the wisdom of the two of them. Let me back up and explain. I have written in here before about being pretty self-contained and motivated since high school. I knew it was the only way I was going to get out of Cottonwood Plains. I had to work to get a scholarship and go to college and get a good job. Mom couldn't help me, and the schools weren't particularly interested in helping a bastard girl from Kansas, so I knew I had to do it on my own. And I did. I made my own way and learned to get what I wanted, to do what I needed to survive, and take care of Bobbie first.

But now, I've come to realize that it's turned me into a person that does what she wants to, or what she thinks needs to be done, with little or no thought to what the implications will be for other people. Like when I decided the girls needed to know about their Italian heritage. That was a good thing, I thought, but I didn't take into consideration what it would mean to them living with Dan and how it would affect their relationships with him. Apparently, they all took a lot of abuse after that because of what I had shared when Cara told him about it. I had never even considered that possibility. I knew he was a petty, hateful man, but I just never stopped to think about the ramifications for them.

As far as pushing his buttons and my guilt about causing him to kidnap and rape Gracie? I keep getting told that it isn't helpful in the long run. This is hard to write and will be even harder to say to Dr. Langston and Beth, but if I don't, I'm just the martyr, and in a way, the victim, and that doesn't solve anything. So, I think I have to find a way to take accountability for what I did but not a blanket guilt, or did I forget to mention this? Or I'll lose everything. Beth will take the girls and move to Wichita, and Kathleen will leave me, and I really will be a pathetic, old woman with nothing. I can't even think or write about that possibility. It's too scary.

Now I have to be persuasive at getting Beth and Kathleen to be patient with me. This learning to be accountable without a massive, unproductive guilt is going to take time, and I'm not going to be perfect at it right away. I think Kathleen will give me time. I know Beth is horribly frustrated with me, even to suggest taking the girls and leaving, but I'm going to hope for her to give me another chance as well. I hope Dr. Langston can help me and can smooth things out with Beth. I don't know what I would do without all of them. That would be devastating.

Chapter Twenty-Eight

Kathleen had three years of experience driving her Pinto on roads that were in town, but she was enjoying this drive out I-70 West for the same reason she enjoyed every other road trip she took between Lawrence and Chicago. The Pinto was a great little car, so much better than that Dodge she had driven before...

"Penny for your thoughts?" Bobbie broke into her reverie.

"Oh, babe, I'm just enjoying the road trip. You know I love driving, especially long trips, so this is just a quickie to me."

"What's so good about this quickie?" Bobbie asked.

"You have to ask me what's so good about a quickie?" Kathleen roared with laughter.

"Okay, okay, Bob Hope, I don't need your tired old humor." Bobbie grinned, too, and blushed almost as red as Kathleen's hair.

Kathleen stole a quick look over at her lover. "It's not old, nor am I tired of it, this idea of a quickie with you. I doubt I ever will be, although the thought of a long, relaxing afternoon alone is even better."

"Eyes on the interstate, Romeo, before you run me off the road or kill me with high blood pressure, whichever comes first. I'm trying to get a solemn piece of business done today. You can have your quickie tonight, back on the highway in some cheap motel." Bobbie watched out the window and fanned herself with the paper she had brought along to read.

"Can you reach the green nylon gym bag on the backseat?" Kathleen asked out of the blue.

"What do you need?"

"I need you to grab the green nylon bag on the backseat and bring it up here." Kathleen kept her eyes on the road.

"Lucky for you this car has an interior the size of a doll's house. Even a shorty like me can reach the backseat." She pulled the bag up onto her lap. "Now what?"

"Now I need you to dig in there and find a Woolworth's bag." Kathleen glanced over at the bag and back on the road. It wasn't an auspicious moment to be doing something like this, but she couldn't wait.

Bobbie dug into the bag and pulled out a folded-up Woolworth's bag.

"Open it." Kathleen's hands tightened on the steering wheel.

Bobbie opened it. Inside there was a white Sears box wrapped with a blue ribbon.

Kathleen waited. Bobbie put the Woolworth's bag on the floor. Kathleen shifted. Bobbie put the green nylon bag on top of the Woolworth's bag. Kathleen cleared her throat. Bobbie held the box in her hands.

"Are you going to open it?" Kathleen asked after thirty full seconds had passed of Bobbie staring at the box in silence.

Bobbie looked up with tears in her eyes. She met Kathleen's eyes, then looked down shyly and shrugged. It was so unlike her that it melted Kathleen's heart. Suddenly the box was unimportant. Kathleen reached over and covered Bobbie's hand with hers.

"Hey, babe, are you okay? I didn't mean to upset you. What's wrong?"

A long sniff. "You nut. I'm not upset. I'm just in love and don't know what to do with you at fifty-five miles per hour on an interstate following a milk tanker. Make that sixty-five, and you better pay closer attention." Bobbie smiled the smile that made Kathleen feel like a chocolate bar in July.

"Well, then open it."

"May I wait for a rest stop? I don't want you crashing the car trying to watch me. It's a tuna can hurtling down a road. Give me a tanker or boat any day. No, I changed my mind. I'll take you in a boat, a tuna can, or a damned roller skate, your choice. Just find a rest stop and make it one too small for the big trucks." Bobbie caressed the box, and the sight of her fingers running over the corners made Kathleen look directly back up at the road and swallow. Hard.

They drove for eighteen minutes on Kathleen's wristwatch until she lucked—truly luck on a Kansas freeway—onto a rest area that had a picnic table at the east edge, far from the restrooms and water fountains, far from the truck parking. She pulled up beside it and stuffed her hair up in a baseball cap she pulled from behind her seat.

"What are you doing?" Bobbie asked.

"Preventing a scene when the profile of two long-haired people kissing gets noticed by some good ol' boy trucker. That's assuming some good ol' boy trucker is looking this way with good enough vision and assuming that one of those long-haired people gets lucky enough to get kissed," Kathleen answered, her Chicago Irish accent thicker than usual.

Bobbie blushed again, looked at the box, and glanced at Kathleen. Kathleen nodded. Bobbie slid the ribbon off the gift and laid it carefully in her lap. She ran her hands reverently over the edges before taking the lid off. Inside lay two silver pendants on chains. "Best Friends" was written on a heart that was broken in half, one-half per chain. It was a favorite gift of girls from high school down to elementary and had appeared around necks and on charm bracelets for as long as Kathleen could remember. She held her breath and waited for Bobbie to respond.

Bobbie smiled. "It's precious."

"They didn't have one that said soul mate, besides that would be a bit obvious. I know this is a tad young for a junior college assistant professor but today is a special day."

"September twentieth?" Bobbie looked up quizzically as she finished putting on her new necklace.

"Don't tell me you don't remember." Kathleen grinned lasciviously.

"Of course, I remember, but I didn't get you anything. I feel bad. I didn't think you would get me something, and I've been so busy getting Beth and the girls settled, and now school starting, and the farm selling at the same time..."

Kathleen waited until Bobbie finished prattling on. "Did I ask for something? You gave me the greatest gift of my life three months ago today when you agreed to be my life partner, my soul mate, and lover. I broke open a ten-year-old shell around my heart when I asked you, and my heart nearly exploded when you said yes. That's what you gave me, and this is just a token of my love. Look beneath the cardboard."

Bobbie pulled out the tiny board and found another one covered in blue felt, boasting tiny diamond studs.

"These are for my girl. I don't know how you'll explain them, if you even need to, or if you'll ever feel comfortable wearing them, but I wanted you to have them. They're almost as beautiful as you are."

As Bobbie looked down at the studs in her hand, Kathleen's apprehension grew. Bobbie's silence scared her. Had she gone too far? Had Bobbie changed her mind? They had been tip-toeing around a tenuous peace after the fight on Wednesday. They needed to talk about it sometime soon, but not right now.

She looked down at the studs and saw what looked like three drops of water. Then another fell. Bobbie was crying on the earrings, for the love of Pete. A knot rose in Kathleen's throat.

She took Bobbie's chin and lifted it for Bobbie to face her. Tears streaked down from Bobbie's beautiful eyes, and one shaky hand reached up to rub at a sniffly nose. "I love you," Bobbie said.

"Oh, babe." Kathleen leaned past the steering wheel and stick shift as best she could and folded her lover into her arms. She rocked her and stroked the long brown curls that fell over her other hand. "Oh, babe. You're the answer to every prayer I ever made to the Virgin Mary. And look, I got my own virgin."

Bobbie laughed and breathed deep. She snuggled close to Kathleen's shoulder and giggled. Kathleen giggled, too, and soon they were laughing so hard they almost put the car in gear.

Kathleen gave in to safety. "Sit up, babe, or we're gonna wreck the ride." She pushed Bobbie back to her own side after dropping a kiss on top her head.

"You're unbelievable, do you know that? You remembered a three-month anniversary, you got me diamonds for it, which you cleverly disguised, and you prayed to the Virgin Mary for me." Bobbie raised one finger to trace the side of Kathleen's face, from the field hockey scar on her left eyebrow down to her dimpled chin.

"Actually, I prayed to the Virgin to disguise me as a boy, so I could have a girlfriend and not go to hell. Then I prayed for the woman of my dreams to become real, for me to find her, and to spend the rest of my life with her. Your mom was Catholic. Didn't you pray to the Virgin?"

"Bastards aren't raised Catholic, and the only time I prayed was when I was taking a test in elementary school. And there were no virgins involved to my knowledge other than myself." Bobbie grinned.

"Well, I was taught that the Virgin intercedes with God and is damned good at it, too. Look what she did." Kathleen sighed and leaned into Bobbie's finger.

"Whatever you say. What I say is look what you did. You came all the way down to Kansas and found me. You spoke to me first and pursued me as a friend when I was just a shy, small town kid. You brought me into your life, you may have kept me in college, and you had a hand in my journey to grad school and my success, so just look what *you* did, Ms. McClintock."

Kathleen took Bobbie's hand during this long recitation and brought Bobbie's fingers to her lips. Taking them gently in her teeth, she nibbled playfully on the fingertips she loved so much, imagining her taste, Bobbie's taste, on them. "It's all for you. And if I'm lucky, your business will take a long time, and the real estate agent will suggest you have one final look at the old family place, so it will run into evening and we'll have to grab some dinner in Oakley and get a motel God-only-knows-where because we're too tired to drive back. Then I'll spend an entire night showing you how much I love you."

Bobbie stared out the front window and took a ragged breath. "If you don't shut up, I'm not going to get that farm sold. Then Beth will kill me, the girls will never be able to afford college, and we'll both come home to a house with the locks changed. So, stop it and drive, lover."

Kathleen looked away with great effort. "You're right. Damn, look at the time. Okay, Cottonwood Plains, you heard my plan. Don't fail me now."

Chapter Twenty-Nine

Bobbie had never done anything like sell a farm, so this was entirely new to her, and she was fascinated by the process, start to finish. The buyer was a rich, older doctor from Denver who was buying his third similar property in western Kansas. He used the existing farm houses as rentals for hunters who would walk in to hunt on government land, a surprisingly lucrative proposition, and build a new house, a bed and breakfast, and a new well. Dustin, the real estate agent, wasn't sure exactly how lucrative this was or if it was just a tax write off for a retired farm boy, but he had the cash to buy the farm, so who cared?

Bobbie and Beth certainly didn't. Cash for the asking price in such a short time shocked and thrilled them. It made the real estate agent wonder if they shouldn't have held out for more, but Bobbie assured him they wanted out of the property business.

"But we'll take you up on one last walk around the farm if the new owner is still some ways out," Bobbie said to Dustin after reviewing the mountain of paperwork the bank and agent had prepared. "I would like to show my friend Kathleen where I grew up."

"Well," Dustin drawled, "he stopped at a phone an hour ago to call and say he needed to purchase a new tire there and would be late. I'm not expecting him for another ninety minutes. You should have time to look around the farm."

Bobbie realized the entire town was aware of what had happened in the barn, but she didn't give a damn. "We'll be back in an hour and a half, either way. Let's have a look, Kathleen, shall we?"

Kathleen followed her out of the office and opened the door for Bobbie when they got to the Pinto. She looked back into the bank window and caught the faint outline of a tall, broad figure watching them through the window. When she got in the car, she asked Bobbie about it. "Maybe I shouldn't have opened the car door for you. I think someone was watching."

"I don't care. This is our last transaction here. Next week we're moving the money to a real bank in Lawrence, and we'll never see them again. Let's go out to the farm, and I'll show you around." Bobbie busied herself peering into the rearview mirror.

"I saw the house and barn the night before the fire. I'm glad we got your mother's furniture out of the barn. We wouldn't have been able to house everyone in Lawrence without it." Kathleen worded her comment carefully as she put the car in first and headed out into the country.

"I still struggle with the way the whole thing went down. I thought it would be a great idea, coming down with a truck for the furniture. Since it had been sitting here for years, I knew Beth wouldn't care, and I didn't care what Dan thought. It didn't belong to him anyhow." Bobbie bit her lip. "Besides, he wasn't going to know. I just planned to slip in and out of town Saturday morning and give them a quick hug. Asshole was always too lazy to come back for something he forgot when he went out to the lake fishing."

Kathleen put the car in park in front of a two-story farm house surrounded by cottonwood trees. She rolled down her window and listened to the wind blowing through the leaves. "Are you sure you want to talk about this, Bobbie? You don't have to say anything at all, or you can just show me your room, or we can leave right now and go back to town and grab some dinner..."

Bobbie waited till Kathleen's voice trailed off. After counting to ten, she spoke. "No, Dr. Langston and I agreed that this would be a good time for me to talk it all through, and that you're a safe listener and someone I can cry in front of, if need be." She smiled bravely at Kathleen. "Do you mind listening to it all, in its gory-ness? It's the part inside my head that's the worst."

Kathleen took Bobbie's hand and squeezed. "I'll listen all night, babe. Lead the way."

Inside the house, Bobbie led her up the narrow staircase. "I've already shown you all the rooms when we scavenged for remaining furniture. This was our bedroom and across the hall was our mother's bedroom and sewing room. She made all our clothing until we graduated high school. Hmm, I probably still have a few things she made me. Isn't that cool?"

"You said your mom was strict?" Kathleen paused at the door to the opposite room like she might disturb the ghost of Mrs. Rossi.

"She was living a tough life in a tough time. A single mom after the war? She must not have had any decent men courting her, and the half-asses that did probably assumed since she had children she would jump at any halfway decent prospect for a husband. She hated the fact that Beth and I were bastards, but even getting married wouldn't have changed that. I think that's why she chose not to get married. I think that's why she didn't go to town any more than she had to, either. She knew it just made it worse for her girls. She had no idea how bad it was for us. Beth and I would cry to one another, but never to her." Bobbie got lightheaded and braced herself with her hand on the wall.

Kathleen touched her hand. Bobbie gave a half-smile. "She was a strong lady to raise us and take care of the elderly couple that owned this farm. They didn't have any children of their own. That's why they agreed to let a nineteen-year-old pregnant girl move in with them, in the first place. She cared for them until their deaths and kept them from having to go to the nursing home in town, and in return, they left her the farm. Mom was a tough lady, threatening to outsiders, and she taught me to be tenacious, also. I guess that's where I got my drive."

Kathleen followed Bobbie back down the stairs. "I suppose I always wondered how your mom ended up owning land in western Kansas when she ran away from St. Louis. And you're right, she sounds like one powerful woman."

Bobbie laughed as she moved to the porch swing. "She would like that you called her that. Powerful woman. I guess my strong lady description pales beside it. That women's studies program certainly changes one's language."

"We can talk about feminism, gay liberation, and the power of language any old day. This is your last time here, unless you're done," Kathleen said gently.

"No, I have more to say. I just wanted to sit and rock in the breeze and watch the sun set a bit. It won't truly set till after seven, but it's pretty, don't you think?"

"Mm-hmm." Kathleen rocked and watched. She looked at Bobbie, just waiting.

Bobbie blew out a sharp breath and rubbed her palms on her knees. "Okay, first, do you have any questions about all of this? I don't want to confuse you more."

"I do," Kathleen said. "Why did Dan hate you so much? I've seen in-law relationships that were antagonistic, but wow, you two really hated one another, and no one ever said why."

"Well, that's awkward." Bobbie coughed once. "In junior high, Dan took special delight in tormenting me. He called me 'that bastard girl.' He harassed and bullied me to no end and made my life hell. In high school, I figured it out. He had a crush on me. He tried, during our sophomore year, to put the moves on me during a tornado drill when we were all evacuated to the gym locker rooms. He and a bunch of his buddies cut me out of a group of girls. I was reading a book and didn't notice, till he tried to put his tongue down my throat. I guess that served as his 'hi, I like you and want to go out,' announcement. But I pushed against him, and when he wouldn't push away, I brought my knee up hard. I racked him so bad he nearly fell on the ground. As it was, he sank onto the bench, cursing me and gasping for air." She paused, a slight grin on her face as she stared into space, remembering.

"But the worst part was his tough gang of ninth and tenth graders fell apart laughing. I threatened to do the same to them and haul them into the principal if they ever did the same to another girl. I told him to stay as far away from me as he could if he knew what was good for him. I guess his revenge was dating Beth. When he avoided me, I thought he had learned his lesson. I didn't tell her because I was embarrassed. By the next time I took my head out of a book, he was firmly ensconced in Beth's heart, and I was too late. I tried once to tell her he was a loser, but she thought I was jealous. So, I backed off and hoped she would figure him out before they got serious. But suddenly, it was serious. To this day, I don't know how much of the story Beth knows, and I don't know how brave I am to tell her."

"She knows he's a jerk. It wouldn't come as any big surprise. I guess the question is, does she need to know?" Kathleen looked up at the pinkening sky through the cottonwood leaves.

"Or do I need to tell her, maybe? No, I don't think I have some burning need to fess up, just because. It would be only if she needed to know." Bobbie felt detached, sleepy almost. Maybe her mind was trying to avoid going through this one last time. She told Kathleen so. "I think I need some of the chocolate we have in the backseat if I'm going to stay awake."

"Are you sure that won't make you sleepy? Sugar gives me a rush for a little bit but then I'm wiped out for good. Do you think we should go for a walk and wake you up that way?" Kathleen offered her best ideas, but Bobbie's face remained pensive.

Until Bobbie jumped up, out of the blue, and began doing an intense Jack LaLanne exercise routine. After three minutes of wild activity and calisthenics, she sat down, refreshed and awake. "Okay, I guess that fitness television show taught me something after all. Back to the story, before the sun goes down and we miss our closing."

"You were there for the action," she said, "when Dan came back, found us, grabbed Gracie, and left. I don't know if I ever told you he had threatened to take all three girls and leave Beth if she even contacted me, all because she suggested leaving him. You saw that happen. What you may not know is my fear. I think Dan attacked Gracie because he was angry at me, and in his alcoholic stupor, confused Gracie with me. He wanted to rape me, not Gracie. But she was there, and I wasn't. She took my place and paid my price. I can never fix that. I can never make that go away. She will never be a whole little girl. She will always have a broken part, no matter how well she heals, and it's my fault."

"Oh, Bobbie." Kathleen took Bobbie's hand and raised it to her lips.

"Oh, Bobbie, what? Go ahead and tell me what those green eyes are thinking," Bobbie said, her voice catching.

"I think you're carrying a lot of weight that isn't yours. Don't take on what Dan chose to do. And as far as fixing it, of course,

you can't. You can't change the rape. You can't change what was
going on before it. No one can, but it's not your fault. It's no one's
fault but Dan's, and he's dead. But don't make Gracie be more than
she is. She didn't pay your price or take your place. She got caught
in the cross-fire. She's a survivor of a war that wasn't hers. But
don't give her the pressure of being your savior, too."

Bobbie looked at Kathleen, feeling some confusion. Was she
doing all that to Gracie?

Kathleen squeezed Bobbie's hand and went on. "And while
you're at it, stop being responsible for everything that happens in
life, good and bad. Magic is good, but over-responsibility is a drag
and unnecessary. You're surrounded by good, strong women and
girls who can pull their weight now. That may not have been the
case before, but it is now. And you have the help of Dr. Langston if
you think something's out of balance. Use her as a resource. And
there's always me, your one-hundred-percent-biased and
on-your-side-no-matter-what lover. I'll always be there for you."

Bobbie's eyes welled up with tears. Kathleen waited for the
first tear to fall, caught it in her hand, brought it to her heart, and
held it there. That caused a fresh shower, which necessitated
Kathleen taking Bobbie into her arms and just holding her.

"You're the best," Bobbie whispered from her muffled
position beneath Kathleen's ear.

"I know," Kathleen said. "But we're even better together."

Chapter Thirty

It was September and the trees were changing their colors. Winter would be gray in Kansas, black branches bare against gray skies, but for now, color still lingered—blue skies, red-streaked sunsets, and many shades of leaves. LeeAnn and Cara were playing in the garden plot on the swing set. Gracie sat on the back-porch steps, avoiding the adults in the house. The girls would leave her alone, but it seemed to her the adults asked more and more questions.

Something rustled under the mulberry bush next to the garage. Gracie ignored it until the cause of the rustle began limping across the yard toward her. A young cat, a kitten really, was covered in dirt and leaves. It was scuffed up, one eye full of pus, probably the results of the first year of fights it hadn't yet learned to win. It hunched down a few feet from Gracie and looked at her with its one good eye. Gracie held out one hand, and it walked up to her.

The porch door opened, and the wounded kitten took off like a runner in the hundred-yard dash.

"Why did you do that? Now it's gone," Gracie said to her aunt.

"What's gone?" Aunt Bobbie asked.

"The kitten."

"What kitten?"

"The one that's gone now. When you opened the door, you scared it. It's hurt."

"Gracie, a hurt animal can be dangerous. It could have rabies or bite you," Aunt Bobbie said.

"Well, it's gone now."

"Okay, I came to get you and the girls for supper. Go inside and wash up."

"Can I sit out here for a few minutes while the girls wash up?" Gracie asked.

"Since you asked, I'll say yes." Aunt Bobbie called the younger girls and followed them back inside. Gracie heard her stop inside the door. She knew Aunt Bobbie was watching her to see if there really was a cat. Aunt Bobbie shushed Kathleen when she asked from the kitchen what Aunt Bobbie was doing.

Gracie walked across the yard toward the bush, sat down, and waited. In just a couple seconds, she heard the rustle again, and the young tortoise-shell cat walked out of the bushes. Gracie held still and was quiet. The cat walked to a couple of feet from her and sat down. The two absorbed one another. Gracie held out a hand, and the kitten walked up and brushed against her outstretched palm.

"Gracie," Aunt Bobbie called through the door. "I'm coming out. Please don't pick up the cat until I can look at it, okay?"

Gracie nodded her head and kept petting the cat, which had crouched down by her knee and was leaning into the affection.

Aunt Bobbie quietly opened the door, walked across the yard, and stopped several yards from Gracie and the cat. "It's not afraid of me now. Maybe it was just the noise before."

She knelt down and stuck out her hand toward the cat. The cat considered her offer for a few moments and looked up at Gracie as if asking permission before it walked over to Aunt Bobbie. Aunt Bobbie gently ran her hands down the cat's body and legs, looking for injuries. The kitten flinched when she touched one hind leg, but other than that, the hurt eye appeared to be the only injury.

"Gracie, I'm going to try to pick it up," Aunt Bobbie said.

"It's a girl."

"Okay, I'm going see if she will let me pick her up."

The cat, once in Bobbie's arms, snuggled against her. Bobbie and Gracie stood up and studied the kitten.

"What vet are we going to take Willie to?" asked Gracie.

"Her name is Willie? But you said it's a girl."

"She is, and her name is Willie." Gracie resisted the urge to use the slow emphasis she would have used with her younger sisters.

"Okay. She does need to see a vet, but we'll have to wait till Monday since it's already so late. If she's still around on Monday, I'll make her an appointment."

Gracie's eyes filled with tears, and her chest felt tight. Couldn't Aunt Bobbie see how badly Willie needed a doctor? "What if her eye gets worse? What if someone hurts her? We have to take care of her now."

Aunt Bobbie studied the ground for a few seconds before she met Gracie's eyes. "Okay, let's see if there's an animal hospital nearby that stays open late. Go get the phone book and bring it out here."

Gracie raced to the house. She was careful not to let the screen door slam and scare Willie again. She ran up the stairs and grabbed the phone book.

"Where are you going with the phone book?" her mom asked as Gracie ran back out with it.

"Aunt Bobbie has a hurt kitten, and if you come out, you'll scare it. We have to find an animal hospital." Gracie slowed her pace to a walk.

With Aunt Bobbie's help, Gracie found an animal hospital open until seven, and it wasn't too far away.

"All right," Aunt Bobbie told her. "Here's the plan. You get a clean towel and my bag. We'll wrap the... Willie, in the towel so she can't scratch you while we're in the car, okay?"

In a quiet hurry, Gracie did what her aunt asked. They wrapped the kitten in the towel and drove to the animal hospital. The kitten snuggled with Gracie the entire trip. A woman met them at the door and took them to a little room where they could wait until the vet could see them.

"What does a Friday night visit cost?" Bobbie asked

"It depends." The vet tech shrugged.

Gracie's shoulders and mouth sagged.

"Oh, Gracie," Bobbie said and put an arm around her, "I just wondered. Willie's important to you, and I'm glad we could get her here."

The veterinarian came in and examined the cat. He told them she needed a leg x-ray. He also worried that Willie's eye had a serious infection.

"Can we get her vaccinations and some antibiotics before we go home?" Aunt Bobbie asked.

"I can't vaccinate her until she's well. The vaccines would make her sicker. She needs to stay here a couple of days until her infection's cleared up. Then we'll give her the shots and send her home." He spoke to Gracie.

"Well, Doctor, you're good at what you do," Bobbie said dryly, drawing his eyes up to meet hers again, "I suppose you should go ahead and do those things that need to be taken care of this weekend."

Gracie gave Willie one last snuggle before the vet took her to the back. The tech gave them some paperwork and asked them to take it to the front desk.

While they waited at the front desk, Gracie slipped her hand into Bobbie's and whispered to her. "Thank you."

During the ride home, Gracie didn't speak to Aunt Bobbie unless she was asked a question, nor did she hold Aunt Bobbie's hand.

"I'm glad you like the kitten. The little girls might be jealous of your new friend. We might need to get them a dog," Bobbie said as they pulled into the driveway.

Gracie didn't make eye contact, but she did smile.

Chapter Thirty-One

Gracie lay on her bed waiting for sleep to come. She liked how dark her bedroom was. It was her very own cave. And her bunk bed was perfect, too. Her mom was so short she couldn't see anything up here when she walked through the room. Not that anything was going on—Gracie just wanted her privacy. Now, more than ever.

She didn't have to protect her sisters from the nightmares on the edge of the bed anymore. Those nightmares were over. Now she had nightmares about those nightmares. Everything that had been cloudy, confusing, or scary was now real and terrifying. She didn't ever want to leave her room and didn't if she had her choice. She would stay in her dark, safe cave and keep the covers over her head where no one could see her or touch her.

It didn't matter that it was hot under there. Day or night, she lived and slept in long pants. Wearing jeans in August and September felt uncomfortable, but they were safer. Safe was especially important at night. She slept in long pajamas with a sheet, a blanket, and her comforter pulled over her.

One part of her mind knew her dad was the dangerous one and wouldn't ever come back. But if her dad could hurt her, other people could, too. At least no one in the house drank beer or whiskey. If she smelled beer or whiskey, she wanted to vomit.

It almost happened that day at the flea market. A man scared her when he walked up beside her and made her remember her dad after he came home from the tavern, all smoky and stinking of beer. It was all she could do not to throw up and run as fast and as far as she could in the crowd. But if she did that, she would lose her mom and her sisters and she didn't know how to get home. The thought made her twice as sick, and she took two steps running, but stopped. She grabbed her mom's arm with her sweaty hands and pulled her toward the parking lot. Her mom came right away, even though the little girls fussed at her. When they got home, Gracie went straight to bed. Her stomach felt better, but she needed the high, dark safety of her cave.

That night, her stomach ached just remembering it. When her mom came in to give her a kiss, Gracie stayed close to the wall and mumbled good night.

"Would you give me a decent goodnight kiss, Gracie? You know I can't reach you there. And we need to talk. I have to go to school early, so you can go with me or have Kathleen walk you over at the regular time," Mom said.

Her mom waited. "I can't make out what you're saying. Pull the comforter down and talk to me."

Gracie delayed until her mom reached up and shook her leg. At her mother's touch, she pulled down the blankets. "My stomach hurts real bad. I'm not going to school tomorrow."

"Oh, Gracie Elizabeth, you have to go to school. I can't just leave you here all day without a babysitter."

Gracie didn't respond.

"Missing Monday is missing the most important day of the week. You know that. You get your Friday folder on Monday, and we must have that. Come on, sweet girl, let's just see how you feel in the morning, okay?"

"I'm not going." Gracie pulled the blankets back over her head. She listened for her mom to leave the room. She finally heard a sigh and her mom going down the steps. She rolled close to the wall, squeezed her eyes tight, and willed sleep to come.

Chapter Thirty-Two

Bobbie heard Beth come tromping heavy-footed down the stairs and into the kitchen, where she got a glass of tea. Kathleen and Bobbie sat at the dining room table grading papers. Kathleen nudged Bobbie and pointed toward the kitchen. Bobbie went and got a glass of tea, too.

"You sure are stirring that a long time. Are you okay?" Bobbie asked Beth.

"I don't know. She'll barely talk to me today. She clammed up. Not that she was talking much, but it was like her barely opened walls slammed down at the flea market. I don't know if she'll ever talk to me again." Beth stared into her iced tea.

"She'll talk to you again. But the doctor says it will take time."

"But it will never be like it was before."

"No." Bobbie paused. "It probably won't be. But it will be okay. She's growing up, so it would've changed anyway."

"Oh, please, no early adolescence problems. I can't handle that now. I just want her to talk to me."

"What happened at the flea market? As exactly as you can remember it."

"I don't know. We were walking, and she suddenly dropped the cat collar she picked out and grabbed her stomach. I could see her throat working as she tried not to vomit. She looked like she was going to run. I was so scared. I wasn't sure I could keep up with her in the crowd, and what about the other two? But she stopped after a couple of steps and waited for me, and I hurried us home. Would you talk with her? Please?" Beth put a hand on Bobbie's arm.

"She's your daughter."

"Yes, but she's upset with me. I know I still have to work things out with her, but this was something big, and I can't wait till then to find out what happened. Something upset her, and she's still up there, hugging the wall and not talking except to say she's not going to school because she has a stomachache."

"Okay. I'll talk with her. Give me permission to do what I need to do or say what I feel necessary? About school or whatever?" Bobbie had the beginning of an idea.

"Yes, anything, Bobbie. You relate to her so well."

"Well, I wouldn't say that, but I love her."

Bobbie wondered if Gracie could hear her struggling up the stairs with the aluminum ladder they used to change lightbulbs. It banged against the wall with a metal ring. Bobbie knew she heard that. She peeked into Gracie's room and saw her roll toward the wall and pull up the blanket. Bobbie pulled the chair out from the front of the desk under the bed and moved it aside. She swore under her breath as she opened the ladder and climbed to the top to sit. Gracie rolled over to look at Bobbie, who braced herself against the wall with one hand.

"Now that I have your attention—don't roll back over, I'm here to talk, and I went to a lot of trouble to do it. Remember, I took Willie to the vet Friday night, and you owe me a favor. I want, no, I need to know what happened at the flea market."

Gracie rolled back toward the wall.

"Gracie Elizabeth, do you want a cat? Because if you do, you better roll over here and look at me."

Gracie rolled back over. She looked at Bobbie but didn't say anything.

"That's better. I like to see those pretty eyes when we talk." Bobbie softened her voice and put her other hand on Gracie's bed. "What happened today, babe?"

Gracie closed her eyes and swallowed. Bobbie waited. After a full minute of silence, Gracie told her. "The man smelled of beer."

"And that made you sick. I'm sorry, hon. I bet it was scary, too."

Gracie opened one testing eye. Bobbie tried to look sincere and waited for her response. "Yeah, it was."

Bobbie's head spun, with no one direction being helpful. She had no idea what to say. Asking why was stupid. Asking how scary was redundant. Finally, she sighed. "You know, Gracie, I can promise you that none of us, no one will drink inside this house, and we will not let anyone bring beer into the house. Or liquor," she added as an afterthought.

Gracie closed the one eye that had been open and whispered, "Thanks."

"From now on, you tell me anything that scares you and I'll see what I can do to help with it, okay?" Bobbie asked.

Gracie nodded, her eyes still closed.

"I know we didn't protect you from your dad. We didn't know what he was doing, and we didn't know what he would do. That's no excuse. Grown-ups are supposed to protect kids, not hurt them. I know we didn't do that very well. But we'll get better, I promise, and if *anything* scary happens, you let me or your mom or Kathleen know, and we'll make it stop. I give you my word. Okay?"

Gracie nodded again. Her eyes were closed, but tears still squeezed out.

"Oh, babe, can I give you a hug?" Bobbie asked.

"Not now."

"All right, but you have one hug waiting for you twenty-four hours a day, okay?"

Gracie nodded again and rolled over to face the wall.

Bobbie sat on the ladder for a little while, her heart in her shoes. All she could do was sit and protect Gracie for a few moments. But what about after she left the room? What about at school? In the yard? At the flea market? They couldn't hide her forever. Bobbie slid down the ladder without any good answers.

Chapter Thirty-Three

Bobbie made sure she was early for the final bell at Gracie's elementary school on Monday. "We have some shopping to do," she said when greeting her quiet niece.

They sat in the car and made a list. "Cat box and litter, food and food dishes, water bowl. What else can you think of, Gracie?" Bobbie wanted to draw her into the process as much as possible.

"A bed?"

"No, not necessary. Cats can and do sleep anywhere and everywhere, unlike a dog. What else?"

"A collar and a comb." Gracie suggested more items than Bobbie had expected.

"Ah, I hadn't thought of a comb, but that's a good one."

"A litter box pooper scooper?" It appeared that even trauma didn't stop this ten-year-old from grinning when she got to legitimately say the word poop.

Bobbie grinned, too. "We will need one of those. Where will we put the litter box?"

"On the inner back porch. I think that should be okay," Gracie said in her serious tone. "And I have an idea. If we put the box on a piece of material, we won't have to sweep all the time. We could take it out, shake it off, and throw it in the laundry."

"Hmm. Another idea. You've been thinking about this a lot, haven't you?"

"Yes. And my friend Abby had a cat that always carried sand on his feet out of the box. But they used a carpet square."

"And what makes a piece of material better?" Bobbie asked.

"They had to vacuum and shampoo the little piece of carpet and couldn't just shake it and wash it."

"So, two squares of material, one for when the other is in the laundry. I think we have those at home already. Good thinking, Gracie girl. I like the way your mind works." Bobbie touched her shoulder.

Gracie pulled away a little but didn't disengage as fully as she had been.

"Let's do some shopping and make it to the animal hospital by five." Bobbie fired up the boat, and they left.

Gracie wore a slight grin but didn't bounce up and down or do any of the other things her sisters would have done. Was that maturity, personality, or trauma? Bobbie wondered.

They went to Duckwall's, lingered over a few toys, and bought the needed supplies. Back in the car, Bobbie had a thought. "You know, this is getting pretty expensive, and we haven't seen the vet bill yet. I was going to hire some neighbor boys to get rid of the leaves this fall and do some of the yard work. Would you be willing to do that instead if I taught you how?"

Gracie nodded from far away.

Bobbie sighed. Even the imminent promise of a kitten wasn't enough to keep Gracie present as much as she would have liked, but then again, it was better than it could have been. "All right," she said. "Let's go get your cat."

When she pulled up at the animal hospital, they were one of several cars, none of which, Bobbie hoped, contained a large dog. They went inside and sat in line. Barbara, the same vet tech who had welcomed them the previous Friday night, greeted them again. "Willie's doing well and will be so glad to see you. Are you ready to come back and get her? Do you have a collar and leash?"

Bobbie and Gracie looked at one another. Whoever would have thought of a leash for a cat? Bobbie was sure the animal hospital would sell them one at an exorbitant price.

All in all, the total cost wasn't as bad as Bobbie had feared. When they got Willie back, her eye looked permanently puckered but less painful, and she appeared more like a playful kitten than the serious animal they had brought in.

"How are her eye and leg, Doctor?" Bobbie asked.

"Well, the eye isn't infected anymore, but she'll always be blind in it. She's very adaptable, so it shouldn't slow her down much. As for the leg, it's fine. No damage to the bone or muscle. It must have been sore from sleeping outside after the fight. She can jump and run and do everything else she'll need to do to entertain you for hours." The vet sounded as proud of Gracie as if she were one of his own children.

"What about off a bunk bed? Can she jump down from a low bunk?" Gracie asked. It was the first time she'd voluntarily spoken to a male since July.

"It would be better if someone handed her down, but she'll be just fine. She'll land on her feet!" The vet laughed at his joke. "She'll need to be fixed in a couple months, unless you want to go through heat, have a risky young pregnancy, and then have kittens. If you want another kitten, we can always find you one to adopt instead."

"No, one will be quite enough, I think," Bobbie said. They carried Willie to the front, paid their bill, and wrapped her in the towel again before putting her in the car in Gracie's arms.

"Gracie, you know your sisters will be excited. They'll want to hold and pet her, but they already know she's your cat. And it looks like she knows it, too. So please don't get too jealous if she spreads a little love around the family. If she's lived outside her whole life, I bet she can take all the loving she can get, right?" Bobbie couldn't help reiterating the lecture she'd given Gracie five different times in four different ways.

"Right," Gracie agreed absent-mindedly, petting the kitten. "But they really need an outside dog for that dog run."

"Oh no, let's not go there yet." Bobbie laughed. "I thought we might put bikes in that dog run."

Gracie looked interested at the mention of bikes. But she had other ideas. "Why don't we make a little fence around that backward corner of the house where the porch goes out farther than Kathleen's bedroom? We could put up the wire and make a square one for bikes."

Gracie's ideas and participation in the conversation excited Bobbie. This cat might be the best thing they'd done so far, after all. "Okay, but we'll need help stretching the fencing and digging the holes and whatever else you do for a bike thingy."

Gracie was lost with Willie's face buried in her neck. "I'll help," she murmured. And that was that.

****

When they arrived home, Cara, despite her mother's instructions, still bounced around the front room. Willie greeted the rest of the family, going to everyone for a little introduction, but returning to Gracie for a lap to sit on and shoelaces to bat. It went well. Bobbie let Gracie tell the family the plans for putting up a little fence between the corner of the house and porch. "We'll need bikes in the spring," Bobbie explained, "and a place to put them."

Cara and LeeAnn looked thoughtful. "How do you learn how to ride a bike?" LeeAnn asked. Cara was stumped. But the thoughtful moment was brief, and they went back to excited chattering.

"What are we going to put in the dog run?" LeeAnn asked.

"Well," Kathleen said, "I had thought about that myself, and I spoke with your mother first. You always have to talk with your mother first about things. The head of the math department will be inheriting a small dog that needs a home. But he won't get her until around Halloween. If you can wait that long, would you be interested in a small dog that's a bird dog-poodle mix? She has long curly hair the color of a bird dog, and her name is Sara Jane."

Cara immediately started prancing around the room chanting, "Sara Jane! Sara Jane!" This frightened the kitten, who jumped and hid behind the sofa, which was a good thing since Cara lost her balance and crashed into her oldest sister.

"Cara!" Gracie yelled.

"It's okay Gracie. Willie will have to get used to the rest of the family," her mother reminded her. "And Cara, you can't bounce in the house. You're getting too big, and you'll hurt someone or something."

"And Willie was hurt like Gracie, so we have to be careful," Cara chanted.

Silence sharp as a fresh-cut wheat field filled the room.

Everyone looked to Gracie to see how she was reacting. Everyone except Cara, who didn't realize she'd said something wrong. Gracie looked behind the couch. The adults sat frozen. LeeAnn saved the day.

"They both were hurt, but they're both getting better," she said, not afraid to go where the adults were reluctant to tread. Bobbie made a mental note to have a chat with the younger two girls about their comments. Maybe they weren't as unaffected by it all as the adults had hoped.

Gracie changed the subject with surprising composure, but a red face. "I need to fix her litter box and food dishes and show her around the house." Everyone agreed, and she went off to do just that.

Chapter Thirty-Four

Bobbie fidgeted as she waited for the others to get seated for the family session. She was restless for no reason and not looking forward to an hour of halting conversation. She flushed at that thought and tugged at her shirt collar. Dr. Langston looked at her for so long Bobbie thought she was going to ask her a question, but she didn't. Instead, the doctor turned to Gracie to begin the conversation.

"Gracie, tell me about this new cat of yours."

"Her name's Willie, and she got hurt in a fight, and she's probably four months old, and she sleeps with me and chases my shoestrings." Gracie strung together more information at once than she usually offered in the first half of other sessions.

Beth added, "I hear her thump down in the middle of the night to go exploring, so she can't be sleeping all night with you. And you have to learn to tie those shoelaces before you fall on yourself and her."

"Maybe a piece of rope with something tied to it would be a good toy," Dr. Langston said. "Do you like having her sleep with you?"

"Yes," Gracie said. "She curls up by my head and purrs."

"I bet that is nice," the doctor said. "Does she ever startle you at night or scare you?"

Gracie sat for a moment. Bobbie and Beth had learned to sit silently with her. Dr. Langston had shown both of them how it was an important skill, even if Gracie didn't talk at the end of it. Today, the waiting grated on Bobbie's nerves, and she blew out a breath of air as slowly as possible. But Gracie surprised Bobbie by going on this time. "She keeps the bad dreams away."

"That is powerful," Dr. Langston said. "What a great gift. How do you think she does that?"

Gracie answered right away. "She takes care of me. Mom and Aunt Bobbie take care of me, too, but she does it in a special way."

"Yes, animals have a special way that no humans have," Dr. Langston said. "Have you ever tried to go to a grown-up during a bad dream?"

Gracie's gaze sank to the floor.

"Bad dreams are scary," Dr. Langston said, "and sometimes hard to explain. But I bet if you went to your mom or aunt, they would try to take care of it. And you wouldn't even need words. I bet they would just let you crawl in bed with them and be safe."

"My bunk bed is safe. And Willie's with me."

"It seems to be safe today for you to talk. Sometimes it's safer to talk in a group than by yourself. Can you tell me something about the bad dreams? Do they happen when you're awake or asleep? Do you remember them?"

"Both," Gracie said, still looking at the floor. "Sometimes I remember them."

"When did they start?"

For a moment, Bobbie imagined being on some bad mushroom trip. She could swear her niece was shapeshifting, right before her eyes, between being a reluctant pre-teen and a crone with a lifetime's worth of pain etched in the peaks and crags of her face. This woman-child sat quietly for a while, again in the supportive silence of the room. "When I was nine," she whispered, startling Bobbie back into reality.

"Can you tell us more about them?" Dr. Langston asked.

"No."

"Please?" And again, Bobbie heard the doctor's words from a distance, like some journalist was reporting "as seen through Dr. Roberta Rossi's eyes." Even at that distance, the gentle tone of the doctor's question rasped at Bobbie like sandpaper.

Gracie stared at her hands in her lap. Her face shut down, and her body language said the conversation was over.

"Thank you for sharing about the bad dreams, Gracie. You know all of us in this room are interested in what you have to say and in what makes you feel things. You're always welcome to talk about any of it with any of us. We'll listen and not ask questions, if that's what you want. But I want to remind you of something. Bad dreams aren't your fault. Grown-up decisions aren't your fault, and it's okay to tell a grown-up they made a bad decision or to tell another grown-up about it." Dr. Langston stopped and gave this information some time to soak in.

After a moment of stillness, she continued. "Have you ever seen your mother or aunt cry, Gracie?"

"Yes."

"A lot or a little?" Dr. Langston kept the questions simple.

"Both."

"Well, you know, and we've talked about this, grown-ups feel all the same things kids do. Sometimes they get mad, sad, overwhelmed, or confused. Sometimes they feel happy, or sometimes they feel more than one thing at a time. Beth, if Gracie wanted to tell you about the bad dreams, would that be okay?"

"Of course, it would," Beth said in a voice as tight as the grip on the fingers in her lap.

"How do you think you'd react?"

"I would probably be sad, or mad, and maybe I'd cry. But I would want to hear about it, and I would hug her if she wanted, and she could sleep in my bed if she wanted."

"And Bobbie, what about you?"

"I would feel all the same things, but I would probably feel angry and guilty the most." Bobbie's words hurt coming out of her throat, and Gracie looked up at her with those damned unreadable eyes. "I feel like it was my fault, Gracie, what your dad did to you. I made him mad, and I feel horrible about it." The words spilled out of her mouth like hot lava, broken and burning.

"It's not your fault," Gracie said, maintaining eye contact with Bobbie.

Bobbie felt hot tears running down her face and realized she didn't give a damn about hiding them. She dropped the tissue she carried in every session and her hands came up of their own accord. Her fingers splayed across her face in some delicate, graceful balancing dance she didn't choreograph, rising and falling with each shuddering breath she took. She closed her eyes until the tears and dance and breath realigned her, then she opened them to meet her niece's scrutiny. "Gracie, can I give you a little hug? I would really, really like a little hug. Could you do that today?"

Gracie stood slowly and gave her a brief hug. Gracie turned to her mother and gave her another short hug. Then she turned to Dr. Langston and gave her a longer hug, surprising Bobbie and, from the look on her face, Dr. Langston, too. All three of the adult women blinked back tears and sniffed. The session was over, but what an ending.

Chapter Thirty-Five

I was rinsing lunch trays this afternoon when I heard a siren. I panicked when it stopped at the school. I dropped the tray in the sink with a clatter, tore off my hairnet, and realized I couldn't find the nearest door.

My supervisor, Linda, who knows everything about Gracie, stopped me. She put her hands on my shoulders. "Beth, it's okay. It was a sixth-grade boy who fell off the trampoline in P.E."

"Are you sure?"

"The principal sent his secretary to tell me, so you wouldn't worry."

But I did worry. All I could think about was smoke and vomit and seeing Gracie lying on the ground, pale and still. The memory was so clear I could actually smell the smoke.

"Are you sure?" I kept asking.

After fifteen minutes of being useless and not knowing what to do with me, Linda told me to take the rest of the day off.

"Take care of yourself," she said. "Hug your girls after school, but don't scare them, okay?"

"Thank you so much," I told her. I hurried toward the classrooms. I peeked in each room. LeeAnn and Cara were fine. Gracie was drawing while her teacher did a math lesson on the board. She hated math. Missing it wouldn't hurt her, would it? Standing to the side of the door's little window so the teacher could see me, I knocked. The teacher finished her explanation and came out in the hallway.

"May I help you, Mrs. Brown?"

"I'm here to take Gracie home early."

"I'm not sure that's a good idea. We heard the siren, and I kept an eye on Gracie. She gave no indication of shock or fear and just kept working on her spelling words. I think if we make it a big deal, it might scare her. Let her finish the day, okay? It's almost over."

I wiped my clammy hands on my uniform. "Okay, I guess it's not that long. If anything happens while I'm walking home, please have the office call my roommate? It's not far, and I can be back in no time."

"Don't worry, Mrs. Brown. We all care about Gracie, and we'll do our very best to take care of her." The teacher smiled.

I sort of smiled and left. Maybe I'd have time to go home and make brownies as a special treat. I'd come back and get the girls. I wouldn't say anything about the brownies until we got home.

At first, the walk felt good. Stretching my legs and swinging my arms helped me feel better. But then, I started to worry. What if something was wrong? What if they called Kathleen and she didn't know how to reach me? Kathleen didn't know the route we took when we walked to school. She might already be at the school, but without being a parent, the school might be reluctant to tell her anything. I'd only walked a block, but I turned and ran back to the school. When I got there, I rushed to Mr. Harding's office.

"Is everything okay?" I asked the school secretary.

She pushed the buzzer for the intercom and told the principal I was there. He appeared.

"Everything's fine, Mrs. Brown. Why do you ask?" He frowned at me.

I told him I thought about making brownies, but then I got scared.

"I see. You're worried we wouldn't be able to find you. It's a good idea for us to know your route in case something happens. Why don't you draw it then go home and make those brownies? Bring me one tomorrow."

I blushed when he teased me. The secretary handed me a sheet of paper and a pen. He walked me to the door and patted me on the shoulder. I headed home again, talking to myself.

I made it to the second block before the school bells rang. I fingered my necklace while my hands and arms tingled. I had to know if they were okay, and I thought that I had to know now! I turned around and walked as fast as I could, but I stopped across the street. The younger kids were at recess—that had been the recess bell. That's all. I took a deep breath and turned to walk the same path home. I reminded myself that the bell would ring again in ten minutes for the kids to return to class.

Nothing to worry about—I was silly. The brownies weren't going to make themselves. I thought about what recipe I was going to use, or maybe cookies.

A bell rang when I was almost at the third block. But almost at the same time I heard the school bell, I heard another siren not too far away. I froze. It didn't come any closer. I ran back to the school anyway. When I saw the school with an empty playground and no ambulance, I cried. What was I doing? When would I learn to let Gracie have some freedom? Am I stunting her growth by being so anxious? I spun around and started home, again.

That sound of the siren was rolling around my gut, but I kept walking. I wanted Gracie to heal, to be whole and happy again. I didn't want to mess it up. My legs felt heavier with each step. I tripped over a crack and sprawled on my face. My knees stung, probably skinned under my pants. As I lay there, it got harder to breathe.

Oh, God, if I can't walk without hurting myself, how will I get back to her if I need to? My baby. It was only a few weeks ago that her father hurt her. What was I thinking? She'll heal in time, but what if she needs me now?

I worked at the school to be close to her, and here I was abandoning her. I stood up and hurried back to the school. I half-walked and half-ran. My lungs pumped hard. My knees burned, and my hands cramped until I had to shake my fingers loose. Tears and snot ran down my face. With each step, my gut got tighter.

When I got there, Mr. Harding was standing on the steps. He caught me as I tried to rush past him and put his hand on my back when I doubled over to gasp and sob. He handed me his handkerchief. As soon as I could breathe, I started through the doors again, but he caught me once more.

"Mrs. Brown, I can't let you go to Gracie's room like this. There are only twenty minutes left of the day. Why don't you come to my office and wait?"

I tried to pull away. "I have to see my baby. I have to hold her and know she's okay."

"She's okay, Mrs. Brown. I checked. You'll only scare her acting like this. Come inside and calm down so you can give her a hug and walk home like you always do." He paused. "Please, Mrs. Brown. You'll frighten all three girls if you don't calm down."

He took my elbow and led me to the nurse's office. She sat me down and handed me a cup of water and a damp cloth, and I don't remember much else. The twenty minutes seemed like an eternity, but I was able to calm down, just as the principal said I should. I walked outside to where I usually waited for the girls.

Even the squirrels were laughing at me. I was looking up into the tree at one chattering when LeeAnn and Cara grabbed me around the waist. Gracie was with them. I burst into tears and scooped them into a giant hug.

"Mom, you're hurting me," LeeAnn said and ducked out. Cara wiggled free. Gracie stood in my arms.

I knelt and hugged her. When she laid her head on my shoulder, it sucked the air out of my lungs. That was the most affection she'd given me since the attack. I held my breath and her, ready to let go when she pulled back. It was a good twenty seconds before she pulled away and surprised me again by taking my hand. We walked home, LeeAnn chatting nonstop, Cara dancing the entire way, Gracie and me holding hands.

Chapter Thirty-Six

Kathleen was drying the last of the dishes when Bobbie came in. She had watched Bobbie pull into the driveway, and a million snarky things flashed through her mind that she could say to let Bobbie know it had been her night to wash dishes. "Nice of you to show up, Ms. Clean-Up Duty." Or, "No, we haven't moved since you went to work this morning. Have a hard time finding us?"

She was out of practice at the verbal sparring and downright snide comments that came with everyday life in her family because this household was just too nice most of the time. But she still got aggravated, especially because Bobbie had pulled this trick before to get out of her least favorite chore. What she wanted to say was, "Have you forgotten how to use a phone?" That's what she settled on and was about to say when Bobbie and her armload of items came bumbling through the back porch and into the kitchen.

"Oh, my God, what happened to you?" She gasped dropped the damp towel on the cabinet, and rushed to her lover's side. Bobbie's upper lip had a huge ice pack on it.

"It's nobbthing." Bobbie sucked in air and flinched when Kathleen pulled the ice pack away to find the lip beneath swollen with a bloody wad of tissue stuck to it. Kathleen braced Bobbie and eased the tissue off. When a surge of fresh, lighter colored blood came with it, she eased it back on.

"You're bleeding, and that is something. No, hold still, I want to pull this off from the top and see if you need stitches. How long have you been bleeding? Why are you bleeding?" A fresh seep of blood followed the movement of the tissue away from the cut. "Oh, dear, this is going to need stitches."

Kathleen grabbed a clean dishtowel and held it up to Bobbie's lip while directing her and her things to the dining room table.

Bobbie followed, stumbling over her own feet. "The police said the swelling has to go down before they can put in stitches, so I have to keep the ice on it."

Kathleen checked the living room. It was empty. All the girls must be upstairs getting ready for bed. "Police? I'm glad your sister isn't here to see you bloody and talking about police, coming from a college campus. Let me get you more ice. You can hold it on the way to the ER, and they can make the decision about when stitches can go in. We aren't going to sit around and wait. But don't try to talk. Every time you do, the blood starts to seep again.

You can explain this to me after we get the bleeding to stop, I guess."

Kathleen got some ice from the kitchen, wrapped it in a fresh dishtowel, and handed it to Bobbie, who sat unmoving at the table. Kathleen went to the stairs and called up to Beth.

Beth's head popped around the top of the stairs. "Yes? I'm running the girls through the shower for school tomorrow."

"Do you have a second? I need to talk to you about your sister. It would be easier if you could come down here."

"Can it wait fifteen minutes?" Beth asked.

"Not really."

"Let me check on everyone and I'll be down." Beth's head disappeared. In less than a minute, she was coming down the stairs, chatting away. "Cara and LeeAnn are in there reading, and Gracie's drying her hair, so I'm free to—what happened to you?" She ran to Bobbie's side and pulled the ice pack off gently.

"I think she needs stitches, so I'm taking her to the ER but wanted to let you know. It's nine on a Thursday, so they may be busy. I'll call if I can." Kathleen was packing up her backpack and Bobbie's purse.

"Okay, dinner was late because of her, so bedtime is late. But they'll be asleep in twenty minutes, and I'll be by a phone. Yes, she definitely needs stitches. What on earth happened?"

Bobbie rolled her eyes and Kathleen shook her head. "She got special dispensation not to talk till her lip stops oozing blood. Then I'm sure we'll have some story. I put the TV on for news, though, and they haven't broken in with anything major, so it wasn't a campus riot as far as I know. We'll be back soon."

Five stitches later, Bobbie was tucked into bed with another icepack, this time one that wouldn't leak. Kathleen couldn't shake the sharp smell of the hospital. She tried to focus on Beth's questions.

"They said she'll be fine, but there will probably be a scar. They gave her a shot to relax her, so they could give her the local injections to numb the lip and sew it up. She's quite squeamish about needles."

"Yeah," Beth said. "She always has been. But what happened? Was she in a fight?"

"Nothing as glorious as a fight, but you won't believe this. While she was getting sewed up, I was looking in her purse for her school ID to see if she had anything about insurance and a ticket fell out. She rear-ended someone coming off campus."

"I made some cocoa," Beth said. "Let's get some and you can finish this at the table." She handed Kathleen a mug of homemade hot chocolate. "Now who and how did she end up in a car accident?"

"All I could get from her was that it was the football coach. He's a total loudmouth who drives a flashy car and thinks he's God's gift to women. I hope she totaled him. Anyhow, she drove the boat home, so there must not be too much damage. Let me run out and check while we're thinking of it." Kathleen moved to get up from the table.

Beth stopped her. "It's eleven thirty and that light in the garage isn't going to show you anything you didn't see when you stopped on your way in. I saw you give it the once-over then. What did you think?"

"I didn't see a scratch. Damned Impalas, built like a tank. Oops, I know. A boat in this case. You're right. I'll check in the morning, but she swears the only damage was to her lip and his car. But the police gave her the reckless driving ticket. I don't know what that means down here, but it was an expensive ticket in Chicago."

Beth squinted her eyes and pursed her lips while she thought. "I've never known Bobbie to drive recklessly. And to rear-end someone?"

"And, drumroll please, it was at a stoplight. How do you rear-end someone at a stoplight?" Kathleen got up and got another cup of cocoa from the pot on the stove.

"She obviously wasn't paying attention. How else do you drive into a stopped car? She's lucky he didn't beat her up. Maybe there were other people there. That boat of hers could total a fancy little car." Beth looked up at the ceiling above them. Kathleen's eyes followed hers. They heard a small thump and then creaks moving toward the upstairs bathroom.

Beth stood up. "I'm sorry, but Bobbie's on her own with this one. Gracie has a bellyache tonight, and that's the second time I've heard Willie jump off the bunk, then Gracie. I think I better go up and check."

"I'll wash up the cocoa pan and anything else," Kathleen said. "You take care of Gracie, and I'll check in with Bobbie in the morning and see what we can find out about Ms. Reckless Driver."

"Thanks, for cleaning up the kitchen twice and for cleaning up my sis."

"You're welcome."

By the time Kathleen cleaned the kitchen and dining room a second time, she was aggravated. To be honest, blood made her woozy. Bobbie wasn't forthcoming with answers or even any good hints. And there was no way to go up and check on her or give her even a good night peck on the cheek without Beth noticing. Damn, but it was hard living in a house this busy and keeping a secret. She had been so scared when she saw the blood on Bobbie, her pulse was just now getting back down to normal. She was lucky Beth hadn't noticed her face being red. Maybe that's the blessing of a boatload of freckles. A boatload. The thought of a boat brought her back to the Impala and Bobbie. Three hours late and bleeding and who wouldn't think of Kent State? Oh well, Friday was a light day for her, so she could do what she needed to about the car. But Bobbie had to lecture. Maybe she should go to bed, so she could drive Bobbie to campus, because Bobbie couldn't help but be sore after a car accident, right? What if lecturing with stitches was too hard? That would have to be settled Friday morning. For now, it was time for bed.

Kathleen lay awake into the wee hours, listening for Bobbie's footsteps in the bedroom above hers, maybe to go to the bathroom or come downstairs for some aspirin, but she never heard them. The last time she looked at her clock was four in the morning, and her thoughts were still of Bobbie or herself getting in a serious car accident and no one knowing about the two of them. Sleep came, but not without a battle.

Chapter Thirty-Seven

Beth's head was already pounding when she came down for breakfast. The girls were still asleep. Monday had never bothered her before, but she wasn't looking forward to a kitchen full of clanking, clanging pots, pans, and lunch trays.

Kathleen stood in the kitchen with her hands laced around a cup of coffee. "Good morning. You don't look like you slept well."

"I slept fine, but I lost my wedding ring. I dropped it and it rolled under the bed. I didn't want to turn on the light and wake Gracie yet."

"May I ask a blunt question?" Kathleen said.

"Any time the girls can't hear."

Kathleen cleared her throat and poured Beth a cup of coffee. "I was just wondering why you still wear his ring?"

Beth stirred her coffee while she thought about Kathleen's question. "First, I wear it because it gives me some credibility as the girls' mom. But more important, I wear it because, no matter what a monster Dan was, that relationship is who I am in a lot of ways. Dan was the first guy I ever dated. The only guy I ever dated, to be honest. I knew he didn't like bastards, and he hated my mom and sister, but he told me that somehow, I was different, I was groovy. I loved being groovy instead of a plain old, Kansas farm girl. I'm not, we're not, even one hundred percent Italian. Did Bobbie tell you that?"

"About your mom and the farm boy? Yes, she did." Kathleen led the way, and the two women went into the dining room to relax at the table.

"That was Mom's big teenage revolt against her parents, and maybe Dan was mine. But I fell in love with him, madly in love. I loved how he made me feel beautiful and special. He was going to be a fireman, so we could go anywhere, to any big city, maybe even Dallas."

Beth's hands tightened on her mug as her imagination took her to Dallas, as it had in the early sixties. Skyscrapers offered dazzling beauty in her imagination. She heard the sound of whizzing interstates, felt the texture of grits and gravy, smelled bluebonnets' gentle fragrance. Wait, did bluebonnets smell? Reality intruded.

"But a few months before we graduated, I had to tell him I was pregnant. Then I had to tell my mom. What would Dan do? What would she do to me? I was terrified. That was when I started living in fear of him leaving me. That's when I started letting him abuse me verbally. I tell you, Dan dying and leaving me was the best thing that ever happened to me. I wear that ring to remind me. Never again."

Kathleen waited so long to speak that Beth feared what she would say.

"Has it worked?" Kathleen asked.

"I haven't looked at another guy yet, so I haven't had to decide if one was good or bad." Beth pulled her shoulders back and breathed the aroma of coffee into her lungs. It rallied around her tongue and gave her courage. "I'll tell you something if you promise not to tell. Sometimes, when Bobbie's trying to bully me, I look down at my ring and twist it on my finger. No matter how much easier it would be just to give in to her, I stand up for myself and say no. So, I think it is working."

Bobbie walked into the room and Beth grinned.

"What's so funny?" Bobbie asked, reaching up to pat ineffectively at her bed head.

"Oh, I was just telling jokes. A college professor walks into a bar and—" Kathleen said.

Beth glared at Kathleen. "No, she wasn't. I was laughing about a high school love affair and how I hope my three girls are old maids well past college."

"Coffee? There's a fresh pot waiting just for you," Kathleen said to Bobbie, keeping up the fast-paced, good-natured banter.

Bobbie shook her head as she looked from her sister to Kathleen and back then headed for the kitchen.

Chapter Thirty-Eight

"We've got to stop meeting like this," Kathleen told Beth as Beth handed her a second cup of cocoa in the same six-day period. "And for the same damn reasons. You tell me yours, and I'll tell you mine."

They took their hot cocoa into the living room this time and sank into the comfy sofas. Beth started. "So how was the emergency room on a Tuesday night and did they remember you?"

Kathleen blew on her cocoa. Over its rim, she considered her lover's sister. She was stronger than Kathleen initially gave her credit for being. She was more of a behind-the-scenes stage manager than a director. For example, tonight she had been in the kitchen with Bobbie when the accident occurred, and her handling of the situation had been flawless. She kept the kids ignorant and occupied, Bobbie calm and collected, and got Kathleen in from the garage, all while applying first aid and making emergency room visit arrangements. Even though Kathleen felt comfortable leaving Beth in charge, tonight had been frightening. The fact that it happened at all left her a strange hollow feeling that made her wonder if her voice might echo as she answered.

"Yes, one of the nurses did and remembered to give Ms. needles-make-me-woozy a shot of something to relax her before the actual stitching of her hand. Tonight had brought twice as many stitches, but it was a hand, so it wasn't right in her line of vision like last week." Kathleen took a sip of cocoa. "It's a good thing I have a strong stomach."

"I can't believe she needed ten stitches from trying to cut up potatoes." Beth pulled the afghan over her legs. "How many would it be if it had been something harder, like a carrot? Twenty?"

"God help us if she ever needs to cut up a chicken." Kathleen was serious, but Beth laughed.

"Oh no." Beth couldn't stop laughing. "My sister, Dr. Roberta Rossi, cutting up a chicken? She would lose a hand. We're both better off if we keep that job between us, and so is her career of typing up lecture notes."

"Explain why you can cut up a chicken and she can't?" Kathleen grinned, too.

"In Cottonwood Plains, all the girls had to take home economics, so she can cut up a chicken, or she could fourteen years ago. She just never had to. Mother never let us cook, so I had to pester her to let me help. Bobbie was diligent about studying to get into college, even as a freshman. Mother wanted us to go to college, but we both knew that scholarships were our only chance. So, at night, I took chicken and she took up Chaucer."

Kathleen agreed. "But she's twenty-eight years old, and she cuts herself cutting up potatoes? She cooked during graduate school surely..." Kathleen knew Bobbie cooked, albeit simple things. She had seen it herself, but she wasn't sure how much Bobbie had shared with her sister of their time together during the past six summers, even as friends before their relationship began.

"You're right. I don't know what's on her mind. I just know I can't count on her right now. Yesterday, I asked her to make sure she gave Gracie her dose of castor oil right after school because it takes four to six hours to work. And she didn't. I was so angry. But now I'm worried about where her mind is." Beth was rolling her neck one way and the other as she spoke, the same way she was rotating her wrists one at a time.

"Now, what is this about the castor oil? I don't know anything about this," Kathleen said.

"That's right, you were over at KU when I freaked out about the doctor's response. Gracie has had a bellyache, and I found out she hasn't pooped in almost a week. I called the doctor right away, and he said to try castor oil every day for a week, keep track of what happens, and keep his nurse posted. If she doesn't poop very soon, her bowels may be impacted. She needs more water, exercise, and fiber, and this probably has something to do with the rape, so I've called Dr. Langston and asked her to bring it up if Gracie doesn't." Beth's explanation sounded like words that had been longing for another adult to hear them.

Kathleen blinked back tears. Was there any aspect of Gracie's life that would be free of the rape's impact? Tonight's feelings of fear and despair were right on the surface, and she reached for some way to express herself that wouldn't leave her open and raw.

"Beth, I have to tell you again, I'm impressed and proud of how well you're managing everything you must do as a single mother of three. I certainly wouldn't be able to do it. I hope we're helping with some of the burdens. That is when one of us isn't whacking her hand with a meat cleaver."

"It was an amazing cut for such a small knife, wasn't it? Thanks. It's a struggle, but you two are a lot of help. You know, I thought Bobbie might have an easier time getting Gracie to take the castor oil, but then she dropped the ball." Beth beamed under Kathleen's praise, and Kathleen wondered once again if Dan had ever said a kind word to her during their marriage.

"Well, she'll be dribbling and catching one-handed the next two weeks, so don't throw her any balls. Maybe tomorrow, after the medicine wears off and the hand begins throbbing again, we can corner her for a discussion about her absentmindedness."

"Yes." Beth stood to gather the cocoa cups. "Maybe she'll explain it to us then."

Chapter Thirty-Nine

Kathleen slammed the lid down with an unsatisfying bang. She grabbed at the handle as the pot jumped and threatened to spill. That was all she needed on top of this day. She let go with a few choice words about the parentage of the pot makers and heard someone clear their throat. Looking up, she saw a very surprised Beth in the doorway between the kitchen and the outer porch.

"Sorry," Kathleen said. "Didn't know you were home already."

"Are you okay?" Beth asked.

"Your sister has me furious. She forgot her lecture notes for the afternoon class and called my dean and asked to have me released to deliver them to her."

"Oh, dear..." Beth bit her lower lip and crossed her arms.

"Oh, dear, my ass. She said to drop them with the department secretary, so I didn't even get to see her and give her a piece of my mind. What does she think she's doing? I take her to the ER twice in a week for stitches, arrive late at work today because she can't drive, then miss half a day's work for her forgetfulness. What's up with her lately? I'm seriously asking you what's up with her?" Kathleen snapped her hands to her hips and waited for an answer.

"May I sit down? I just walked home from school, but I agree, something's up, and I think we need to figure out what to do about it." Beth led the way to the dining room table.

Kathleen followed, her blood pressure still rising. Her jaw hurt, and her heart ached. How was she supposed to function, apparently for herself and Bobbie, under these conditions? She tried to focus, but even being balanced and reasonable was beyond her control.

"I tried to give her the benefit of the doubt. She had to handwrite these, and it wasn't in her normal habit to put three-hole notebook paper in her notebook. But these are typed notes she dated last week for today's lecture. She's just not thinking."

Beth jumped in. "And the car accident. Don't forget the car accident. I can't let the girls ride anywhere with her right now because I'm worried." Beth brushed her pageboy back. "In family therapy, she's not saying much, at least about how she feels. Dr. Langston is kind of on her about her lack of participation. I wonder what's going on in her private sessions. Maybe she's feeling overwhelmed and is just checking out."

"I guess that could be, although that makes it harder for me to be mad at her. I was kind of enjoying being mad." Kathleen's emotional balloon deflated, and she gave a half-hearted, lopsided attempt at a smile.

"I could tell from the drum riff in the kitchen as I walked in. Maybe you should be talking to Dr. Langston, too. You're living here with all of us, and we're getting the benefit of having someone to listen to us and help us figure out things, I wonder why no one thought that you might need the same chance?" Beth rested her weight on her elbows and relaxed onto the old oak table.

An icy wind hit Kathleen, and her remaining anger dissipated to nothing. She needed to keep her voice balanced. "I appreciate it, but Dr. Langston sent home a journal for me, and I've been keeping track of things and getting my emotions out in there. It's been more helpful than I expected it to be."

Kathleen smiled, a brittle smile this time. She dared not share the things she had written in her journal, especially without Bobbie's permission. They'd never talked about keeping their relationship a secret; it was just a given. The girls were too young, and one little slip to the wrong playmate who had a parent who—

"I still think since you're really part of this family, the family session, at least, should include you. Maybe just part of the time, but boy, would it be nice if you were there today, so we could work out this thing with Miss Bobbie."

"Bobbie won't be there for family therapy. She has a meeting with her dean she can't rearrange. Do you think she's in trouble at school? She could be slacking, and we don't know about it. Or maybe she can't pay attention there either." Kathleen began to speculate.

Beth said, "That's okay, Gracie and I have some talking to do and sometimes it's easier without Bobbie. Speaking of which, maybe it would be easier for you and me to corner Bobbie and force her into a discussion about what's going on without the girls there. Do you have time tomorrow? Do you think we could get one of your students to take them to the park or something? Maybe even a movie? Assuming Bobbie is home."

Kathleen went to the living room and returned with the paper. "I have a great idea. Let me call Sabrina and see if she can take the girls to that movie." She hesitated as she shuffled papers a moment. "Here it is. There's a Disney movie, *The Absent-Minded Professor*, showing. That's the ticket. We can say it's a grown-up night at home and just 'forget' to tell Bobbie. She never makes plans without telling us anyhow, and she can't drive with those stitches. Ha! We've got her cornered, now what do we do with her?"

Beth twisted her hands on the table and chewed on her lower lip. "We aren't supposed to talk about what goes on in therapy unless we have permission from the others to do that. But this may be an important time to break that promise. I'm really worried about her, Kathleen, I am." She took a deep breath. "One of the big deals in the family therapy is that I'm the only one who will talk easily about my feelings. Bobbie will talk in circles around hers and then totally avoid them. Dr. Langston says she's going into her head and not feeling them. Gracie won't talk about hers hardly at all, and she never cries. Bobbie cries but she won't talk about what she's feeling. Maybe she does in her private meetings with the doctor, but when she's with us, the only thing she'll talk about is feeling guilty for causing the rape and she won't talk about that much. So, if she won't talk to Dr. Langston, what are we going to say tomorrow? What are we going to say tomorrow without the doctor?"

Kathleen closed her eyes and tried to come up with a plan. "What you're saying is that she doesn't want to feel the emotions about what happened. It completely makes sense to me that if she's trying to hide from a pile of feelings, she may have to disappear inside herself. I'm not her therapist, but I've been her best friend for ten years, and I've seen that before."

Beth's shoulders sagged. "What can we do?"

"My best guess is do a couple of things. Maybe we can remind her that we're here for one another, and we're all in this together. Also, we can insist that she has to pull her head out of her...back pocket and deal with things. It's obviously not safe for her to hide inside, and it's not safe for the girls or even us. What if she started a fire by not turning off the burner when she made cocoa? What if she, well, it doesn't matter, it's just not okay for her to disappear inside. After we tell her those two things, I think we can insist she tell us something about what's going on right now, and we all make a plan for how we're going to deal with it."

"We're going to do this tomorrow night?" Beth sat up a little straighter.

Kathleen nodded. "That would be my suggestion."

"Okay. I'll talk with Dr. Langston about it in my private session today, and maybe I can get some ideas to share with you." Beth looked at her watch. "But for now, I have to get the girls and hurry back, so I can drive Gracie and myself to Dr. Langston's office on time."

"Tell you what, let's drive up to the school in the Pinto and get the girls. When we get back, you and Gracie can take the truck. The little girls and I can hang out like usual until it's time to get the ten-stitch wonder woman. It will be quicker, and they always like being sandwiched in my car. It's a treat."

"Yeah, at least you aren't likely to rear-end someone on the way," Beth said.

"Only if her name is Bobbie, and even then, only if I thought it would help," Kathleen said with a sigh.

Chapter Forty

Bobbie twisted the gauze around her right hand. It was almost impossible to write clearly. Dammit, it was starting to itch, really itch. She hoped she'd be able to write again and type, especially type, before her ten-days-worth of pre-typed lecture notes were exhausted. Maybe she could tape new ones on a cassette tape and give them to the secretary to type up. She leaned back in her desk chair in frustration. It was growing dark out, and her clock only showed six thirty. Standard time, daylight savings time, it was all a crock of—

"Bobbie, didn't you hear me? Dinner's ready." Kathleen's head popped into the office. "I've been yelling for you since I was at the foot of the stairs. Wake up, woman." She grinned at her partner.

Bobbie helplessly smiled back. That grin of Kathleen's was delicious. She had a beautiful partner and wished they had more time alone together. Someday when this was all—

"Bobbie, you smiled, so I know you heard me. Get your butt down here. Dinner is special tonight." Kathleen headed back down the stairs.

Bobbie smiled even bigger. It was far too quiet for there to be three children in this house and far too dark for them to be outside, thus, dinner just might be an affair for two.

"What's for dinner?" she called down the stairs before she started putting away her books and incomplete notes.

Kathleen's voice wafted up the stairs. "My mom's shepherd's pie, if there's any left when you get down."

Bobbie hurried to join her. It was definitely too quiet for the girls. "Is this a meal just for us?" she asked as she came around the central staircase, through the living room, and into the dining room.

"Yes, it's a Saturday night for adults, a treat for sure," Kathleen said.

Bobbie entered the dining room with fewer lights than usual and some James Taylor on the stereo. She practically purred in anticipation. Then Beth walked out of the kitchen carrying the shepherd's pie. Bobbie looked down and saw three place settings.

"What were you expecting?" Beth said. "That I would be sentenced to a movie with the kids, also? I'm an adult, too, you know and deserve a little time with other grown-ups. Sabrina took the girls out for pizza and to a Disney movie."

"I'm sorry, I was. I'm still thinking about *Wuthering Heights* and was picturing a meal for two. Sorry about that. I didn't get a lecture done, and it's lingering—"

Kathleen walked in with a salad. "And now you're babbling. Just sit down and enjoy a dinner without someone saying, 'Eww, gross.'"

Bobbie regained her composure. "Oh yes, we do hear something's gross at every meal, don't we? Well, this looks delicious, and it's great to get to spend time with you two. I love the girls, but I love big-girl time, too."

"Woman time," Kathleen corrected her.

Bobbie lifted an eyebrow. "Hmmm, maybe we're going to talk about the women's studies program tonight? It certainly has shaped your vocabulary."

"No," Kathleen said, "we have something else planned, but pass me that pie first. And just in case we all survive this pie, we have apple pie with apples fresh from today's trip to the orchard." Kathleen grabbed the main course and took a good helping.

"Someone went to the orchard today?"

Beth rolled her eyes. "Yes. Apples, pears, and pumpkins are in season, and it's cheaper to pick your own than go to the grocery store. We went this morning."

Bobbie tried to look like she was on top of the conversation. "Well, we do go through a lot of fruit."

Kathleen interrupted. "But the important thing about what you just said was that you didn't notice that four of the six people living here were gone for five hours today and brought back three huge bags of fruit. You've missed a lot of things lately, and we wanted to talk with you about that."

Bobbie went cold inside. She gave Kathleen a cautious stare. "I'm not sure what you're talking about. I know I've been distracted by all the itching on my hand and my inability to write or type my next lectures, but that's no reason to pick on me."

"No reason to get defensive. We just wanted to talk," Kathleen said.

"You've had a car accident, a knife accident, and a forgotten notes accident all in the last week," Beth said. "Those are all pretty big things. We're worried about you."

"There's a reason the word 'accident' is attached to each of those events. They were accidents and just happened to fall in this same time frame. I'm about to get my period, and you know that always makes me a little klutzy anyway. What's the big deal? Are we counting now?" Bobbie scratched her hand.

"Stop scratching the bandage, and yes, in this case we are keeping score—" Kathleen said.

"And you just finished your period like we all did, so what is worth lying about?" Beth said. "You just aren't here right now. You're lost inside your own head, and it's scary."

Bobbie threw up her hands. "Scary? You're making this bigger than it is. Scary?"

Beth sat up straight and folded her napkin on her lap. "Yes, scary. From now until this is resolved, you're not allowed to drive the girls anywhere."

"I can't drive the girls? You've got to be kidding."

Kathleen put her elbows on the table and leaned into the argument. "You rear-ended a stopped car. How much more dangerous a driver does someone need to be before they're told they aren't allowed to drive children? I'm not riding with you either."

"Or me," Beth added, her face flushed.

"I don't have to listen to you two gang up on me in my own house."

"Yes, you do, if you want roommates, and it's our house, too," Beth said quietly. "It's our house, too," she repeated a little more loudly.

Kathleen cleared her throat. "I think the simplest thing to do is figure out what's going on and resolve that, then you'll be your old self again. This isn't something bigger than us. We just need to work it out together. Will you do that? Talk with us?" Bobbie was almost grateful Kathleen was speaking, since Beth was coming straight for her jugular.

"It's talk with us or drive no one till Dr. Langston gets back from vacation on Monday," Beth said loudly.

Bobbie looked at her, speechless.

"I've hidden your car keys," Beth said.

Bobbie sat, face flushing bright red, hands in fists on the table, shoulders tightening up. How dare they talk to her like this? She pushed back in her chair and...and...and...

And began to cry. Cry hard.

Her shoulders shook, and she brought her fists to her eyes to cover them, bending forward in shame and pain. Her torso swayed ever so slightly as the sounds came up out of her gut into the evening's blankness where the record had finished on the stereo. She had never cried like this in front of anyone. Had she ever cried like this before at all?

Kathleen was sitting on her end of the table and got to her first. She simply stood behind Bobbie, one hand on either side of her shoulders and let Bobbie lean back into her stomach and cry.

Beth sat across from her sister, opened her hands, and reached across the table.

Bobbie peeked through her fists long enough to see the look on her face, the same look she wore in the hospital when Gracie was attacked—lost and aching. Bobbie felt her across the table, across a mile at the same time. Behind her, she could feel the warm body of her lover pressed against her head and neck. Kathleen's hands, fingers spread over her shoulders, held her down so she wouldn't spin off into the stratosphere and never find her way home.

With a shuddering gasp, she took in one belly breath then another. She rubbed her fists on her eyes, feeling the two women who loved her the most in the entire world, feeling them in the room, at the table, keeping her safe while she cried and felt. Felt...felt, whatever. Something she wasn't used to feeling, or maybe she was. Maybe she was and was too afraid to name it.

"What is it, Bobbie? We're here. You're okay. What's going on?" Kathleen asked her.

From across the table where Beth sat, she heard a strangled moan that might have been her name. She opened her eyes again to see tears streaming down Beth's face, also.

Kathleen's fingers closed on her shoulders, holding her tight and safe. She was safe. It was safe. She started to tell them what she was thinking about, just starting to think about. How she didn't need anybody, and maybe that was because she was afraid there wouldn't be anybody there when she did need them. But when she started to think about it and to journal about it, it stole time away from focusing on other things. Maybe, maybe that's why she had been so forgetful. She started to tell them, she wanted to tell them, but just when her resolve was good, when she felt safe, the back door flew open, and LeeAnn ran in, shouting.

"Cara peed her pants. Cara peed her pants in the restaurant, and we didn't get to go to the movie. Cara's a baby!"

Chaos ensued with a crying six-year-old, an embarrassed and frustrated twenty-year-old, a tired ten-year-old, and, of course, LeeAnn, the broadcaster. Beth stood up, torn between her twin and what might be nothing or might be a real mothering moment. Sabrina rushed to explain. The girls all headed to their bedrooms, and Kathleen whispered that she would pay Sabrina outside, so she wouldn't see Bobbie in such a condition. Bobbie relaxed a bit. Then a bit more, then back into the oblivion. Well, at least halfway into the oblivion from which her sister and lover had tried to rescue her before the night went bad. With any luck, she could escape upstairs into her room as well, and call the Kansas inquisition done.

Chapter Forty-One

Gracie's Top-Secret Journal Entry

One reason I wear my long pants and stay under the covers in my bed all the time is I'm embarrassed by my butt. There. I wrote it. But only because I already said it out loud. My butt has no privacy. It's not like Mom or Aunt Bobbie or Kathleen run around telling everyone, but there are people they think need to know and when they tell them what happened, that person knows that dad put his pecker in my butt. My whole butt, from my belly button down to my legs, shrivels up, and burns red hot, and I can barely walk, and I have to hide because I'm ashamed. That's another of Dr. Langston's words. Ashamed and shame. She says it's not my fault, and my body is mistaken when it feels that way. That's how Dad should feel.

It's terrible. I can't even poop right. His pecker went in my butt, and now the poop won't come out like it used to. One time, I went a week, and my belly hurt so bad my mom threatened to take me to the hospital. I still have to drink this gross stuff every day to make me go. Then when Dr. Langston and I talked in our private session, we talked about shame and how my butt was ashamed to poop. I cried when we looked at the butthole on the baby doll, and she talked to the baby doll who got raped, and I threw the doll across the room. Dr. Langston asked if I was angry at my butthole for letting Dad in. I wouldn't talk. But I'll tell you, being angry is better than crying. Anything is better than crying. Dying is better than crying.

Chapter Forty-Two

I know I don't write in this journal much, but this Friday in family therapy, I saw how helpful journaling was for Gracie and Beth, so I thought I'd try.

When I go to bed at night, it's silent in my room and the house. It seems that Cara can hear even the quietest radio through the wall we share and will wake up just enough to go back to bumping against the wall continuously. So, no music. In my night's silence, there are voices. There's Beth saying, 'No, Bobbie, this is serious, you can't come visit till I work this out, or Dan will kidnap all three girls, and I'll never see them again.' Only now do I hear how anxious and certain she was.

There is Dan's voice. "I don't care which little bitch it is, you'll never see her again." And Gracie's voice. "Why, Aunt Bobbie? Why did you bully Mom and come to town? This would never have happened to me. Why couldn't you listen for once?" Except she never said that. That's my voice, the voice that never hushes, putting words into her mouth every time. There's nothing for me to do but listen. Kathleen says I've lost weight. But I don't know how. The only exercise I get is running from those voices.

Chapter Forty-Three

Family weighed heavily on Bobbie's mind of late. Since the confrontation and ensuing emotional outburst earlier, Bobbie had dreaded today's family therapy. While she hadn't admitted it, she had come to agree that Beth and Kathleen had her dead to rights. She wasn't feeling her emotions and was shrinking from them and from life in general, and probably wasn't safe for herself or for others.

But the great whimper when there should have been a bang, was that nothing happened. There was no significant follow-up. Of course, Bobbie had been far more intentional about being safe and present in her interactions with family, the world, and all metal implements, but all the things she feared? They never came to pass. Her keys reappeared Friday morning on her desk. She expected Beth had put them there. She could see Beth being reluctant to push what had felt like an angry agenda after it became apparent that Bobbie was in so much pain. Kathleen on the other hand...

Kathleen wasn't someone Bobbie would have expected to let something like this go. But let it go, she did, and if Kathleen didn't want to, Kathleen would have made that perfectly clear. So, what else was Bobbie to believe? It was all convoluted and frightening enough to Bobbie that she didn't want to approach it either, so it would remain frightening and unexamined. She was just glad she had her keys back. Nothing was said, including when Beth and Gracie joined her in her car for the ride to and from therapy.

When Bobbie pulled the Impala into the driveway from their family therapy appointment, Kathleen and the pickup truck had disappeared, and one of Kathleen's math students pushed Cara and LeeAnn on the swings in the fading sunlight. Gina had babysat for them before, so they weren't worried, but she would give out no information about Kathleen and the truck, or her destination.

"Fine," Beth said, laughing. "But if she doesn't come back, the Pinto's mine!"

After dinner, Kathleen returned. Bobbie could see what she was doing outside the window but kept the others occupied indoors. Kathleen bustled around outside the house a bit while the others were washing up. When the tarp and other assorted things were hidden away in the garage, Kathleen came in to hear about everyone's day.

Cara and LeeAnn had long stories about school to share. Beth didn't say much but looked happy. Bobbie told a far-out story about her early morning English class that was getting ready for midterms. Finally, Gracie said she'd had a good day. That was enough to get Kathleen into action.

"Well, that's good, Gracie, because I'm going to need your help. With all this good cooking, I am getting too big for my clothes. I need to get some exercise, but I don't want to do it alone, I need a helper. Now, girls, you're all getting one of these for Christmas, so, Cara and LeeAnn, you'll get one, too, but I'll need you there to pick out the right kind for you. If I wait till Christmas, I'll be as big as Santa Claus, so I figured I'd start now. Anybody want to see what I bought today?"

Cara and LeeAnn didn't know about the movement in the garage, so they looked around the room. Kathleen smiled and led the entire family out to the garage. As she entered through the side door, she flipped on the light and walked across the double garage to where a few assorted boxes stood in front of the work bench. She pulled a tarp off two odd shapes, and there sat a woman's bicycle and a girl's dream bike with high, split handlebars, a hot pink banana seat, and matching pink tassels off the handlebar grips. Gracie's eyes widened, but she didn't say anything.

"I haven't ridden a bike since I was a kid," Kathleen told her. "And if I fall or hit something and get a flat tire, I need someone who can ride back to the house and get me help. Would you be willing to ride with me? I hear you're an awesome bike rider."

Gracie grinned a little. "Yeah, I can teach you some things."

Bobbie watched as eyebrows went up around the room. Gracie hadn't sounded that cocky for months. "All right then, tomorrow morning we ride," Kathleen said.

Cara and LeeAnn were excited. They always were excited about new things but didn't appear to feel left out. Neither of them knew how to ride a bike. They didn't know how Gracie learned but probably figured they would have to be older, too. They bounced back into the house, chatting about the color of the seat.

Beth grabbed Kathleen and Bobbie as the girls went into the house. Her face was red, and her words grated like they were squeezing out around a hot pink banana seat stuck in her throat. "You two can't be spoiling her like this. You can't make her happy by buying things. It just won't work. She's used to nothing. Now she has a cat and a bicycle? We can't do it this way."

"I'm sorry, Beth," Kathleen said. "I should have asked you first. But we're all getting bikes for Christmas, and I really do need the exercise and company now. And Gracie doesn't run, play, or swing on the swing set with her sisters. She needs it, too."

"I'm sorry. I know you meant well," Beth said, "but I guess I'm just worried that we're buying her healing right now. She had a good day in therapy, at least in family therapy, because she talked some, mostly about the cat again. And now a new bike?"

"Do you want me to take it back?"

"No, it's too late for that. Next time, just ask me first, okay?"

"Okay, and I'm sorry. You're the mom, and I'm not. You two can ride the big bike, too, and take your turns with her," Kathleen said in awkward apology.

"It's all right. We'll figure out something."

Kathleen hung out in the garage when the others left. Bobbie came back outside looking for her. Kathleen was putting the tarps back over the bikes. Bobbie walked up behind her. "Hey, we have cookies. Are you coming in?"

Kathleen turned around slowly. Bobbie saw tears on her face. Moving to hold Kathleen, Bobbie felt her pull away. "What's wrong, babe?"

"Nothing."

"Yeah, right. What's wrong?"

Kathleen leaned against the workbench and thought for a minute. "I just want to be part of the family. I didn't realize how much I miss my big family in Chicago. It's not the same here, no matter how hard I try. The little girls accept me, but they accept babysitters just as easily. Beth is polite but not warm. And Gracie..."

Bobbie stood on her tiptoes, trying to peer into Kathleen's green eyes. She had never seen Kathleen like this before, and it made her heart hurt. Time to wheedle her back into good spirits. "You have me."

"Not openly."

That was a dead end. Bobbie didn't know how to answer that one, so she went back to the family thing. "I don't know how much Beth realizes what your commitment to the family is. I know she deeply appreciates all you've done for her, and she probably feels a little funny about it since she just met you a few months ago. The little girls adore you. You're not just a sitter to them. And Gracie, well, Gracie thought you walked on water when you taught her all those math shortcuts the first night you met. Give her time. She's barely relating to her mother right now."

Bobbie put on her best charm school smile and then stopped. That wasn't working. Only genuine would work. She hoped Kathleen would hear the difference in her voice, even in this distracted state. She focused and continued. "As for me, you've been my best friend and soulmate for ten years and now my lover for four months. I love you and adore you and I'm your family for now and always."

She counted to eight as she breathed in. "I'm sorry it's not open enough at work and in front of Beth and the girls. I'm still trying to figure out how to do that without getting a huge, dangerous problem going for all of us. The little ones talk, and Beth has never met a lesbian that she knew was a lesbian. Gracie would probably be the most accepting of all right now." Bobbie coughed a little at that realization. "I don't care if the school knows, as long as we can still work, but I'm not sure how that would pan out. I want the whole world to know, Kathleen. It's just I'm new to this and figuring it out. I'm sorry if that has hurt you, I surely didn't mean for it to cause you any pain."

"I know." Kathleen scuffed her shoe on the ground. "I've been waiting for this for so long, to be with you and have a family with you. I guess I want more than I can have."

"You have my whole heart and soul and being. I can't pick between you and Beth and the girls, because you all are family. But if or when she moves away, I'm staying with you."

"And if I wanted to go back to Chicago?"

"Well, I don't know. Do they need English teachers in Chicago?"

"Probably not ones with your overqualifications." A tiny smile cracked the gloomy mask on Kathleen's face.

"Oh, gee, thanks." Bobbie smiled back. "Let's navigate these waters together, Kathleen. When you feel this way, tell me."

"Well, with Gracie so—"

"Gracie is a different issue. You're my lover and my partner and my heartbeat. Don't lock me out because of someone else."

"Okay."

Bobbie flipped off the light and wrapped Kathleen in her arms. Kathleen's taller, larger frame snuggled down close and leaned the two of them back against the workbench. "Mmm," she said, her voice muffled against Bobbie's hair. "Your hair always smells good."

"Thanks. Think I could sneak down for a couple of hours tonight?"

"Now you're the lascivious one." Kathleen grinned.

"No, I just want to be with you. However that works out."

"I love you, Bobbie."

"I love you, Kathleen." A long pause. "I saved you leftovers."

"Now that's real love."

"I saved you the dishes."

"Now that's real family."

Chapter Forty-Four

Dear Journal, Gracie's happiness got bought again today, and it made me angry. But today, it wasn't my sister, so that's a new one. I don't remember Kathleen doing this before. I wish we could all get our acts together. Even I do it sometimes, so I can't blame them totally. But it doesn't help her get any better. She's going to have to find her own way, and we can't bribe her to be well. Grr, this makes me so mad!

Okay, enough. So, to take my mind off that, I will write about what else is going on right now. Things are a little stressful. Kathleen and I had that intervention with Bobbie, and it was successful in some ways. She's focusing more on slicing food items, at least, and hasn't cut herself again accidentally. What surprised me so much was how she cried. And cried and cried. Nothing was resolved. I was afraid she was going to come apart at the seams, and I had to leave so I could clean Cara up and put the girls to bed. I just hoped Kathleen was able to put her back together again. I need her together.

We still need to come to some out-loud resolution about this living together stuff. Since I told Bobbie to get her crap together or I was leaving, she has done better, but we still haven't sat down and talked about it or talked with Dr. L's help. I think that would be the best. This walking in the hen house stuff is nerve wracking. One wrong step and you have goo on your shoe!

But other than that, things are going well for me in therapy, and I'm feeling some changes. The best one is how I don't feel like a monster so much anymore. I still feel really bad about what happened to Gracie, and I still feel horrible that it happened when I was supposed to be protecting her, but I'm not taking responsibility for it anymore either. The asshole I married was a terrible man who made some evil decisions. I still don't understand how he did what he did to our daughter, but Dr. L says I don't have to understand, I just need to grieve and grow. I don't think I will ever stop grieving in some ways, but I definitely am growing.

It's only been three-and-a-half months. I
can't believe how much my world has changed in
three months. Even more, I can't believe how
much Gracie's world has changed in three
months. If you had asked me four months ago if
I could grow this much in a year, I would have
said, dream on. But I have. I've grown in
those almost four months. I'm not a doormat
anymore. I don't let Bobbie walk all over me.
She doesn't mean to, but sometimes she does it
out of habit, or she used to. But no more.

Dan used to do that. I guess he was the
monster in the relationship, not me. He was
the one who did monster-like things to Gracie.
I worry if she will ever be the same. But the
growth I can feel in me is this—I feel more
confident that we'll find a way, no matter
what happens to her. It will be okay. Her
sisters and I are going to make it. We have a
good place to live here, and a good new family
with Bobbie and Kathleen, and we can work out
any problems that come up. I'm looking forward
to Thanksgiving this year because I'm feeling
thankful for all I have, considering all
that's happened. I mean, the girls and I could
be stuck alone out in the country, trying to
manage this by ourselves. That would be hell
on earth.

Another thing that was almost hell on
earth was the last time I wrote in here, back
when I kept hearing the sirens and was trying
to walk home. I was freaking. I was going to
lose my mind for sure! But look at the
difference between that entry and today's
entry. I'm feeling good today and have a good
assignment from Dr. L. You can tell I'm
feeling good when I write this much before
getting to the assignment. I'm supposed to
think of three descriptions of myself that
don't involve anyone else in my family. Like,
I can't say mom or sister. I can't even say an
employee, I know because I asked.

So, my idea is to say, and don't laugh,
journal, I'm going to call myself a fabric
artist. That's just a fancy way of saying I
like to sew, and I think I'm pretty good at
it. I'm making the girls' Halloween costumes
right now. My mom and home ec taught me that.
Besides fabric artist, I'm going to say music
lover (which will surprise everyone since I
never listened to music before, but Kathleen
has turned me onto it this fall) and dreamer.
Dr. L gave me that one back. So there, those
are my three. I know Dr. L will like them next
week. I can't wait to show her.

Chapter Forty-Five

Kathleen took a deep breath and released it, letting her chin fall to her chest. Vertebrae popped, and her left cheek twinged. It might not be too smart to let Cara and LeeAnn out of her sight long enough to stretch well, and besides, it was too cold to get a good stretch. Everything would just tighten back up in a matter of seconds. How did she get stuck with this duty? Oops. She meant, earn this honor? She grinned and looked up the sidewalk to see Cara removing her coat again to show off her dog costume. She waited till Cara was halfway back before calling, "Hey kiddo, where's your fur?"

Cara looked down at her costume, remembered the coat, and ran to retrieve it.

LeeAnn shook her head. "I'm sweaty. If I wear it when we cross the street or walk long distances, would you carry my coat between the close-together houses?" she asked.

"Nope, I told your mom you would wear your coat over your costumes and wear them you will. If you get tired, or sweaty, or cold, we can go home anytime." Kathleen shifted her weight from one foot to the other while she waited for Cara. She saw the grandmotherly woman who owned the house they were at put her arms around Cara's shoulders and give her extra candy.

"Cara, come on, girlie, we need to keep moving," Kathleen called.

Cara picked up her coat and pillowcase and ran down the sidewalk. "Look what that lady did! She's going to bed, and she gave me more candies. But she said I needed to share with my sister, so I told her I had two and one stayed home to give out candy, then she gave me the whole bowl!"

"Yeah, we saw." Kathleen grinned.

"Why didn't Gracie come?" Cara asked.

"You mean why didn't Gracie come trick-or-treating with us?"

"Uh-huh." Cara pulled Kathleen's hand to the corner and waited.

"Because she doesn't like people, dummy." LeeAnn grabbed Kathleen's other hand.

"We don't call people dummies, and why do you say that?".

"Because she's afraid of people she doesn't know. She didn't want to dress up and go get candy with us," LeeAnn said.

Kathleen stopped at the car. "Let's get in."

Cara yelled, "I don't want to go home."

"We aren't going home. We're going to warm up and talk for a minute." Kathleen shut the door behind Cara.

"You're right," Kathleen said. "She isn't fond of strange people and places, right now, so she stayed home tonight. That's perfectly all right. Either one of you could have stayed and helped, too."

The look of horror on Cara's face almost made this conversation worth it. Apparently, candy-gathering was a sacrament to her. Then Kathleen grimaced. Of course it was. Having grown up in a family with nothing for extras, Cara would think free candy was worth anything. Compared to teaching, this parenting stuff was a whole extra bucket of worms.

"I'll tell you what. If you agree to stop when I say stop with no arguing, I'll drive you over to the big houses by the college and we'll see what the fancy people give out for Halloween. How's that?"

"Yeah!" LeeAnn yelled.

"Yes! Yes! Yes!" Cara chanted.

Kathleen put the car in gear and wondered how buying the little girls with candy compared to all their attempts to buy Gracie some safety in her own home.

Chapter Forty-Six

Bobbie woke Saturday morning after dreams of all the pets she ever had while growing up on the farm, both approved and hornswoggled—those she had gradually worked from being only outdoor animals to being indoor members of the family. They might be inconvenient at times, but in her mind, pets, the joys and sorrows and even expenses of them, were a part of the rites of passage. She was almost as excited about the day as the children.

That morning, Kathleen took LeeAnn and Cara over to her friend's house to pick up the small dog. A great deal of coordination had gone into this as well. First, the girls made a shopping list. Next, they swept out the dog run and put clean straw in the new dog house, both items compliments of Jimmy, the landlord. Finally, they discussed the requirements of having a dog.

Beth sat with them at the table throughout the discussion. Bobbie joined them as Beth gave the rules.

"You'll have to scoop poop out of the dog run and wash it down on a regular basis. You'll have to scoop the poop out of the yard, also. You'll have to take her out of the dog run and play with her or walk her every day, even when it's cold and snowy. If you don't, we find another home for her. Feeding her and giving her fresh water every day is your job, as well."

The girls thought for a moment. It was obvious they had just realized that a dog was a lot of work. It was also obvious that their desire overcame their hesitation. Beth told them to wait to do their shopping to see what items came with the dog and that Kathleen would take them over in the boat to get her.

When they got back, Bobbie fell in love. Sara Jane was a beautiful little dog. She looked like a spotted cocker spaniel, with long wavy hair instead of curly poodle hair. Kathleen told Bobbie and Beth that the woman who had owned her suggested getting her shaved in the summer. "It gets the tangles out and helps her to be much cooler. Then she looks like a miniature bird dog. Right now, she looks like a mop and by the end of winter, she *will* be a mop."

Dog dishes and half a bag of food, a pooper scooper, and several toys had joined the rug Sara Jane used as a bed. The dog was a bundle of joy in the backseat with the girls, bounding around as much as Cara did. She wagged her tail so hard she almost spun around in a circle.

"You'll have to keep her on a leash until I can buy a chain

since we don't have a fence," Beth said as they disembarked at
home. Beth and Bobbie had joined them in the backyard to look at
the new dog. "How old did they say she is?"

"Three years old, fixed, and up-to-date on her shots," Kathleen
said.

"Good. That's one less worry." Beth sounded relieved. "A dog
and a cat are enough. We don't need puppies or kittens. Kathleen,
are you and Gracie going to ride this morning?"

"Yes, of course," Kathleen said. "How long should we ride
for?"

Bobbie was a bit surprised at the abruptness of the question.
Beth must have some agenda with the younger girls.

"At least a half hour, if you don't mind. We have some
chatting to do here," Beth said, confirming Bobbie's suspicions.

"Okay, I'll get Gracie," Kathleen said.

Beth laughed. "She's putting a rubber band on her pants leg,
so it won't get caught in the chain, and is looking for one for you.
She'll be out in a second."

Kathleen grinned. "See? I need a good instructor."

Gracie came out of the house and met the dog before they took
off on their bikes. While she and Kathleen were getting them out of
the garage, Beth told the younger two to put the dog in the dog run
so she could get used to her new house, and then they should come
inside to talk.

As everybody sat down at the dining room table, Beth snagged
Bobbie's arm and directed her down, too. "I may need your help,"
she whispered.

"Okay," Beth said, "back about a month ago, on the Monday
night when Willie came home from the vet's, Cara, you said Willie
and Gracie both had been hurt. And LeeAnn, you said both of them
were getting better. This morning, when I came to get you for
breakfast, Cara, I heard you ask LeeAnn how long it would take
Gracie to get all well now that Dad was gone. Can you tell me what
you meant by that? And I don't mean Dad or Willie, I mean
Gracie," Beth said.

"Dad hurt Gracie," LeeAnn said.

"Do you know how?"

"The night the curtains caught on fire, he beat her butt. And I
think he hit her that day he took her to the farm and burnt down the
barn."

Bobbie was confused. "He hit her? What are you talking
about? When some curtains caught on fire, you saw him hit her?"

"I was going to the bathroom, and I saw him beating her butt
with his belt and yelling at her." LeeAnn's demeanor changed.
Bobbie thought she looked like a young, sad Gracie. "She always
told us to be good because he would beat our butts if we were bad.

I thought she had been bad and didn't want to tell you, so I didn't tell. I went back to bed."

"Did you know about this, Cara?" Beth asked her youngest.

"No, I guess not. I sleep pretty good. But she always did warn us." Cara played with her fingers rather than meet her mother's eyes.

Beth was getting angry, and Bobbie jumped in to calm her down.

"Tell us about the last day, the day the barn burnt down. What happened then?" Bobbie asked.

Cara answered this time. "You were there. Dad came in and yelled bad words and grabbed Gracie and took her away. He hurt her because when you came back you took her to the hospital. She looked like she was going to cry all the time except when she wasn't doing anything. Maybe her bottom hurt from getting hit with that belt again."

"Did your dad ever hurt you?" Bobbie said.

"No, but he yelled a lot when you weren't home, Mom. We stayed out of the way. But he spanked us when he thought we did something bad, even if we didn't. Then Gracie warned us, and we were big girls and didn't get in trouble, and he didn't yell so much then," Cara said with an odd pride to her voice.

"He grabbed my arm once when I got in the way of the TV, and he spanked me a few times, and he hurt my feelings yelling at me, but that's all," LeeAnn answered.

"Will Gracie ever be better?" Cara asked. "I miss her playing with us."

The adults sat silently for a moment. Bobbie was formulating an answer and expected to be the one to deliver it, but Beth cut her off.

"Girls, your dad was a very angry man, and yes, he did hurt Gracie. She's scared and angry and sad and confused right now. She will get better, and she'll be Gracie again. It's just going to take some time and work."

"Can we go to the talking doctor with you guys?" LeeAnn surprised Bobbie.

"Yes," Bobbie said. "I'll see if she can meet with the four of us, just to talk about what happened with you two and see how you feel about it and your dad."

"He was bad. I hate him. I'm glad he died," LeeAnn said without showing a great deal of emotion.

"I hate him, too. I hope Mom gets us a better dad. Or maybe we just stay here with you and Kathleen forever, and we don't need a dad," Cara added. "Can we go back outside and play now?"

"Yes," Beth said. "Put your coats back on, and next time you come in, you hang them on the hooks in the back room that

Kathleen put up. Don't just drop them on the floor. You understand?"

"Yes, ma'am," they said together, as they ran for their coats and the back door.

Beth and Bobbie heard the back door slam. They sat at the table looking at one another. Bobbie didn't know what to feel.

"I suppose we should've guessed earlier," Bobbie said. "What's this about the curtains?"

"One night, I came home from a late shift and Dan was drunk, and one of the floor-length curtains was burned halfway up, all balled up and thrown in the garbage can. I assumed he'd dropped his cigarette and put it out himself."

"You never mentioned it."

Beth exploded. "I never mentioned half the things that asshole did. Or ninety percent of the things that asshole did."

Bobbie flinched. "Why not?"

"Because you were always telling me what a jerk he was. What was I supposed to do, Bobbie? I had three little girls, no way to support them, and an asshole for a husband. But I couldn't tell you that. I had to defend him to you, so you wouldn't get on me even worse. I was stuck trying to make the best of a rotten situation, and your bitching about him didn't help." She had risen to her feet while yelling and fell back into her chair when she ran out of words and steam.

Bobbie sat stunned. She had never considered it that way. She thought for a few moments before she answered. "Beth, I'm so sorry. Without thinking, I just spoke my mind. I didn't realize what a bind it was putting you in. I am so, so sorry. Sometimes, a lot of times, I guess, I get so caught up in being right that I just announce things without thinking it through. I pressured you, and it made things worse for all of you. I'm so sorry."

"Thanks. I appreciate the apology."

"Do I still do that?"

Beth stared up at Bobbie with a half-pained, half-humorous look in her eyes. "Since you were eight years old and to this very day."

"Shit."

"It's just you."

"No, it's not just me. Well, it is, but I don't want it to be. I don't want it to hurt the people I love. I don't want it wrecking things here in this house for you and the girls and Kathleen and me. You're my sister. They're my nieces. And Kathleen is my best friend of ten years. We all have to live here as a family, and I can't be a jackass like that without hurting you all and myself. Please promise me that if I do something stupid like that again—"

"You mean when."

"Okay," Bobbie said. "When I do something like that again, promise me you'll tell me. I'll pay attention, but I don't want to hurt any of you. I've been the queen of my old life for so long, this is new to me."

"I'll tell you. Speaking up is good practice for me, I guess. Dr. Langston keeps pushing me to do more of that."

"Well, you did beautifully with the girls," Bobbie said.

"Yes, and I saw you starting to answer, so I cut you off. Bobbie, you are the dearly beloved aunt, but I have to be the mom, okay? You have to let me be the mom. Even in large families where there are many extended parents, there's one mom."

"What?" Bobbie was confused.

"Kathleen and I have done some talking about how children are raised in extended families. She has some good ideas, but she reminds me, I'm still the mom. So, respect that."

"I promise. And you can tell me every time I step over the line."

"I know." Beth sighed and slumped farther back into her chair. "This is new to all of us."

"I didn't know you and Kathleen talked that much. What do you think of her?"

"I like her. The girls love her. I understand why she's been your best friend. You two are like twins in so many ways, half of the other's personality. There's something different about her, but I can't figure out what. And it's not different enough to bother me. Maybe it's the Irish influence. I figure if she were a man, you'd get married."

Bobbie coughed. "Can we move this conversation up to my bedroom?"

"Why?"

"Because I need to talk to you about some things I don't want the girls stumbling into the middle of."

"Okay, I guess. If they holler, though, I'll need to go to them."

"Deal."

Chapter Forty-Seven

They walked up the stairs in silence. Bobbie opened the door and motioned Beth onto the chair by the dresser. "About me and getting married. It's not going to happen. You'll never have a brother-in-law."

Beth leaned forward. "After my daughters' confessions just now, that's not hurting my feelings any."

Bobbie walked over to the window and looked down at the yard to see if she could spot Kathleen and the girls. "By the way, you handled that well, and I do think a trip to Dr. Langston's is a good idea."

"We came up here to talk about Dr. Langston?" Beth wrinkled her forehead.

"No." Lazy Saturday morning sounds came up into the room: neighbors driving off for shopping and dogs barking at who knew what. Bobbie waited. "I'm nervous about telling you something."

"You can tell me anything. What's wrong?"

Bobbie sank onto the side of the double bed and picked at the colored thread on the quilt. "Nothing's wrong. Something's very, very right. I guess you could say I'm in love."

"But you said you would never get married. Oh, my God, is it a married man? Who? Another teacher?" Beth's eyes widened.

"No, not another professor, and marriage isn't the deal killer. Well, kind of."

Beth crossed her arms. "I've never heard you this confused. Just say it. We'll deal with whatever. What could be worse than what's already happened to us?"

Bobbie took a deep breath. "If what I say bothers you, promise me we'll work it out before you jump to any rash decisions." All those years of finishing one another's sentences, set way back in the memory recesses of childhood, wasn't happening now. She couldn't even read her sister.

"What has you so scared?" Beth was saying when Bobbie broke from her reverie.

Too many deep breaths, and she would overdose on oxygen. Just do it. "What if I told you I was gay?"

Beth was quiet a moment. "Well, to be honest, I wouldn't be surprised. You've never been interested in boys or men. I've never even known you to date. In your life, there's only been Kathleen...Kathleen?"

Bobbie nodded, holding her breath.

Beth's voice went up an octave. "Oh, my God, Kathleen?"

Bobbie nodded, still holding her breath. She felt like she would pass out before her sister answered.

"Oh, Bobbie, I don't know anything about homosexuals except that you shouldn't have them around children. But you would never hurt the girls, and Kathleen?"

Bobbie rushed to answer. "Would never hurt the girls either. She loves them. She loves you, and most of all she loves me, and I love her."

Beth sat silent for a few moments. Then a few more moments. "I don't know what to say. I really don't. Their father raped one of them. Her own father. How can I trust anyone around them?"

"Don't you trust me?" Bobbie scooted forward on the edge of the bed.

Beth leaned back in her chair and didn't quite meet her eyes. "Yes."

"And haven't you trusted Kathleen to this point and my judgment about bringing her into our home?" Bobbie asked.

"Yes." Beth scuffed one shoe on the floor.

"Then just keep trusting me. I'm serious. A few nights ago, she was crying in the garage because she wants so bad to be a part of our family."

"She's done so much for us, from that first week..."

"You're a part of me, and she loves me, so she automatically loved you all."

"But what about the girls? Are you going to cut off your hair and sleep together and tell the girls?"

"No, I'm not going to tell the girls or cut my hair off. I'm the same me I've always been." Bobbie smiled and stopped, with effort, bouncing her knees.

"I have to tell you my head is going in circles right now. When Dan called you a dyke, I never believed him. How could he have known?" Beth asked.

"He didn't. He was just throwing out the worst insult he could call a woman. I didn't even fully realize I was gay till this summer."

"You mean you haven't always..."

"No, it was early this summer that we talked about how we cared for one another and decided to be together forever. I've known she's the other half of me since college, but I didn't understand it till six months ago." Bobbie didn't know what else to say so she stopped there.

Beth closed her eyes and rocked in the chair.

A dark cloud passed over the sun outside Bobbie's window, or was that just inside? What would she do if her twin didn't accept her lover? They'd grown up alone in the world, except for their mother who had died two years ago in a car accident near the farm. Without one another, who would they be?

"I need to think about this," Beth said. "Maybe sleep on it. Can we talk tomorrow morning, over coffee, just you and me, without Kathleen?"

"That's fine. I'm going up to the university today with Kathleen, for a presentation she's making tonight at an art show. Something about women's studies, I don't know." Bobbie tried to relax her shoulders and swallow normally, something she hadn't done since they came upstairs. "I'll even bring donuts for the whole house."

"Thanks. The girls have homework, and we'll be just fine," Beth said.

"All righty then, coffee tomorrow. Now, let's see what the girls are doing with Sara Jane." Bobbie's too-hearty voice filled the small bedroom and spilled over into the hallway and office. Beth avoided her eyes, her pinched face pointed toward the floor just as it had been when Bobbie witnessed an altercation between Dan and Beth. Her heart ached. She didn't want to be the cause of that, but she couldn't live a lie much longer. The ball was in Beth's court now. Bobbie would have to wait.

* * * *

When they got downstairs, Kathleen and the girls were teaching the dog to come into the back porch and kitchen.

"Look, Mom," Cara said. "She's smart and knows how to stay off the carpet already."

Beth smiled a brittle smile. "Well, that's a great relief. I wasn't sure how we were going to handle that."

"This way, if she gets excited and pees, we can wipe it up and not have to wash the carpet," LeeAnn said.

"LeeAnn," Cara said, "she's a good dog. She wouldn't do that."

Her big sister smiled and cocked her head to one side. "Why not? You did when you were little."

"I did not," Cara said, indignant. She looked around the room for confirmation but found only stilted laughter.

Chapter Forty-Eight

Bobbie sat staring at her coffee cup. It was full, but the coffee was cold. The house was silent. She thought she heard the shower upstairs, but that may have been her overactive imagination, considering how long ago that had been and how little time it normally took Beth to get ready. Kathleen was cooling her jets in her room. She had said it was okay. She would sleep in or read a book, but it bugged Bobbie nonetheless. Wait. Finally, she heard sounds on the creaky stairs.

She waited.

And waited some more. The milk looked nasty on the top of the coffee. She went to get more and passed Beth coming in with her cup.

"Good morning," she said to Beth's still pinched face. She didn't look like she'd slept well.

Bobbie got fresh coffee and came back. "I'm glad you slept in. I'm also surprised. I noticed LeeAnn and Cara weren't home last night. Did they sleep over with a friend?"

"All three of them are sleeping over at a friend's house."

"Gracie never sleeps over."

"She did last night." Beth's quick-fire, matter-of-fact comeback made Bobbie's eyebrow go up. Several automatic responses came to mind, but she bit back every one. This already had the feel of some of the meetings she had lived through during her pursuit of her doctorate—pointless trajectories full of no potential for good and great potential for misunderstanding at best and insult or attack at worst.

She tried to change the tone and direction of the discussion. She looked at Beth's coffee. "Can I get you a donut? You must have missed them next to the coffee."

"No, I'm not hungry," Beth said and added as an afterthought, "Thanks."

"Okay, you might as well just be not talking this morning," Bobbie said. "Hello. I'm me, your twin sister speaking. Can we talk about this?"

"You aren't my identical twin."

Bobbie snapped back from the punch she'd taken to her mid-chest that left her reeling. Beth had never hit her with that one before. Neither one of them had ever questioned the twin bond. They fought but had never done that. She made her decision quickly.

"Where was so enticing that all three girls wanted to sleep over? And why are you acting like a monosyllabic grunt? Why lead with what you know is a direct hit?"

"I thought it might be best if we had this conversation without little ears." Beth folded her hands.

"That, out of everything else, almost makes sense, but do you think my donuts are going to poison you? I got your favorite, chocolate cake."

"Why do you take everything personally, Bobbie-center-of-the-universe? Maybe I slept poorly, and maybe my stomach feels queasy with that news you dumped on me yesterday."

"My news made you feel queasy?" Bobbie asked, her voice no longer quiet. "Go ahead and say what you want to say, no one's stopping you. What did my news do? Did it make you sick? Did it disgust you? I'm still the same person I was. Nothing has changed, nothing at all—"

Beth shot up to her feet, disrupting Bobbie's words. She shook her head. "No, no, you're not. You're playing some terrible trick on me. Why would you make up some horrible lie like this? In my own house?" She stepped to the side of the chair.

Bobbie took a deep breath and tried to calm herself. This could get out of hand fast, and she was hurrying it along. It just seemed beyond her control. "Beth, listen to me. I'm the same person I was a day ago, you just know more about me now—"

"I know more about you, is right. I know you've been influencing my girls right in my own house without me even knowing it. What else have you been teaching them?"

"Get serious now." Bobbie felt her shoulders rising and tried to release the muscle tension. Her getting upset would only upset Beth more. Standing up would only threaten her. What the hell was she going to—

Beth bent forward at the hips and waved a finger at her like she would at Cara. "I was married to Dan for ten years, and look what he did. How can you expect me to trust you and some dyke I've known for four months with my babies? And sending Gracie off to sleep-away Girl Scout Camp this summer. What was that about? Should I worry about that, too?"

Bobbie stood up, her hips bumping against the table. In the back of her mind, she was glad for it and the physical distance between them. "Get real already. I didn't go with her to the camp. I just paid her way. Hundreds of girls were in that camp and came back healthy and happy, just like she did. Just settle down, and let's talk about this like adults."

Beth's eyebrows almost shot through her hairline. "Like adults? Queen Bobbie is going to tell me to act like an adult? The woman who has only been out of school and in the real world for two years is going to tell me how to act? I've been working full-time and raising a family for ten years, and you've been playing in graduate school, getting overeducated and getting funny ideas in your head. Look what it's done to you. You were bossy before, but now you're bossy and crazy and maybe dangerous!" She turned and headed for the door to leave, but Bobbie was around the end of the table like a flash and grabbed her wrist.

"Wait, you're overreacting," Bobbie said, her voice shaking.

Beth turned, and the outrage on her face was beyond what Bobbie had ever thought possible. She jerked her wrist out of Bobbie's hand and spat out the words. "Stop telling me what I'm doing. I'm the mother here. You. Are. The. Pervert. I'll decide what the right type of reaction is. And let me tell you this. If either of you dykes has touched one of my babies, I'll report you to the cops and to the schools where you teach, and you will never work with a kid again, as long as you live, I promise you."

Bobbie backed off physically. "Don't threaten me."

"It's not a threat. It's a promise. And this is a promise, too. I'm taking the girls and moving out. Ms. High and Mighty Homosexual can just have a house with her lover. I don't care. If living in this big town has corrupted you, I'm taking my girls back to a small town. Maybe Cottonwood Plains isn't so bad. At least, I know people I can trust there. Maybe I can get my old job back."

Now we're back in the land of reason and logic, Bobbie thought sardonically. "Good grief. Lawrence has a population of, what, fifty thousand? This isn't New York City. Cottonwood Plains has less than eight hundred. How are you going to support the four of you?"

"Now, don't you go threatening me. I'll do what I need to do. I don't care. If it's a one-bedroom house that's safe, that's better than this. I don't care if some high school friend gets me a job with their great aunt Sally on the farm. I'll figure it out." Beth's face was red, and her hands were shaking, but her voice was steady.

"Fine. Do it. Maybe Kathleen and I can afford a four-bedroom house without you. You won't be hurting us. You'll be hurting the girls. You'll be hurting Gracie most of all. You uproot her now, drag her across the state into an unknown situation, and she'll shut down for sure. She may never even graduate junior high, let alone pass high school math, at that rate. Just condemn her to the life of a victim." Bobbie pressed forward, punching point after point into her left palm with her right hand, driving her advantage.

Beth shrank back a bit, but ran into the wall and stopped, pinned there. "Don't blame me for what you're making happen. I'm not the one who's destroying the first real home she's ever had. You and your sick ideas..."

Bobbie had this picture of Gracie, back in Cottonwood Plains, stuck in her head and it drove her onward. "Think about it, Beth. Think about what you're threatening to do. If you're so damned convinced that life in the town where she was raped is better for your daughter, then why not wait till spring? You've got the proceeds from the farm sale. Keep working and put your check in savings. Let the girls finish the year. Then they'll have a full grade without being uprooted from one school to another, you'll have a nest egg to start with, and maybe Gracie will have gotten far enough in therapy that she'll be able to cope with the memories there. I promise Kathleen and I will keep our distance from the girls, have as little contact as is humanly possible when we're living in the same house. Don't destroy their lives just to justify your prejudices, Beth. Don't do it."

As she finished speaking, she consciously stepped back and sat down on the nearest chair again. If she frightened Beth out of the house now, would she ever see the girls again? Would she ever know if Gracie was okay? Maybe not.

Beth shifted uncomfortably. "You can't promise for her. I want to hear it from Kathleen herself. I want to know the name and phone number for both your bosses. If I even suspect you've broken your word, I'll report you quicker than a hawk hits a field mouse. And don't you forget it. I was a different person when I came here. Dan had me beaten down, but I've gotten a lot tougher, and you won't beat me down, Bobbie. I know who I am now, and I'm a mother first, dammit, so you mess with my girls, you mess with me."

Bobbie took a deep breath. "Truce then. I'll talk with Kathleen, and the three of us can talk together. We'll make it work, or we'll come up with a new plan. Just don't get crazy, sis, give it some time." She tried to give Beth a big smile.

Beth wasn't smiling back. "You're one to talk about crazy. Just don't mess with my girls."

"No messing." Bobbie prayed that her face and body language hid her fury and instead showed what she desired, honesty and commitment.

"Yeah, I'll be watching."

Bobbie stood and stared at her twin, feeling the most awkward she had ever felt around her sister. "When will you go get the girls?"

"When will you get me a paper with your bosses' names and numbers on it?" Beth shot back.

"Right now."

"Then I'll think about picking them up after I see that."

Bobbie watched her turn and walk away. She'd never been sick with anger and fear before, never to this degree. She gathered the coffee cups and her untouched donut.

Chapter Forty-Nine

Beth pulled the pickup into the parking lot of the medical building and let the engine die. She rested her head on her hands on the steering wheel. Just for a moment. She rested and let her pounding heart quiet a bit. The heavy truck door closed with an ominous slam behind her, and she headed inside.

She climbed the stairs, arrived too quickly to the office, and darted inside the waiting room. She was still ten minutes early. What if Bobbie comes in for an emergency appointment, too? The doctor wouldn't let that happen. What if Bobbie drove by, headed who knows where, and notices the truck here? She took a deep breath. Then let Bobbie notice. She was only doing what she needed to do to take care of herself and her children. Her hands were trembling. Her short, red fingers were unsteady, and it wouldn't—

"Beth?" Dr. Langston called gently. "I'm sorry. I didn't mean to startle you."

"It's okay, Doctor Langston. I was woolgathering." She picked up her purse and coat, went into the inner office, and sank into a soft armchair.

"You called me for an emergency appointment this morning, and then you're deep in thought. Was the weekend okay?" Dr. Langston didn't waste any words.

Deep breath. "No, Doctor, it wasn't. But before I can tell you what happened, I have a very important question to ask you." Another deep breath. "Are you a...a homosexual?"

"I get the feeling this is a very important question to you. What would it mean to you if I were a homosexual?"

"It would mean I couldn't keep coming here," Beth answered in a rush of breath.

"Why so?" Dr. Langston sat up in her chair.

"Because you lied to me."

"Beth, you remember when we met, and we were talking about family therapy, I told you I was married to a psychiatrist and that I'm the mother of two boys. I haven't lied to you. But it sounds like this is very important to you, and I'd like to know more about why. Can you tell me more?"

Beth exhaled. "Bobbie told me that she's gay, and she and Kathleen are lovers. She told me this Saturday like it was the most natural thing in the world. I don't know what to do. I can't afford to

move out with the girls, but I can't risk them getting abused or
molested or turned into perverts."

"That's a big concern for a mother to carry. I'm glad you
called me. Let's see if we can work this out. You said Bobbie told
you she and Kathleen are gay. Is this the first hint you've had of
this? And what did you do when she told you?"

"Yes, that's why it's been such a horrible shock. I didn't know
what to do at first, but then I got scared and angry, and I yelled at
her. I said all sorts of things I regret, like that she's a pervert." Beth
felt the familiar irritation that meant her neck had turned a blotchy
red, and she scratched at her collar before she went on.

"It made me think all sorts of things like, what about me? Am
I gay, too? And why didn't I know before this? What did I miss?
Did something happen to Bobbie while we were growing up? But
all that can wait. What's important right now is my girls. Doctor
Langston, I don't know what to do about my girls. Living in the
same house with them and all, you know."

She watched Dr. Langston while she spoke. The doctor was
quiet and held her hands in her lap. Dr. Langston gave her time to
finish speaking but didn't make her wait for an answer.

"I have some good news for you. Just last year, the American
Psychiatric Association declassified homosexuality as a mental
disorder. We don't think of it as a mental illness anymore. It's just
the way some people are. Lesbians and gay men are no more likely
to assault a child than a straight person is." Dr. Langston stopped
there abruptly.

"Well, Doctor, pardon me if I don't find that comforting."

"I'm sorry, Beth. Given what happened with Dan, I'm sure
that wasn't a reassuring thing for me to say. What I meant is, gay
people aren't intrinsically dangerous to children. And it appears
that women are less likely to molest children than men are, in
general. Has Bobbie ever scared you or have the children ever
acted reluctant to spend time alone with her? Or to spend time with
Kathleen?

Beth thought. "No, the girls love both of them dearly, and I
haven't seen anything wrong. I just don't want it to happen before I
see it."

Dr. Langston cocked her head so far that her neatly cut hair
touched her shoulder. "Can you really do that, Beth? Can you
protect your children from everything? I know they've been
through a terrible trauma, and so have you. It's natural for you to
want to protect them from the big, bad world. But is it possible to
do that? And at what expense?"

Beth hung her head. "I don't know. Yes, we've talked about
not smothering them and letting them have normal childhoods,
even with what happened. But it's terribly hard, and it's like now

it's inside my own house. Or Bobbie and Kathleen's own house. They had it rented before we moved up here, so it's not even my house. It's theirs."

A wrinkle crossed Dr. Langston's brow. "If I remember correctly, Bobbie and Kathleen both had other living situations before moving into this house. They rented the big house, I thought, because they were hoping you and the girls would leave Dan and move up here even before the attack took place. So, in a way, it's even more your house than their house. What do you think about that?" Dr. Langston sat back in her chair in the way that Beth had come to recognize as her way of giving Beth time to think.

They did rent it for Beth and the girls to come live with them. Otherwise, they could have gotten a little duplex, and no one would have been any wiser. Maybe they were trying to be helpful, and that's it. They just happen to be helpful lesbians. Lesbians. Could she let her children live with lesbians?

Dr. Langston answered her unspoken question. "Maybe the question is, can you let your children live with these two specific women, Bobbie and Kathleen? Not can they live with some unknown lesbians."

"Was I thinking out loud?"

"Yes, Beth, you were." The doctor smiled.

"Then I guess the question is, can I let the girls live with Bobbie and Kathleen?" Beth heaved a huge sigh. "I've trusted them in the worst time in my life, and they were my best friends and my only family. Still are. I guess I have to."

"I hate to say this, but 'have to' isn't going to cut it. This is a big deal. A slip by you could cost them their jobs and their careers. It could keep them from getting good references and jobs in the future. You have to choose to let your girls live there, not just be forced to let it happen."

"Yeah, yeah, the whole passive thing. It's a choice of mine, not someone else's. Okay, I'll make the choice to stay there, but I still want their promises not to mess with or influence my girls, and their bosses' names and phone numbers. And if they hurt my girls, and I can prove it, I'll protect any other children by reporting them. I don't care if they lose their jobs forever. They shouldn't be working with kids if that's true." Beth's fingers dug into her knees, and she released them with the realization that she might have caused a bruise.

Dr. Langston's voice brought her head up. "What you said about being able to prove it is very important. Reporting them based on fear or a rumor could ruin them, so be very careful. You have a great deal of power in your hands, Beth, but I trust you to use it wisely."

The clock on the desk beside Dr. Langston's chair ticked away an entire three minutes, and Beth didn't speak. So many thoughts flooded her mind that she didn't know where to start.

Once again, the kind therapist seemed to read her mind. "I see you're having some trouble. Do you have too many questions to ask? You brought your journal, as usual. You're so good about that, better than many of my clients. Why don't we start by listing all of them out in whatever order you think of them? Then we can pick out which are the most important ones to talk about and which ones you can journal about at home and bring back Friday. How does that sound? We have another twenty minutes, and we might be able to organize at least some of those thoughts."

"That would be great." Beth picked up her journal, took a pen out of her purse, and began to lay out the pile of problems in her mind in some semblance of order.

Chapter Fifty

The straight-back chairs in the dining room couldn't have been any stiffer than the backs of the three roommates sitting in family therapy that Friday. Bobbie jumped when she heard her name.

"Bobbie, dammit, you aren't even listening to me," Beth snapped.

Bobbie's sigh was deep and dramatic. "Do we have to start this way?"

"No, but we may finish this way if you don't get your shit in gear. I'm not wasting my time on someone who's—"

Bobbie stepped on her sister's sentence. "I'm putting my thoughts together. We've only got an hour and a half to make some pretty major agreements, so if you want me to be concise—"

"Oh, yes, be concise since you obviously only listen to yourself talk—" Beth had her fists on the armrests of her chair, pushing down as though she could make holes in the leather.

But when Beth interrupted Bobbie right back, Bobbie's face grew red and she tried to speak over her twin "But, no, we're wasting time doing this—"

Kathleen took a deep breath and leaned forward as if to separate the sisters physically.

"Beth," she spoke over her lover's rant, "what could I do that would make you feel more comfortable about having me in the house with your daughters?"

"Move your perverted self out?" Beth spat.

"Dammit, Beth, that is not okay. Dr. Langston are you going to let—" Bobbie jumped up but made no move toward her sister's chair. Yet.

"Please sit down, Bobbie. Beth, name-calling isn't a helpful way of expressing yourself or getting what you want or need. Do we have to establish ground rules again for fair fighting?" Dr. Langston spoke like Muhammad Ali boxed, light on her feet but firm and brooking no disagreement.

"We did those while Bobbie was staring out the window, so maybe we should waste time doing them again, Doctor, unless you have handouts," Beth said in a sing-song voice.

Beth sounded like the high school cheerleaders that taunted Bobbie for being a bastard. She'd always hated that tone, and her twin had never used it with her, until now. So many things had never happened between them, until now. Dammit, she wasn't going to cry in front of her, not today. Bobbie steeled herself to protect the wound her sister had created.

"And she's gone again," Beth said loudly enough to break into Bobbie's thoughts.

"Bobbie, you seem to be having a hard time staying in the room today. Can you tell us about it?"

"No, Doctor, I don't think I need to be abused any more than I already am." It came out more pathetic than facetious.

"I don't want anyone to feel like they're being abused in this room," Dr. Langston said.

"And I don't want to feel like my girls are in danger of being abused in their own home," Beth said loudly. She lifted the front of the chair up with her feet and let it drop back down again. The thud reverberated through Bobbie's chest wall.

"I'm sure that has to be every mother's worst fear," Kathleen said slowly. "Especially considering it happened just this summer. But Bobbie and I are not Dan, and we're willing to do what we need to do to make you feel more comfortable about that."

Beth made a loud harrumphing sound and looked at her nails.

"We're here," Kathleen said, "as a show of good faith. I think Bobbie offered to give you our bosses' names and phone numbers, and we promised what you asked for, but if there's more we can do, please tell us." She looked directly at Beth the entire time she spoke, and only the slight reversion to her Chicago Irish accent gave away the sheer amount of stress she must be feeling.

Or so Bobbie thought. She was proud of Kathleen. She watched her try to mediate and knew how hard she'd worked to build a relationship with Beth.

"Sorry," Bobbie broke in. "I'm just thinking about what Kathleen said. And I don't think I'm willing to give my boss's name or phone number to Beth. I don't work with minors, for one thing, and it's none of her damn business, for another. And for a third, if she wants it so goddamned bad, she can just call the switchboard and ask. Or look in a course catalog. It's public information. But what does that have to do with the price of tea in China? I don't want her flying off the handle and calling my boss, telling God-only-knows-what-kind-of story and having me prevented from ever teaching again."

"Bobbie, I—" Dr. Langston began to say.

Kathleen said, "I'm willing to take the risk and to offer something that could be found the hard way, if it will prove to Beth my willingness to work with her in fashioning a family." Kathleen sounded reasonable again, and it irritated Bobbie.

"What do you mean, family?" Beth's words tumbled out. "You're not, and will not be, family to my daughters. My daughters don't have any family but me and one another. If I have to move to

Alaska and raise them alone to protect them, I will."

The doctor tried again. "This is all becoming a little unreasonable—"

"Unreasonable? Who are you—" Beth leaped to her feet and yelled at the doctor.

Bobbie raised her voice and slid to the edge of the couch. "Sit down and shut up, before you embarrass yourself in front of the one person in the room on your side. She didn't say you're unreasonable, she said—"

"I don't have to take this kind of talk from them, Dr. Langston, and you're going to start it, too?" Beth had tears in her eyes.

Kathleen sank back into the couch and looked for all the world like she wanted to be swallowed up in the throw pillows piled in her corner. Dr. Langston was pale, and her Muhammad Ali butterfly wasn't floating. Beth was doing all the bee-stinging for now. Bobbie watched in sheer amazement at the raging grass fire sweeping along in front of her. If Kathleen was Bobbie's soulmate and the other half of her soul, then Beth was the other half of Bobbie's heart. And it was tearing her heart apart to watch Beth do these horrible things. It never occurred to Bobbie to wonder if Beth was feeling as wounded as she was.

Bobbie. Just. Exploded.

"You are the most self-centered, obstinate, thoughtless, high-horse bitch I've ever seen. You aren't my sister. I don't know what you've done with her, but she's not here."

"Don't let the door catch you on the—" Bobbie heard as she slammed out of the room.

Chapter Fifty-One

Kathleen was thinking about a spot of good Irish whiskey when she spied the yellow Impala in the parking lot. There were days when she felt like the relationships she had with it and her little red Pinto were her most stable here in Lawrence. Why did she leave a good teaching job in Chicago to live in a little hick town? She sighed.

"Grad school was number three," she whispered in her head, "and teaching at the junior college came in at number two." Her heart softened as she saw number one sitting behind the steering wheel of the car.

"So, was the rest of it as bad as the part before I left?" Bobbie asked.

"Ah, girlie, you have no idea." Kathleen climbed into the passenger seat.

"Then I don't know why you stayed." Bobbie folded her hands in her lap and looked out the driver's side window.

"I stayed because the art of compromise demands you be there," Kathleen said, suddenly angry. "How do you expect us to come to some agreement if we don't stay at the table? It's about give and take. By walking out the door, you made your demands permanent. That's not how it works."

Bobbie sat like a cool stone. "Not when she's irrational."

"Maybe she's not."

It was Bobbie's turn to stare.

"For her, maybe these are rational fears. Rather than help reduce them, you're inspiring more. Your storming out mid-session, unwilling to listen to her side, really isn't helpful. As of right now, she and I have a tentative agreement, brokered by the two of us and the doctor, without your participation. Either you agree to it, or Beth goes out of state to a location I know about and where I can contact her in case of emergency. You won't be able to harass her, because you won't know her whereabouts."

Bobbie's eyes grew larger and her pupils smaller. "You're kidding."

Kathleen shook her head. "Also, you will turn over your boss's name and phone number to her, the same as I will. I know it's random information and public knowledge, but it's also a good-faith gesture on our part of our conviction that she's wrong about us being dangerous to the girls—"

Bobbie jammed the car into drive and began pulling out of the lot. "I don't want to hear the rest. I don't give a flying—"

"Maybe you should," Kathleen interrupted right back. "Why don't you stop the car? I don't think this is a good conversation to have while we're driving." A dump truck whizzed by the hood ornament, too close for comfort and an obvious punctuation of her thought.

"I'm dropping you off at home and going back to the office. I don't have time for this shit."

"This shit is what's going to save your relationship with your sister and your nieces, so you better make time." Kathleen was finally as mad as the sisters had been at one another during the beginning of the session. Bobbie's accusing Beth of small-minded prejudice right off the bat only earned a volley about protecting Beth's girls from whatever dangers lurked in their own home and family. Not an auspicious way to begin a peace accord. To be honest, it got easier once Bobbie left.

"Did you hear me? Do you want a relationship with your nieces? They're going to move to a city and be swallowed up, and you, their only living relative, will have no way to contact them."

"I'll believe that when pigs fly. Beth is chicken-shit. She would never do that on her own, not even as close by as Kansas City."

Kathleen sat quietly for a moment, listening to the building noon traffic. "If you don't get your crap together before the kids finish school at the end of the year, we're going to look for a place for her to live. She'll have her share of the farm sale as a nest egg to get started. Once settled, she'll enroll the kids in new schools and get a job."

"We, schmee," Bobbie mumbled, pulling around some slower cars. "We? What do you mean, we're going to look for a place for her to live?"

"I mean, I'm helping her as much as she'll accept."

"She wouldn't accept help from you."

"She would if it's the only help she has in the world and her only family has turned her back on her and walked out on her."

Bobbie ignored that comment. "How? How are you helping her?"

"I have some contacts from my family in Chicago and from the Dykes Circle that meets at the womyn's bookstore once a month in KC. I'll help her find something." Kathleen breathed a silent prayer to St. Mathurin, patron saint of idiots and fools. Those idiots and fools pressed all around the Impala, driving like they were on the Autobahn. The boat slowed imperceptibly at first, just like it had run out of gas or lost power and entered a steady death glide. Drivers of all ages and ilks coursed around the yellow vehicle, swallowing it in a sea of metal and rubber parts.

Then Bobbie slammed on the brakes. The Impala screeched to a halt. The car behind them swerved into the right lane, and the driver leaned on its horn.

"Dammit, Bobbie. We're in traffic. Put it in gear!" All Kathleen's anger changed to fear and adrenaline, shooting through her nervous system. Her fingers and toes tingled, her hair stood on end, blood rushed in her ears, and she feared her life was about to end any second.

Bobbie left the car running and simply sat back in the seat, looking straight up at the ceiling. When she turned to Kathleen, her expression was tight, her face pinched, her shoulders raised. Kathleen shrunk back before Bobbie ever opened her mouth.

"Whose lover are you? You're going to help her? She called us perverts and child molesters."

A delivery truck downshifted and moved around them while the men in it yelled obscenities out their windows. Kathleen cringed and thought about her chances if she jumped out the passenger door and ran for the side of the road. Lunch traffic wasn't heavy enough to be backed up and slow but was busy enough to keep her pinned in the car. Bobbie seemed oblivious to the vehicles piled up behind them causing their own traffic jam, complete with honking horns and furious voices.

"And said we were dangers in their own home. Now you want to help her get away and make a new start? Are you going to bankroll this? Be her sugar mama? Let her get away with calling us evil things?" Tears flooded Bobbie's eyes, and she pounded the steering wheel with her left hand. Kathleen might have been drawn into the rhythm of it, if the volume hadn't been at screaming level, with a background soundtrack of the snarl of angry traffic.

That was her snapping point. If she was going to die, she was going to die honestly. "Roberta Ann Rossi, sometimes you're insufferable, and this is one of those times! Can't you see she loves you, but she's terrified? Look what happened to her daughter by her own father's hand. What's to make a mother think that a relative stranger, like me, wouldn't do things just as cruel? Get your head out of your ass and think for a minute. You know your sister inside and out. You know what she's capable of, for God's sake. You're twins. She's no more capable of being cruel or evil than you are. Now get us out of traffic before you kill us!"

Bobbie was having none of it. With eyes glazed over, she barely stopped to listen to Kathleen's admonitions, keeping on with her accusations. "How could she turn against me like this, just take my heart and break it into a million pieces? Well, we'll see how that ends...you want to run off with my sister, I won't be there to watch it, dammit. I won't be there. You can't hurt me like this..."

Bobbie shoved her car door open onto the double yellow and stepped into the median between the four lanes. She looked behind the Impala and ignored the oncoming traffic as if she didn't see anything at all.

Kathleen screamed her name over and over and fumbled for her door handle. The traffic, speeding past from behind them, kept her effectively pinned in. She took one deep, shaky breath and slid across the car seat. Bobbie had disappeared behind the car, whether she was now in oncoming traffic or the snarl that remained beyond Kathleen's vision was unknowable from the driver's seat. It didn't sound like there had been any accidents across the double yellow but who the hell knew for sure?

What the hell do I do now? I'm going to get her or myself arrested as crazy women if I let this car sit here in noon traffic. But I can't leave her here.

She spun her head around again, trying to see her lover, but Bobbie was lost in the traffic or distance or who knew what. Oh, God, she'd never pulled a stunt like this before. Kathleen didn't know what to do. She nearly gagged. She closed and opened her eyes again to balance her stomach with a sense of what was up and what was down.

Bobbie made this decision. I didn't. So Bobbie will have to live with it.

Kathleen steadied her sweaty hands and shut the door. She put the Impala in gear and drove away, praying to the Virgin Mary that she would meet Bobbie at home and in one piece, at least physically. Their relationship was another matter.

Chapter Fifty-Two

It was past eleven, and Kathleen sat in the dining room, the only one in the house still awake. She wrapped her arms around herself and stared out the dark window. Headlights came down their street. So many had slid past that she'd given up hoping until she noticed that these slowed. The lights stopped in front of their garage, so she listened closely to hear a door slam, holding herself back from running to the porch door. She waited to see what sort of condition Bobbie would be in when she entered.

Bobbie looked so good that Kathleen reached down and braced herself on the edge of the oak table. If Kathleen were honest, she looked a little rough. Bobbie was windblown and had bags under her eyes, but to Kathleen, she was a vision of beauty. They looked at one another for a long moment. Bobbie pulled out a chair and dropped her light jacket but remained standing, staring at her lover. Kathleen was resolved not to speak first. It didn't take long for her to swallow that resolve.

"Would you like some hot cocoa?" When Bobbie hesitated, she added another enticement. "We have left-over shepherd's pie."

"You've always known I can't resist that." Bobbie's words came out as more of a croak. At Kathleen's alarmed look, she said, "I may have walked a few hours in the cold today."

Kathleen gritted her teeth. "I'll get you a plate." Returning, Kathleen deposited the food in front of Bobbie. "It may be a bit dried out."

"I'm grateful. The warm pie will be nice."

As Bobbie dug in, Kathleen returned to the kitchen. She was sipping a cup of cinnamon tea when Bobbie brought her dirty dishes to the sink.

"Leave them to soak," Kathleen said. "They'll be no big addition to breakfast."

"No, I can do them." Bobbie moved stiffly to stick her hands in the hot, soapy water Kathleen already had the pan soaking in. Kathleen didn't comment further.

She watched as Bobbie washed and dried her few dishes. As she put away the last one, Kathleen gave in. "This is awkward as hell, and I never have been as stubborn as you, so you win. I cave. Where have you been all day, what did you do, are you okay, and can I kick your ass tonight or tomorrow morning?"

Turning from the cabinet with tears in her eyes, Bobbie

wouldn't meet Kathleen's gaze. "I am sorry," she half-whispered, half-croaked.

"Oh, babe." Kathleen took three big steps across the vast kitchen and wrapped her arms around Bobbie. "I was so worried."

Bobbie mumbled against her shoulder, "I was so stupid."

"Yes, you were, and I'm still pissed, but are you okay?" Kathleen pulled back and held her lover at arms-length as if she had X-ray vision and could see any injuries.

"I'm fine. I just caught a cold." Bobbie coughed. "I didn't have my scarf on. I think it's in the backseat of the boat." She still had that hangdog look and would barely make eye contact with Kathleen.

"Look, if you want to go on avoiding my eyes or really talking to me, I'll just go to bed. You know where the cough syrup is. But Beth is worried sick. The only reason she's asleep is because Cara will be up at six, Saturday or not. I was worried half to death, and nothing is resolved except that you're trying idiot stunts that prove you're willing to not only risk your own death but mine as well. I've got to tell you, that's not boding well for your canonization investigations. So, spill it or I'm out of here."

"Okay," Bobbie whispered. "Can we sit in the living room?"

Kathleen followed her and waited patiently while she wrapped up in a soft-as-snow afghan. Bobbie cleared her throat.

"Wait," Kathleen said. "I don't even want to hear about that stunt, reason, rhyme, reaction, anything. I might listen to the history of it tomorrow. As for tonight, we need to hammer out a few things about the living arrangement you so condescendingly walked out on in therapy today. How are we going to live together as a family if Beth, hell, if Beth and I can't trust you to act like an adult?" She stopped and took in a deep, slow breath. "Yeah, I'm angry and don't even try those baby eyes on me. Play it straight tonight, Bobbie, or I just might walk on you."

Bobbie swallowed, visibly gathering herself, and sat taller. "I have the world's biggest apologies to make. To you, Beth, Doctor L, and the traffic of Lawrence that didn't kill me." She lowered her head. "Us. Later, though," she added and looked back at Kathleen.

"Today," she said, "I spent hours thinking about what you told me. Assuming I got the basics right, despite not paying attention to all the details, I think I'm pretty lucky if you two let me live with your plan after what I did. I was so angry. When you told me you were going to help her, well, I refused to hear the part where you said, 'if you don't get your crap together.' That sounded too much like what she threatened me with before, so I acted like an ass. After several hours of random near misses, I finally woke up. I worked out you'd be doing what I wanted in the long run. What I always wanted was that Beth and the girls be safe and happy. The reality is if I wasn't able to get my shit together and you did that, you wouldn't be betraying me, you would be protecting my interests, to look at it one way. I owe you everything. You love Beth and me enough to risk doing the thing that might, probably would, threaten me the worst. You're amazing, and I don't deserve you."

Kathleen studied her lover for the longest time, as she gauged her sincerity. After what she went through in the car and nearly twelve hours of terror at what had had happened to the missing Bobbie, she wasn't going to be quick to forgive. Their future as a couple depended on the outcome of this conversation. Beth's future might depend on the outcome of this conversation. Three harmless children certainly relied on it. She stood up and paced.

After a good two minutes of pacing, time that part of her secretly hoped might feel like hours to the errant Bobbie, she stopped at the far end of the room. Kathleen looked at the tired woman before her and tipped her head. "How am I ever going to trust you in the driver's seat again?"

Bobbie's face broke into an uneven, somewhat tenuous smile.

"Don't get me wrong." Kathleen raised her voice slightly to make her point. "If you ever pull a stunt like that again, I'm out the door before you come home, and I'll take Beth and the girls with me. You and Sara Jane may be sleeping together for quite a while. That's up to Beth, and you better take her decision with good grace. As for me, if you can live with the very basic version of the agreement Beth and I hammered out, which, by the way, is typed up and waiting on your typewriter for your return—I had to give Beth some promise that you were returning, so I suggested she prepare it for all three of us to keep as a reminder of our commitment and the details we committed to. Anyhow, some of the details on that list may make you squirm a bit. Tonight, I just don't care. If you can live with them, I'll stand behind you, and between you two if necessary." Abruptly ending her long, rambling talk, Kathleen stared at her speechless housemate. "And by the way, I love you, too."

Bobbie stood up and crossed the room. She took Kathleen's hands in hers and brought Kathleen's long, slender fingers up to her lips. As she did, Kathleen noticed Bobbie's scraped and bruised knuckles. Kathleen cringed and willed herself not to ask, not right now.

Bobbie kissed Kathleen's fingers gently. "I give you my word, and perhaps more valuable right now, the keys to the boat until I can earn your trust back. I never want to see that questioning look in your eyes again. That cut me to my bones."

Kathleen sniffled. "Okay, I accept your word of honor and the keys. You'll get them back, but there will be pop quizzes involved." They chuckled, and the mood lifted a bit. "Would you like to visit my room for a few minutes before you go upstairs?"

Bobbie sighed. "I have only regrets, but no, I really can't. I need a hot shower. I hurt all over, and I'm still chilled through. Besides, my sister has an extra sense as to when I'm around and when I'm hurt, and that would be more than awkward—it might put an end to the détente."

"Okay, Professor Rossi, I'll let you slide this time because I know what you mean. But you need to heal quickly and stop using big words when there's no one to impress but me, and you know you've already impressed yourself on my soul."

Kathleen gave her a quick smile, brushed her hand along Bobbie's cheekbone, and turned and locked herself in her bedroom. She leaned against the door and listened as her lover grunted her way up the stairs. She was thrilled Bobbie was home and worried if, indeed, the awkwardness would bring an end to the fragile peace. So much was riding on so many fragile details. She was mentally and physically exhausted, but she moved for the rosary she kept hidden. She wasn't sure she, the radical lesbian feminist, believed anymore, but she was sure they could use any and all help they could get.

Chapter Fifty-Three

I am so mad at Mom right now. I hate my boobies. Why did they have to grow? They just get me in trouble. The older boys tease me about them, and Mom doesn't believe me. She thinks an undershirt will keep them from getting noticed, but they still show. The boys notice them. Dad noticed them. That day that Dad took me for a ride with him in the wheat truck, I was so proud to be working harvest, too. We laughed and sang on the way back from the farm to the grain elevators until I realized he wasn't looking at my face. He was looking at my boobies. It made me, well, when we finally got back, I threw up. How was that my fault? But somehow it was my fault just for having them. Dads aren't supposed to look at their little girls like that. Dads aren't supposed to rape them. Dammit, I need bras, and I need them now!

Chapter Fifty-Four

Gracie lay in bed, petting the ever-purring Willie. Willie's engine soothed her and helped her not think so much. Thinking always hurt. Well, except tonight. Tonight, thinking made her mad.

Today's bike ride made her mad. She wanted to ride fast and feel the wind blowing around in her hair. But she had a hat on, and Kathleen was with her. Kathleen couldn't ride that fast for very long. She didn't know for sure how old Kathleen was because she hadn't asked. But Kathleen was as old as her mom, and that was old, so it seemed silly to ask.

But that wasn't all that made her mad. The last time she had taken a fast bike ride was to the grain elevator in her hometown. She could ride the nearly empty streets by herself there. Here in a big town, she couldn't. And she didn't know where she could ride. And there were lots more cars and big streets to cross. She missed Cottonwood Plains.

Who would have thought that? Stupid old Cottonwood Plains didn't deserve to be missed. But she did. She missed the quiet little town and the school librarian and being able to go all over by herself when there was someone else to watch her sisters. She wasn't sure what all she missed. But she missed something. And she was mad. Mad that she had to move. But at the same time, she sure didn't want to stay there after, well, after what happened. She didn't miss sharing a bed with both sisters. She didn't miss the smell of cigarettes and beer. She didn't miss her father.

Or did she? Part of the time she was happy he was dead, but part of the time she felt bad because it was her fault. She wasn't his babysitter. She shouldn't have to make sure his cigarette was out when he passed out. He had lit one fire before, and she saved him from that. Why was it her fault? Especially after what he did.

What he did. Why did he do that? Was she so horrible she deserved that? Dr. Langston said no way. She said her stupid old father made that choice, and that it was okay to be mad at him. Well, she felt really mad, and at everyone else, too. She was mad at Kathleen for being nice to her. She was mad at the girls for what they said about her being hurt. Who told them what happened? Had it been their mom? Aunt Bobbie? She was mad at them, too. Mad at everyone except Willie. Willie was the only good one in the house.

Deep inside, her heart ached and tears filled up every crevice of her being. But she wouldn't allow them out. If she started crying, she would never stop. She would drown in them and die. Just like the nightmares. She gritted her teeth and pretended it wasn't real, and if a few tears squeaked out, well, she couldn't help that. But she didn't dare let that ocean of tears get touched by anyone or anything.

Everyone wanted something from her right now. Her sisters wanted her to play. The doctor wanted her to share. Her mom and Bobbie wanted her to talk and hug them. Even Kathleen wanted her to go bike riding. Couldn't they all just leave her alone? She just wanted to stay in her room with Willie. Maybe she and Willie should run away.

But she knew better. If she got hurt by her own family, running away would be stupid. And Willie was still a baby and not able to protect herself yet. She needed to live inside till she could take care of herself better. Gracie wondered when that would be. Even ten wasn't old enough for girls. Cats might never get there.

All this swirled in her head. Mad and sad and hurting and confused. It never got better. It was almost November. Three whole months had passed, and she was still confused and all those other things. She wanted to kick her sister Cara at dinner when Cara mentioned something about her mom getting them a new dad. She wanted to kick the dog when it scared her cat. She wanted to hang a DO NOT ENTER sign on her bedroom door, but she couldn't even do that because her mom had to walk through it to get to her bedroom. Maybe she could hang a rope across the room with a sheet on it, so no one could see in her part of the room or come in. Yeah, her mom would love that.

And her stupid mom still hadn't bought her a bra. The boys in her class teased her and one other girl about their boobies when the teacher wasn't looking. She thought about telling Dr. Langston and seeing if she would tell her mom for her but gave up on that thought. Maybe she could tell Kathleen. Kathleen made her the least angry this week. And Kathleen didn't try to fix her like all the other grownups.

She ignored the knock at the door and pretended to be asleep. It didn't work. Aunt Bobbie came on in and hauled out the ladder for their nightly talk, or rather talking on her part. Gracie didn't want to listen tonight. Her jaw ached, she was so mad.

"Hey, Gracie, just wanted to check in with you tonight before you go to sleep," Aunt Bobbie said. It didn't even do any good to fake sleeping anymore.

"I want to talk to Kathleen."

Aunt Bobbie almost fell off the ladder. Gracie felt just mean enough to be pleased by that. "Okay, I'll get Kathleen."

Gracie listened to Bobbie climb down and go out into the den and speak softly to Kathleen. Kathleen walked into the room but didn't climb the ladder. Instead, she was tall enough just to fold her arms on the side of the bunk bed.

"This wooden rail is in the way of us talking. Do you need it to stay up here, or is it just in your way, too?" Kathleen asked. That board made her mad, too. It made it look like the bed belonged to some baby who would roll off the edge.

"Please take it down." Easy enough to take down, it just slid down into slots on either end of the headboard and footboard and needed to be taken out to change the sheets.

Kathleen took it down without comment. She didn't even say something annoying like "Now this looks like a big girl's bed." She did say, "What can I do for you?"

Gracie got straight to the point. "I've got boobies now, and my mom won't buy me a bra. I've been asking since last spring, and she always says no. I need one now. Would you get me one?"

Kathleen answered right away. "Yes, I'll try. I had the same problem. I'll have to explain it to your mom, but I'll try to make her understand. Do you want to pick it out yourself or just have me get a couple?"

Gracie was shocked. Kathleen treated her like an adult and didn't give her any crap. "I guess you have to try them on?"

"It usually works best that way, but if you don't want to, I can bring a couple of different sizes home, and you can pick the one you like best. Either way, your choice."

"I guess I can go with you."

"Will Monday after school work?"

"Yes."

"It might be more than just you and me. Maybe your mom will want to come, too," Kathleen said.

Gracie wasn't sure what to say except, "Okay."

"Okay, it works for me. You need anything else, you let me know."

"Thanks." Gracie breathed a sigh of relief.

"You're welcome. Good night, Gracie."

"Good night." That went better than she thought it would. Kathleen didn't ask her why or a bunch of silly questions or try to hug her. Well, that was one thing off the bad things list. Maybe she could find ways to get rid of the rest of them. But she doubted some of them would ever go away.

Chapter Fifty-Five

Bobbie sat at her desk and faked interest in some unread papers while Gracie and Kathleen spoke in voices so low she couldn't hear them. She was about to give up her pretense and stand beside the door. Gracie couldn't see her, and Kathleen wouldn't rat her out. But just then, Kathleen came out of the room, crooked a finger at her, and beckoned her to follow downstairs where Beth sat watching television and folding laundry.

"Can we talk for a minute?" Kathleen asked.

Beth stopped sorting socks and turned off the television. "What's up?"

"Gracie just asked to talk to me."

Beth looked at Bobbie. "She asked me and didn't say why, so I got Kathleen," Bobbie explained.

"It was a big deal, at least to her. She needs a bra, or more than one," Kathleen said.

Beth nodded. "She's been asking for a bra for months and knows I'll tell her to wear an undershirt. She's just a little girl. Besides, what were the two of you doing deciding who would talk to her? I thought we were limiting contact."

"I didn't know direct requests were to be ignored," Bobbie answered quickly.

Beth stood up. "Maybe not ignored, but did you think of clearing it with me or having me there with you?"

Beth looked like she was building up a head of steam, but Bobbie couldn't keep her mouth shut. "This could get really tiresome really fast."

"As could us all arguing where the girls can hear," Kathleen said. "Why don't we sit down and keep the focus on them, where it belongs? And next time, I'll come and ask you, even if she asks for me specifically."

"Thank you. But like I said, she's just a little girl. She doesn't need a bra yet." Beth's words were stiff, as was her back.

Bobbie intentionally relaxed her own posture. Come on little fishy, relax. That stiffness was probably evidence of how she was thinking about the new agreement beginning to be worked out.

"Have you looked closely at her lately?" Kathleen said. "She's developing young. The boys are probably teasing her in class, and she's uncomfortable. It happened to me, and I hated it."

Beth stared at her then looked at her feet. "Oh."

"I never noticed," Bobbie said, "but now that you mention it, she is pretty mature looking for a fifth grader. I don't think I got my first bra till sixth grade."

"I told her I could bring back several sizes or she could try them on at the store, but I would have to ask you first, Beth. Can I take her Monday after school?" Kathleen asked.

"No!" Beth almost shouted. Then she blushed and fell silent.

"Oh, wow." Bobbie turned to Kathleen. "Don't forget..." How was she going to deal with this? Especially, as Kathleen said, while all three girls were asleep right upstairs? Surely Beth was kidding, threatening to go off the deep end like that. Or was Bobbie the one overreacting? She wondered which one her lover would say. She couldn't predict Kathleen's loyalty anymore in this case, and the damned thing about it was that Kathleen had the far more sensible head than she did, and they both knew it. She sighed and listened to hear how much she'd missed.

"Of course, Beth," Kathleen said. "You can take her if you want. I agreed because she asked for me by name, like I said."

"Yeah, okay, right. You try dropping everything to take one child out of three on a shopping trip someone else promised on the next possible school night. We don't even all fit in the truck at the same time," Beth said, her shoulders hunched up.

"Back off, Beth," Bobbie said. "You know you're always welcome to take the boat." Kathleen caught her before she could get too heated.

Kathleen's eyes threw darts at her. "Why don't you go back upstairs and let Beth and me finish the conversation?"

Bobbie bristled with anger. How dare Kathleen try to cut her out of the, oh, well, dammit. There Kathleen went again, being right. "Why don't I just listen and stop being myself so much?" She tried to grin.

Beth didn't grin back, but she apparently accepted the stepping-back momentum of the comment, because she turned her body slightly away from Bobbie and went on in her conversation with Kathleen like Bobbie hadn't even spoken. "Just yesterday, we agreed you two would have minimal contact with the girls. I knew nothing of this, and I don't know how to tell them about yesterday's agreement without alarming them, but this feels wrong to me."

Bobbie rolled her eyes, but in her supreme wisdom, kept her mouth shut.

"Listen," Kathleen said, "if it would be more comfortable, why don't you come with us, or meet me there? What's important is that she gets something that feels imperative to her. And it is imperative. As I said, I developed early and just a few boys teasing me made me feel obvious all the time. I hadn't noticed it particularly, but you know how she pulls her shirt down in front? That's probably to stretch it out, so it's not so obvious."

"I never had that problem, I always wished for more," Bobbie said.

"Me, too." Beth glared at her sister. Looking back at Kathleen, she added, "And you know this because it happened to you?"

"And from teaching. The well-developed younger girls tend to get a habit of pulling their shoulders together in the front to minimize their breasts. It's really bad for your back and posture. I never talked with them about it, but I would call their mothers and leave the moms with some things to consider. It's hard enough for girls to feel good about their bodies when they're changing every ten minutes, but when the boys are making fun, or older boys notice, it's really difficult."

At the words, "older boys notice," Beth went white.

"No," Bobbie said. "If Dan did notice, it's not your fault. He was a sexist bastard, and it's not your fault. Those were all his choices, all his fault."

Beth was still white. "You're right," she mumbled under her breath. She looked at Kathleen and sighed. "You're willing to get her fitted? I'll pay for it."

"Of course, I'm willing. I made the offer to Gracie, and I was serious. If I weren't, I would have told her I would just talk you into it." She smiled at Beth.

"Does it feel, well, funny?" Beth fumbled for words.

"You mean being a lesbian and helping a young girl? No. I'm not attracted to children. I'm not even attracted to the junior college students I teach. I like my women aged and mature." She looked at Bobbie, but Bobbie understood and smiled, too.

Kathleen continued. "Beth, I want to say something to you. It was very hard for my mother when I told her I was a lesbian. But she already knew me and trusted me. And she knew Bobbie and loved her. She figured out about Bobbie before I ever told her. I just want to reiterate that I've found my soulmate, and I'm not attracted to anyone else. I've found the woman I want to spend my life with, and I promise, I'll never look at you or any of the girls as anything but family."

"Okay," Beth said. "I don't know why that makes me feel better, but I guess it does a tiny little bit, maybe. Bobbie promised if I had any questions I could ask either of you. I don't, but if they come up, I'll ask."

"Good. You are my sister-in-law." Kathleen gave a small smile.

That made Beth frown. "That's pushing it. But, getting back to Gracie, she must be angry with me if she had to ask someone else."

Bobbie bristled at Beth's frown and even more at Kathleen's

apparent disregard of it. Kathleen spent all that time in her feminist persona telling everyone not to take sexist bullshit, not to take comments just sitting down, and yet here she was, taking crap from Beth. How could she do that? Bobbie would never have stood for that if she weren't going to kick her out of the conversation. It certainly seemed like a double standard.

Kathleen took this all in and scratched her chin. "Maybe so. She sounded mad at the whole world tonight. Actually, she sounded mad all day, including the bike ride this morning. I thought it was just because I was old and slow, and she's got to be a lot more limited here in her riding than she was in Cottonwood Plains."

Beth sighed. "Yes, there were no major streets, not much traffic, and she could go anywhere safely back then."

All three women grew quiet, each one lost in her own thoughts.

Where on earth can be safe when home isn't? Bobbie wondered. And what can I do to make sure home is safe here?

She wanted to tell the other two how she thought they should all handle the situation but remembered her discussions with Beth and swallowed her words. They were both capable and wise, and this was their discussion, not hers anyway. She must be learning if she could catch her tongue before she caused anyone, Beth especially, any emotional fallout.

Kathleen broke the silence. "Okay then, Monday after school, I'll take her to TG&Y and get her set up."

"Bring me the bill?" Beth asked with a sigh.

"Will do."

"Is her being angry a good thing?" Beth wondered aloud.

Bobbie jumped back into the conversation. "I think so. Dr. Langston would probably say that means she's dealing with it and not in shock or denial anymore. It may be a bumpy ride, but whatever it takes." Any emotional movement on the part of her niece was a good thing. Wasn't that obvious?

"Makes sense to me," Kathleen added.

"Okay," Beth said. "I just hope the ride isn't too bumpy for the rest of the family."

"We'll make it," Bobbie said. "Whatever it takes, we'll make it through."

Chapter Fifty-Six

Bobbie woke before dawn on Sunday, but that wasn't unusual for November. She had slept poorly all night and finally decided to stop tossing and turning and get up. In the kitchen, she began heating milk for hot chocolate. She choked out the dreams that filled her brain and focused on measuring out the cocoa and sugar into the hot milk. She was stirring the mixture by rote before she looked up at the clock. Two thirty-six. Two thirty-six? How could that be? Surely it was six or seven by now. She'd lain in that bed, fitfully rolling about for at least nine hours. Perhaps not. She ladled out one large mugful of cocoa and set the rest on a back burner.

She curled up on one sofa with an afghan that had been crocheted by Jimmy's wife and looked at it as if the stitches of variegated golds, oranges, and greens might hold the answer to her sleep deprivation. A shadowy, vaguely threatening daydream on the edges of her less-than-awake consciousness snapped her out of it, and she pulled the afghan up like a talisman and took a deep drink that would have scalded her throat if so much time hadn't passed. It wasn't like her to waste time in woolgathering. Or at least it hadn't been before this summer, had it? She found this disturbing, as much as she found the night's lack of sleep disturbing. She would be hurting for it by Sunday afternoon for sure, so she should be using this quiet time productively.

All this productive woolgathering blanketed her hearing, and she jumped when Gracie padded into the room in blue pajamas and black mule house slippers, two sizes too big. "Where did you come from?" Bobbie asked, after nearly spilling her half-empty cocoa.

Gracie looked at her like that was the silliest question she'd ever heard.

"Would you like some cocoa?"

In the kitchen, it only took a minute for the gas burner to bring the cocoa back to temperature. Bobbie handed a mug to Gracie. "Sit at the table, please, so you don't spill it."

Again, those eyes. "Okay, you can sit on the loveseat, but please don't spill it and don't tell your sisters." The absurdity of Gracie prattling on about sitting on the loveseat with a drink made Bobbie feel really stupid. She tucked Gracie in under a throw blanket, and they sat and sipped in companionable silence.

After the longest five minutes Bobbie had ever known, longer even than the same length of time in family therapy, Gracie got up, having not spilled a drop, and put her mug away. She returned upstairs in those too-large slippers. Bobbie sighed in relief. Gracie hadn't stared at her, but Bobbie had felt under a microscope just the same. The silent voices from her dreams returned. "Why weren't you there for me?" Gracie's disembodied voice asked.

Beth's voiced followed, demanding. "Why did my daughter need Kathleen instead of her aunt, to ask for bras? Can't you be trusted with anything?"

"No," Bobbie said aloud. "I'm glad she trusts Kathleen and feels comfortable with her, which was one of my hopes."

But... said the inside of her head. *Why was Kathleen safer than me? Why wouldn't she trust me with a question that big? Did she think I couldn't handle it? That I would lecture her or take her mom's side? That I wouldn't understand her pain? I thought she loved me best.*

That mental statement brought Bobbie up short. "I thought she loved me best?"

What on earth did she mean by that? Did she want, need Gracie to love her best, and what did that mean? Better than Kathleen? Than her mother? Than the therapist? It didn't make sense. But the rejection surely reared some ugly head inside Bobbie. Maybe not ugly in a mean way, but ugly like someone had ripped out her heart and hope and walked away with it.

Bobbie sighed a great theatrical sigh, but no one heard. Kathleen didn't emerge from her room. Beth didn't come downstairs to see why Gracie had come down. Bobbie was left with only the inside of her own head, and she didn't like the company very well tonight.

Chapter Fifty-Seven

Monday started well enough. Gracie seemed relieved when Kathleen picked her up to go bra shopping, as Kathleen later described the trip to Bobbie.

"She was scared and shrank away from the actual trying-on of the training bras. I tried to be gentle but firm. I showed her over her shirt how to snap a bra and slide it around frontwards, then I sent her into a dressing room with three that we picked out as likely candidates. When the second one fit all right, we cut the trying-on short, grabbed five of the style and size Gracie chose, and got out of there."

By the time they got home, the fury had begun. It lasted all week, sliding out in small and large ways. Gracie slammed doors. She said no when asked to do things. She called LeeAnn a brat and Cara a baby. She acted like she was going to kick the dog, and when Beth raised her voice, Gracie called Beth a better mom to the dog than to her. The entire family, except Kathleen, crumbled into tears more than once.

****

Like that last horrible two weeks in July, Kathleen was everywhere and everything to everyone. Her new relationship with the family seemed to give her a protected distance. That and several years of working with adolescents as a career helped her keep her balance. One day, the principal's office called Beth in when Gracie called the teacher a name. Kathleen didn't have to teach that afternoon, and Beth needed her to come and pick Gracie up for an afternoon's worth of writing apology sentences at home. It appeared to Kathleen to be the only instance in the week that got through to Gracie, shaming her a tiny bit. The rest of the time she was a tornado unleashed.

By the time Friday's family session with Dr. Langston came around, eggshells didn't even begin to describe the psyches of Beth and Bobbie. Kathleen sent the younger girls over to Gina's for a couple of hours and came to therapy with the family, in case Gracie walked out of the session. About halfway through the hour, Gracie came slamming through the door out into the waiting room. She was alone with Kathleen and made a move for the outer office door. Kathleen jumped up and stood in front of it with her arms crossed.

"Oh no, I don't even think so," Kathleen said.

Gracie didn't try again.

When Bobbie and Beth finally left, they found Kathleen had Gracie corralled in the waiting room. Kathleen heard their unison breaths of relief that she was still there and safe. The eggshell walk continued until bedtime. To their relief, Gracie's anger seemed to exhaust her, and she went to bed early of her own volition. Beth retrieved the younger girls, who were full of pizza and television, and put them to bed, as well. Then the adults collapsed around the dining room table.

"What happened in there? I've been waiting all day to find out," Kathleen asked.

"The session was a nightmare, as expected," Bobbie said. "Gracie was totally silent for about ten minutes then she started yelling. She ranted and called everyone names. She told Dr. Langston she was stupid, to stick her advice up her butt, and that the private sessions were over. She called Beth a horrible mother and blamed her for Dan's abuse. She blamed me for her rape, repeating my fears that my presence incited Dan's anger. She said her life was a nightmare and it would never end, and she stomped out of the office. Dr. Langston let her go, because we had already clued her in that you were outside. We needed her services to put the two of us back together."

Beth picked up the thread. "We both cried. And talked about how guilty we feel. Dr. Langston told us she doesn't think Gracie can maintain this level of anger for long. She told us not to provoke her too much—"

"But not to let her walk all over us," Bobbie added.

Beth continued the explanation. "She said it would be a really difficult balancing act. She said the three of us need to check in with one another, LeeAnn, and Cara each night to make sure we're all okay and still hanging in there."

Bobbie broke in again. "And we need to listen carefully to anything Gracie says, even if it's ugly, because it might give us some insight or clue as to what's going on inside her head." She paused. "How ironic, us looking for clues into Gracie, Girl Detective."

Kathleen listened as they shared more of Dr. Langston's advice and helped make plans to keep the younger girls occupied and out of Gracie's hair for the weekend. They also built in some respite time for each adult. It was a strategic plan worthy of national notice. But they ended up not needing it.

Saturday morning, Gracie wouldn't get out of bed. She didn't refuse; she just didn't. She didn't care what anyone said to her. She didn't eat or drink anything all day. Even her precious cat was ignored. Katherine felt tossed on her head. Everyone was ready for her rage, but this degree of depression blindsided them.

Beth broke first and dialed Dr. Langston's emergency number. "We don't have any idea what to do with Gracie. It's really bad."

Dr. Langston was concerned. "If she doesn't get out of bed to urinate once during the day, and if she continues refusing liquids, she'll have to be hospitalized."

Thankfully, it didn't get to that point.

Bobbie sat at her desk outside Gracie's bedroom while Kathleen walked into her room Sunday morning and told her she had to get up and go to the bathroom and drink some water and a shake.

"You don't have to eat," Kathleen said to her. "You don't have to get dressed. You don't have to do anything but drink some and pee."

Gracie slid down out of the bunk and complied. But she crawled back up and under the blankets until Kathleen gave her the same directions that night.

Beth and Bobbie were beside themselves on Monday. They raged and wept in turns. Kathleen finally arranged for LeeAnn and Cara to stay with Jimmy and his wife for a couple of nights, fearing that the emotional states of their mother and aunt would frighten them to death. Dr. Langston came out to the house and spent some time on the ladder in Gracie's bedroom. When she came down, she had some news for the women.

"I think she's full of grief and won't let herself feel it or cry, so she's depressed instead. Just like the anger, this can't go on forever. You'll get your Gracie back, I'm positive. I think she's better off here than in a hospital, even if there was a good place for her. Just keep her drinking water and milkshakes, listen when she's ready to talk, and find excuses to be in the room checking on her. I think she's sleeping a lot, so don't be surprised if that's true. This is delayed trauma, and while I can't say with one-hundred-percent certainty what will happen, I can say with all my heart that I believe she'll get through it all right. If you want to call another psychiatrist that deals specifically with rape only, I'll understand, but I can't think of one here in Lawrence who specializes in sexual trauma in children."

Finally, she asked, "Did she say anything that might help us understand what's going on?"

Kathleen and the twins were at a loss.

"I had hoped for more. If you think of something I didn't, don't hesitate. Trust your guts. You know her better than I do. I hope she'll let you get her ready and to my office on Friday. And don't neglect the other girls. It will frighten them. Kathleen told me they're staying with friends, and that's fine, but see them every day and remember they're going through this trauma with you. Oh, and do you have a church or spiritual practice that Gracie follows? That might be helpful."

"She went to vacation Bible school once when she was very young," Beth said, "but nothing else. Our mother didn't raise us with anything like that, and her father's family didn't go to a church, either. A minister's wife told her this summer at the county fair that her name means the love of God for people who don't deserve it."

"That's interesting, Beth. Well, maybe that's not an avenue that would have meaning to her, after all. I have to go, but do call if you need to tell me something, all right?"

"Thank you, Doctor Langston," Beth said, with Bobbie and Kathleen echoing her words. Kathleen looked at the sisters who appeared to find hope in the doctor's words. She only wished she'd found as much.

Chapter Fifty-Eight

Kathleen walked the doctor to her car and enjoyed the crisp darkness of the evening for a moment before returning to the warmth of the dining room. The last thing Beth had told the doctor preyed on her mind. She guessed this was what the Catholic Church meant, but somehow, hearing someone raised outside any faith reducing the concept of grace to "the love of God for humans who don't deserve it," lacked the beauty, promise, hope, and well, grace, that she had come to associate with the word. Of all the things Gracie now needed, beauty, promise, and hope certainly remained high on the list.

But enough deep thoughts for a Monday night. Tuesday morning was coming, and it would require many things of her. As she returned to the dining room table, she gave a deep sigh and straightened her shoulders.

"Beth? Why don't we draw up a calendar for the next week and put down what hours we can be here with Gracie, since school isn't going to work out. I can move some of my tutoring appointments into the front room, and you may have to take some time off work. If you're here with her during the day, I think you should go over to be with the younger girls at night and leave her to Bobbie and me for the evening."

Beth nodded. "That's a good plan. I was going to ask for the week off work because I'm too distracted to be there safely anyhow. But I'll need a break from this house, and I can take clean clothes to the younger girls and help with their homework and, well, whatever." She shrugged.

"Okay, let's see how this week goes." Kathleen rubbed her eyes.

"Good plan," Bobbie said. "I don't know how to pray, but I'm about to find out." She headed upstairs to bed. Kathleen heard her footsteps in Gracie's room, checking on her. For a moment, she wished she slept on the same floor, so she would have the excuse to pop in. But in reality, having the only bedroom on the first floor was a gift. She was close enough to get the aroma of bacon wafting in as she awoke in the morning, but the true bonus was a tiny bit of emotional distance from everyone else. It was as close as she was going to get for a long time to having her own apartment. But living with Bobbie was worth it. She smiled. Sleep called.

****

Gracie sleep-walked through most of the week, moving to the bathroom when they directed her, drinking, and eating a little bit. She even sat in the sun on the porch for a while one warm afternoon. But she never spoke or reacted. She could have been a giant doll. And she never cried.

Kathleen gritted her teeth as she watched Bobbie once again hovering near Gracie as much as her teaching schedule would allow. "Thank goodness Thanksgiving break is just around the corner, and I won't have to go to campus," Bobbie announced Thursday evening in their nightly check-in.

"Why?" Kathleen knew the answer but was annoyed with it enough to push Bobbie on her reasoning. "Beth and I are fully capable of managing the situation while you're teaching."

"I know that, of course I know that. I just feel better when I'm here," Bobbie said.

Kathleen couldn't argue with that. At least not in front of Beth. Every night, it only took a few moments of discussing the next day's schedule for Beth to get exhausted.

"I'm going to bed," Beth said. "You two sleep well. I wish we could all sleep well." She went to her room and left her sister and Kathleen in the office.

Kathleen and Bobbie agreed and said good night. Bobbie slumped onto her desk chair with a sigh. Kathleen just watched her, until Bobbie noticed. "Now what?"

"You're sleeping downstairs tonight."

"I'm not Gracie."

Kathleen put down the stapler she'd been fiddling with. "What do you mean by that?"

Bobbie straightened up in her chair. "I don't need someone to tell me when and where to sleep."

Kathleen stood up and started down the stairs.

"Wait, I'm sorry. You were trying to help."

Kathleen slowly took the step back up to the den. "You're right, I shouldn't boss you around, but I won't take verbal abuse when I'm wrong."

"What do you mean by that?"

"I mean you need to...I'm asking you to give it a rest tonight and sleep downstairs with me. I don't think you're sleeping. You aren't eating any more than Gracie is. If you don't take care of yourself, you'll be in the hospital and what will we do then?" Kathleen finished with a sigh.

"You're exaggerating." Bobbie's act wasn't convincing Kathleen.

"Maybe not. Really, I'm worried about you and Gracie." She ran her hands along the railing that led down the stairs from the office directly to her bedroom. *It's not so far. Just one foot after another.*

"What about Beth?" Bobbie played with her hair, curling it around one finger.

"She talks to me about what she's feeling. She plays with Cara and LeeAnn. She eats and sleeps. She's getting through this. I'm not sure you are."

What a change, to think that she, the potential child corrupter, would within such a short time become Beth's confidant and backup woman again. Sometimes life happens when you least expect it. It made Kathleen proud, a little relieved, and to be honest, a tiny bit angry, but that too was life, and it was better than the alternative.

Bobbie sat back and let out a deep, long breath. "I don't know if I'm getting through it okay, either. I'm so glad next week is our November break."

"Speaking of that, Bobbie, I have an idea. I think you and Gracie need to go on a trip."

"A trip? With zombie girl? Where on earth can I take her to make her better? I can't take her away from her family right now." Bobbie pushed back from her desk and right up against the bookcase behind her.

"You can take her anywhere. She seemed to be the angriest at you, and you look guilty as sin. She can read that. If you're guilty and weren't even there, why shouldn't she be even guiltier? You both need to put the guilt where it lies. And she hasn't cried yet."

"Oh," Bobbie said and swallowed hard. Twice.

"She's bottled it all up into depression. If she doesn't let it out, what will happen? Will it eat her from the inside out? I don't know. I'm not a doctor, but I know that until I have a good cry, I can't let go of the things that hurt me."

Kathleen stood up, came around the end of the desk, and perched on the phone table between the two desks as she searched for ideas. "Why don't you go to St. Louis? I know you need to go there for research. You could consider this a reconnaissance mission. Stay in a motel where it's just the two of you. Drive around and look at something, anything, historical sites even. Don't let her spend too much time with other people, just be with her yourself. Talk a lot. Hell, I don't know what to do with her, just be with her. Force some contact."

Bobbie stared at her. And stared. And stared a little more. "It sounds crazy."

"Give it a chance. Some time with you in a different place might help her snap out of it. It might help her connect with a different part of herself than we can offer right now. As far as we know, the trip-taking part of her was totally free of the abuse, right?"

"Right," Bobbie said slowly. "But I still don't understand."

"I'm not sure I can explain it. It's just a gut thing, but it's worth a try, don't you think? And you'll both be off school. Two days driving and two days over there would give the other girls four days at home with undivided attention with their mother and their dog, who's pining away in a very smelly dog run."

"You just don't want to shovel dog shit."

"Listen, I wipe Gracie's butt. Don't make me do the dog's, too. Wait," Kathleen said and paused, "That came out wrong. I don't regret anything I do for Gracie, but I think... I don't know where this came to me, but I had a dream last night. And you need to go."

Bobbie twisted on her office chair and thought before answering. "I'll ask Beth. The change of scenery might be good for both of us. And I would love to see St. Louis. I'd love to see if I could track down mother's family, if any of them are even living, and if not, perhaps I can find a family cemetery. I can't do much there with her in this condition, but maybe a trip would be good for us."

"I think so. You need the time and space with just Gracie. We'll plan another trip with Cara and LeeAnn later." Kathleen held out her hand. She wouldn't beg, but she would provide every opportunity for her lover to join her.

Bobbie thought for one more minute. "I guess I will sleep downstairs tonight. But what if I can't sleep?"

"I was kind of hoping to keep you awake for a little bit, but if my mind isn't playing tricks on me, you're going to crawl into bed and pass out," Kathleen said.

And Bobbie did.

Chapter Fifty-Nine

When Beth and the girls moved to Lawrence with them, Bobbie found her time stretched thin. With individual and family therapy, home life, and teaching, she felt her joints, physical and emotional, pulled out of their sockets. At a friend's suggestion, she started working again on her family genealogy project, a favorite leisure activity that had been swept aside in the summer. She hoped that having something just for her would make her feel more centered and relaxed. She never got much time to work on it at once, but even the bits and pieces of research she'd been able to do about her mother's origins and her father's possible identity helped her feel more alive and less two-dimensional. When she had something else on which to focus, she felt like she wasn't just in survival mode. Kathleen's solution for Gracie's anger problem was tantalizing in its design and appeal. Bobbie didn't want to think about whether accepting the challenge made her or her roommate more of a mercenary.

The three adults decided that Bobbie and Gracie should drive to St. Louis on Sunday and drive back Wednesday before the weather turned nasty. That would give the two of them two full days in Missouri, using up much of Gracie's Thanksgiving break from school. Bobbie called the St. Louis Visitors Bureau and Chamber of Commerce for recommendations on where to stay, what to visit on Sunday night and Tuesday, and how Bobbie could use her few precious research hours on Monday to the best application of her genealogy project.

When they told Gracie about the trip, her reaction surprised them. She opened her eyes for a second, gave a quiet "okay," and drifted back into her slumberless-yet-not-waking state. Bobbie interpreted that as a sign of interest. Beth said she was less impressed, seeing it as the path of least resistance. Kathleen just took it at face value—acceptance of their request. But Kathleen's insistence on four full days suggested to Bobbie that she hoped the trip would be much more before it was over.

Bobbie planned to drive Kathleen's Pinto to St. Louis. She and Gracie didn't need Bobbie's boat, and the Pinto would be cheaper. A blasting heater promised to be another benefit. As Kathleen and Bobbie loaded up the car, they discussed their hopes for the trip.

Bobbie handed Kathleen the car first-aid kit. "I just hope a change of scenery helps a bit—maybe catches her attention and pulls her out of the funk."

Kathleen shifted a bag of cat litter in the trunk of the car. "You don't sound convinced."

"I guess I'm not." That must be the greatest understatement of the year. Bobbie crossed the fingers on her right hand and pulled them up into her jacket sleeve.

"I'm hoping for more." Kathleen grabbed the snow shovel that Bobbie was staring at but not picking up.

"Like what?" Bobbie asked.

Frustration and what must be a little anger colored Kathleen's voice in many shades of gray. "I don't know—maybe that you two chew one another up, maybe that you have a sob fest, maybe that you just get inside one another's heads and work some things out. I know, I know—that's a lot to ask of a four-day trip. But if Gracie's depression is hiding guilt and anger, it has to come out somewhere and it isn't happening here. Maybe she'll let go with just you."

"Dr. Langston might be a better person for that attempt." Bobbie caught herself shifting from one foot to the other and forced herself to remain still.

"Gracie knows you. You two have a special relationship. Beth has talked to me about it. I've seen it. Use that somehow and pry her lid off if you have to."

Bobbie noticed Kathleen showed less and less sympathy as time progressed. She still acted with compassion but took fewer and fewer excuses from anyone.

"Okay, okay, I'll pry her lid off. I'm sure Dr. Langston will like that one." Bobbie tried to make it a joke, but Kathleen wouldn't laugh.

"Yeah, well, make sure yours falls off in the process." Kathleen tugged Bobbie behind the garage door, gave her a hard, quick kiss, and walked away.

Bobbie completed the loading. Two small bags and winter driving gear all fit easily into the Pinto. Kathleen returned with extra antifreeze and double-checked the fluids and tire pressure while Bobbie poured Gracie into the front passenger seat and buckled her in.

"If you get tired, pull over. Or roll down the window and sing loudly in the cold wind. That helps me," Kathleen said. "Take care of yourself and Gracie, okay? I want to hold you in four days."

"Okay," Bobbie agreed. "We'll be careful and stay safe."

The family waved them out of the steep driveway, and Bobbie had a sudden image of the hero's quest in the English literature courses she taught. This contained all the hope of a miraculous cure or at least a vision of who Gracie was to become with time. She saw Gracie as much more of a hero than herself, but the quest was the same.

For the next four hours, Bobbie fidgeted inside the car. Molasses must flow faster than the red Pinto traveled to St. Louis. Gracie spent most of the drive in her shutdown state. Eating when told to eat. Going to the restroom when prompted. Looking out the windows at miles and miles of unchanging highway.

November was bleak in Missouri. Though the weather still hung above the worst of the seasonal marks, shades of gray already decorated the landscape. Bobbie had wonderful memories of her winters during her college years in Lawrence, for the first time away from the limitations and abuses of her prejudiced hometown. The hometown that shamed her mother for being an unwed pregnant teen right after the war had tried to shape her and her sister in their own image of slut, whore, and bastard. But on her own, she was free to be who she created herself to be. She'd forgotten the stark imagery of the black-and-brown tree branches, bare against the gray skies. Those memories came flooding back to her on the drive, and even inside a car with a good heater, she could smell the cold rain of winter in the air as she walked from her dorm to her classrooms. It was unforgettable.

Despite her good memories of bare tree branches against gray skies, this wasn't college and she wasn't walking with Kathleen, her best friend and roommate since their freshman year. This was her hero's quest, and she was a companion to Gracie on the road. She became more and more like Gracie as they drove. The first hour, her excitement about the trip kept her chatting at Gracie. The second hour, her determination about the quest fueled her as she sang and talked to Gracie. During the third hour, she pointed out the occasional unusual item along the way. For the rest of the trip, she drove in silence.

They had left Lawrence so early that it was still light and dinner time hadn't yet come when they arrived in St. Louis. The secretary of the visitor's bureau had recommended a motel on the highway and made reservations for them. Bobbie grimaced inwardly at the idea of spending a long evening with an unresponsive ten-year-old. A second later, she felt guilty for grimacing.

She didn't realize how tired the driving made her until they reached the motel. They grabbed burgers and fries from a stand near the motel and took them back to eat in their room. Neither of them ate much. They watched the local TV and went to bed early.

"Gracie? Tomorrow we're going to have breakfast and then go to one of the county historical buildings to do some research," Bobbie said.

Gracie grunted and threw the rest of her dinner in the trash. She dropped her shoes, lay down on the bed fully dressed, and pulled the blankets over her. Bobbie's exhaustion left her too worn down to be upset at this response. She, however, changed into pajamas before she went to bed.

The next day, Bobbie took Gracie to the Department of Vital Records building with her. She didn't need to worry about her niece as she put in her feverish hours of research. Gracie sat in a chair, ignoring the conversation of the employees. A little bit of embarrassment and a great deal of relief flooded Bobbie when she didn't have to explain or supervise Gracie's interactions or conversations. She just shrugged her shoulders in a universal I-don't-understand-I'm-sorry movement and kept on with her research. She tried not to feel guilty for the joy she found in her hobby as she gathered the information she would need for her next section of work. A bitter moment choked her when she realized she had far more conversation with her past in silent papers than she did with her future sitting next to her.

Chapter Sixty

Tuesday nearly drove Bobbie to distraction. Gracie was silent. Not exactly sullen, she didn't respond at all as they visited the places the visitor's bureau had suggested. On Monday, Bobbie had been occupied by her genealogical passion, but Tuesday, she was ready to pull out her hair as they moved quickly through the list. Their final stop on their last night in the motel was going to be a cemetery outside Fenton, Missouri, where it was possible her father's family was buried. This was exciting to her. On the subject of Gracie, however, her thoughts were less than gracious. If she could just drag the day out, it would be time to clean up for supper and tomorrow they could get out of here and go home.

She had given up on Kathleen's dream that spending time with Gracie would bring them together. Anytime she tried to broach the subject of feelings or what had happened, Gracie shut down and refused to listen or talk. There definitely was a hint of anger in her eyes and, dammit, Bobbie was going to let it go. She didn't feel equipped to handle an angry ten-year-old by herself.

With a deep sigh, she drove them to the last site. It was easy to find, but she'd expected more. They got out of the car and walked to the cemetery, which sat in an area that was surrounded by plowed-under fields, probably wheat in the summer.

"Come on, Gracie." Bobbie tried to keep her frustration out of her voice. "Don't you want to see the headstones? Some of them are really old and interesting."

"No, I don't want to see it." Gracie stomped off in the opposite direction.

"We don't have to see it if you don't want to. Do you see something in this direction worth checking out?" Bobbie ran to catch up with her, and her annoyance grew.

Gracie said something under her breath.

"I didn't hear you. What did you say?"

"I said no, I don't see anything, and stop following me." Gracie walked faster.

"I can't just let you take off by yourself. You might leave the parking area and get into farmland. What if I lost you?" Bobbie's shaky grip on her anger began to unravel.

"That would be fine with me. Just leave me alone." She stopped about ten yards in front of Bobbie, who also stopped, pummeled by Gracie's anger.

"I can't do that." Gracie's intense anger had caught Bobbie by surprise and frightened her a little. She spoke louder, to make sure Gracie could hear her across the distance.

"No kidding. You've been bothering me for months. Just leave me alone!" Gracie's voice rose at the end of the sentence.

"What are you talking about? Are you mad at me? Did I do something wrong?"

"Yes. I'm mad at you!" Gracie yelled. "Just leave me alone."

"We have to talk about this."

"We sure as hell don't." Gracie still refused to face her, although her shouts were crystal clear.

"Don't use that language. Just tell me what's wrong." Bobbie crossed her fingers, for what, she didn't know.

"I'll say what I damn well want to say. I know words you don't even know I know."

Bobbie's mind raced over the advice the therapist had given them over the last months. "Babe, tell me what you're angry about."

"Dammit, don't you know already? How stupid can you be?"

Bobbie was stung by Gracie's words. She stood without an answer as Gracie tromped away from her again, over the broken ground. "Gracie, I—"

"I don't care about whatever you're going to say. It doesn't matter. just leave me alone."

"No, I love you, and I won't leave you alone. It's dangerous out here." Bobbie followed her farther into the field.

"Dangerous?" Gracie turned around and stared at her, a small angry woman instead of a ten-year-old girl. Her shoulders were hunched in visible pain and shook with pent-up feeling. "What do you know about dangerous? You came to town after Dad said you couldn't. Didn't you know that was dangerous? Did you care?" She picked up a dirt clod and threw it at Bobbie.

"Yes, I cared." Stunned, Bobbie barely managed to duck. "I'm so sorry."

"Sorry doesn't make it not happen." Gracie threw another clod, closer to Bobbie this time.

"I know, babe. Nothing will make it not have happened."

Gracie picked up another handful of clods. "Nothing will ever make it better, either. And all you do is try to make me feel better or do this or do that. Well, it doesn't work." She threw two clods at once.

Bobbie made a move toward her. Gracie threw a rock that narrowly missed Bobbie's head. Bobbie decided not to push her by going any closer.

"What do you want me to do, Gracie? I can't leave you alone out here. What do you want me to do to make you feel better?"

Bobbie was yelling now, too.

Another clod whizzed by Bobbie.

"Babe, time will..."

Gracie's face grew even redder. "Stick your time up your butt!" she screamed.

This left Bobbie speechless. She knew Gracie's anger, turned inward, looked like depression. Dr. Langston had told them that. What she didn't know was how to handle it with no support when it exploded all over her in the middle of the Missouri prairie.

Gracie turned away and ran. Bobbie ran after her. Gracie stumbled and fell over a large clump of dirt. "Leave me alone!" she screamed as Bobbie got close.

Bobbie ignored her. She fell to her knees and grabbed Gracie's arms to prevent point-blank missiles. "Dammit, Gracie, I'm trying to help."

Gracie thrashed and looked as if she might cry. Then her face grew rigid with determination, and she struggled harder.

"Can't you tell me?" Bobbie begged as they fought.

"No!" Gracie screamed.

"Why not?" Bobbie yelled back.

Sudden silence. "Because I might cry! Now leave me alone!"

Shock rocked Bobbie yet again in this tirade. "It's okay to cry. I'm here." She dropped her voice to a normal level.

"You don't understand!" Gracie screamed.

"Then tell me!" Bobbie refused to let go of her arms as they shouted, face to face.

Gracie started to cry. She fought harder and almost broke free. Bobbie held on with all her strength, afraid of what might happen if she lost her hold on Gracie now.

Gracie's tears erupted. Bobbie's mind raced, coming up with nothing helpful.

"Dammit, let go of me! I have to get away!" Gracie was still yelling.

"Why, babe? Why can't you cry? Just tell me."

"Because if I start, I'll never stop."

Bobbie could see the panic on Gracie's face, overlapped with the anger.

"It's okay. I'm here," she told Gracie. "Cry."

"No, it's not...it will eat me up." Gracie's struggling landed a blow to Bobbie's left cheek.

Bobbie spread her legs apart on the ground and wriggled to maintain her balance as she tried to pull Gracie between her legs where she could hold her, or pin her, or something.

Gracie continued to thrash, her breathing ragged, as she cried and fought. She cursed Bobbie with words only Dan could have taught her. Bobbie realized that she was crying, too. She also felt the need to stop crying, to get away from the powerful feelings that threatened to overwhelm her. The thought of Dan had touched on all her sorrow and pain and left her weak with guilt. She held on with fear for Gracie and for herself. With strength she didn't recognize, she pulled Gracie on top of her and fell over backward onto the rugged ground. She wrapped her arms around Gracie and held her close.

"I don't want to cry either, babe, but it won't kill us."

"Yes, it will," Gracie said as she wept. "If I start, I'll get sucked up into it and I'll never stop. It's just too big."

Bobbie's tears blurred her vision. It hurt to breathe, hold on to Gracie, and talk at the same time. "No, it won't, babe. I'm here, and I won't let anything get you."

Without warning, Gracie's body went slack. Then it began to shake in huge, heart-rending sobs. "Why?" she cried, the only word discernible. "Why?"

Since Gracie wasn't fighting her anymore, Bobbie moved one hand to stroke her hair and cried with her. "I don't know, Gracie. I don't know, but I'm so, so sorry." The uneven ground beneath her served only to jab into her back, each point a punishing reminder of her failure.

"He hurt me," Gracie moaned. "I hate him."

"I do too, babe. I do, too." Bobbie gasped out her response between gulps of air and fresh streams of tears.

If anything, Gracie sobbed louder and her body shook harder. Was she right? Bobbie wondered. Will her sorrow and pain eat her up and never let her escape? But somewhere in Bobbie's gut came the reassurance that it wouldn't. Her own pain and grief felt like a huge lake that threatened to drown her, but she had to trust that it wouldn't. She kept on holding Gracie, stroking her hair and rocking her, singing as women have sung to heal pain for hundreds of generations. Gracie wailed out her pain, fear, and whatever else she was feeling. Several times, it came close to that edge that Bobbie also feared, that place where she was afraid Gracie would be lost. Bobbie just kept rocking and stroking and crooning to her, not knowing what else to do.

Then, it happened. The intensity of Gracie's crying eased, and a hurt little girl, crying her eyes out, reappeared. Bobbie pulled her closer and cried along with her, her sorrow and guilt mingling with Gracie's. They cried there for what seemed like forever.

And when every tear in that vast reservoir had been poured out, Gracie moved closer to Bobbie, closed her eyes, and drew something from her aunt. Her stiffness evaporated. She lay there and took in huge breaths of air, her body still convulsing now and then.

Bobbie felt her own fragility and the frailty that belonged to

Gracie. They lay there for a long, long time. But outside of that sacred, shared time, it was late November and the darkness came early. She had to get them up before the cold immobilized them.

"Gracie?" she whispered. "We have to go back to the car. Can you do that?"

Gracie nodded, and they struggled to push up. Drained, they leaned on one another as they stumbled back across the field and the tiny cemetery, past the headstones they had never viewed. Bobbie led Gracie to the passenger side of the Pinto, opened her door, and buckled her seat belt. She sagged for a minute against the side of the car, stood again on wobbling legs, went around to her side, and got in.

"Do you need to pee?" Bobbie asked Gracie for lack of any other words.

Gracie's voice came back small. " I think I already did."

"We'll take care of that." Bobbie turned over the engine and headed back to the motel. She wondered what they would do and say when they arrived. How would they go from such intensity back to regular life? She had no answer, decided it would happen as it happened, and tried not to plan it or worry about it. She refused to be the professor here. Students didn't have to have all the right answers. She and Gracie would find them together.

****

When they got back to the motel, the clock read six, but it was already dark outside. Gracie could feel little shudders in her breath now and then even though her tears dried awhile ago. She felt like she was lifting concrete limbs as she changed her clothes while Aunt Bobbie just sat on the bed.

"Are you hungry?" Aunt Bobbie asked when Gracie finished.

"No." Gracie's body hadn't thought about food in months.

"We should eat something, so we don't wake up hungry in the middle of the night. Can you eat a little something if we get dinner? We could bring it back here."

"Probably eat here." Gracie didn't say much, but at least she responded to the question.

"Okay. Let me get washed up, and we'll get something to bring back to the room." Aunt Bobbie went into the bathroom and shut the door. Gracie heard the water in the sink start. She kicked her pants in the direction of her suitcase and sat down on the bed to wait.

She was lost in her thoughts. It didn't kill her. She fell into all the tears and didn't drown. Her heart didn't start thudding again, even though she was thinking about such hard things. She still hated him, and still felt horrible, but it didn't kill her. Dr. Langston told her that, and Aunt Bobbie told her that. They all told her that someday she would feel better. She wondered if that could be true. She thought about the anger that filled her. She hadn't spent thinking time under a tree since she was attacked in July. Maybe she could do that again, too. Far away in her musing, it took the sound of silence to bring her back to the room. What made her aunt take so long? She stood on wobbly knees and knocked on the bathroom door but heard only water running. She knocked again.

"Aunt Bobbie? What's taking you so long? Are you done yet?" Aunt Bobbie didn't answer her, and Gracie turned the unlocked doorknob.

At the far side of the small room, sunk to the floor between the tub and toilet, huddled Aunt Bobbie. Gracie turned off the water in the sink and went closer. Aunt Bobbie had her fists up to her eyes, but Gracie could see the tears escaping from beneath them. She heard deep gasps for air as Aunt Bobbie cried.

"Aunt Bobbie? Are you okay?"

"No," Aunt Bobbie wailed. "That bastard...raped you...hurt me...you instead..." Tiny groups of words broke through her sobbing, enough to let Gracie know what she was thinking, but not enough to be sentences. "My fault...never right."

Gracie came closer and sat down on the toilet. Silent tears fell from her eyes now, too.

Aunt Bobbie leaned toward her, held on to her legs, and cried harder. "I'm so sorry, so sorry...what to...don't know..." She stopped trying to speak.

Gracie didn't know what to do. She sat there and touched her aunt's hair, the way her aunt had touched hers in the field. She listened while Aunt Bobbie cried.

Maybe Aunt Bobbie has her own ocean of tears that wants to drown her, too. Gracie's tears hadn't swallowed her up when she cried in the field, even though she was afraid they would. She took a deep breath. "It's okay. It's gonna be okay."

Aunt Bobbie looked up at her and grabbed Gracie's hands. "No, it never will be. I hate myself for making him so angry." She kept crying.

Gracie shrugged. "I don't hate you."

Aunt Bobbie cried harder, unable to take in this tiny slice of forgiveness. "But what he did to you—"

"It was horrible, but he did it, not you. Don't cry, Aunt Bobbie. I don't want you to feel bad."

If anything, Aunt Bobbie cried even harder for another minute then drew two sharp breaths. Her tears began to subside. She cried herself out and got the hiccups. She let go of Gracie and wiped at her eyes with the backs of her hands, leaving stripes of mud.

"You didn't wash your hands," Gracie said. "You look like a raccoon."

Aunt Bobbie smiled a little. "I feel like a worm."

Gracie stood and took Aunt Bobbie's hand to pull her up. The difficulty in getting out of the wedged-in position required Aunt Bobbie to push off the toilet to get up. Her hair hung limply, curls hanging loosely around her shoulders in messy disarray. She looked like she had been through the same hell Gracie had gone through in the field.

"Can you forgive me?" Aunt Bobbie asked, with a wavering voice.

"Yes." Gracie felt like a small, but grown woman.

"I am so, so sorry. I would do anything to make it not have happened." Aunt Bobbie's tears threatened a second time.

Gracie wrapped her arms around Aunt Bobbie's waist and squeezed hard. She didn't have any words. Luckily, her aunt seemed satisfied with the hug. Gracie felt her take in a huge breath then let it out slow. "Oh, babe," Aunt Bobbie said. They stood holding one another, both depleted, but stronger for having had a little piece of healing.

Chapter Sixty-One

Gracie tossed and turned. The covers weighed her down, held her down, pushed her against the bed, and she fretted beneath them. The motel room was too warm for everything on top of her, but she was wearing long pants and sleeping with all the blankets she could find. She had done so since she got out of the hospital in July. It was safer that way. It had been comforting until tonight. After what seemed like a whole night of sweating and struggling, she felt her eyes grow heavy and she let go and slept.

The monster came almost immediately. Her body had barely relaxed when her mind tightened around her. She opened her eyes but saw only blacks and greys, with brown and blue streaks marring her vision. She couldn't see the monster until he was on top of her, just like usual. But unlike those previous visits, this time she saw him clearly. He was tall and blond, with a square chin that worked over and over. Somewhere in her inner ear, she knew now what the monster's mouth said. It was screaming loudly.

"Bitches! Fucking Bitches! How dare they...I'll show them—" Her inner ear blanked out again so that the scene played out in silence as it did every night.

In his fury, Gracie wasn't sure if her father was yelling at her or her Aunt Bobbie. Aunt Bobbie? How did she know that? Nothing made sense. He'd gone crazy was the only coherent thought she had. Confusion controlled the rest of her mind. Escape, she must escape. She tried to push away and run, but he tripped her onto the hard-packed dirt floor of a barn. She tried to crawl away, but he kicked her, knocking her over onto her back. She sucked in air, not sure what would make things better and what would make them worse.

Then he was standing over her, unbuckling his belt, and shouting. She couldn't hear him, but she knew he was screaming something about dyke bitches. It terrified her. But unlike freezing, unlike closing her eyes and disappearing into the recesses of her mind, she continued to see the scene as it played out. She was angry. She hated him for hating her aunt, for hating her mother, for hating her. She tried to decide what to do until he fell on his knees and ripped her cotton shorts and panties in one wild grab. She didn't have to decide then, she fought to escape.

She tried sliding away from him, but pushing didn't work. She hit at his chest and yelled at him to let go, but it made him laugh.

She rolled out from under him as he straightened up on his knees, but he caught her by her hair when she got up to run. He threw her back down on the ground and yelled more.

Terror filled Gracie's chest, like a hundred-pound weight on her lungs. So far, she had fought him like a boxer, but the adrenaline made her attack him like a tiger. She fought for her life this time. One of her fists caught him upside the head, and he cursed. Her nails scratched at his face, and he cursed again. She was kicking, too, and must have hit him between the legs, but he didn't curl up like the boys at school did, he reared up and roared at her. "Now, you're going to get it!" And his huge fist came down on the side of her head making everything go slack and gray...

Suddenly, Gracie sat up in the motel bed, wide awake. She remembered the nightmare in agonizing detail. She remembered the whiskey and beer stench filling her nostrils. She remembered the light coming through missing slats of the roof, painting patterns on the hay on the ground in front of her. She felt his weight pin her to the old hay, which poked her and felt both sharp and soft against her legs. She remembered the rest of the attack, every moment. From the fire burning through her bottom up to her stomach, to the cigarette smoke she smelled later when she woke again. She remembered feeling sick and knowing she had to get away. She looked up and saw him leaning against a bale of hay a few yards from her, drinking whiskey and smoking, his fury spent.

"Dumb bitch," she heard him say. "You smashed my smokes."

She remembered pushing up to her knees and crawling, then grabbing her shorts and standing to stagger out of the barn and into the first shelter she could see, the stand of cottonwood trees, where she could hide and vomit. But the remembering, the knowing, didn't terrorize her the way it had before. She had fought back. It didn't stop him, but she had fought back.

Gracie reached up and felt the tears on her cheeks. The bed was shaking silently. She touched her chest as it heaved with her shallow breathing and pounding heart. In the pale light of the bathroom door, she could see Aunt Bobbie's outline sleeping in her bed. Gracie's nightmare hadn't even woken her. She wondered. Could she? Should she?

She waited until her breathing slowed, slid out of her bed, and crossed the short distance on wobbly knees. Her hands wobbled, too, as she reached for the blanket that covered Aunt Bobbie. Gracie tried to slide beneath it without waking her but failed.

Aunt Bobbie rolled her head toward Gracie and blinked her dark, sleepy eyes. "Gracie? Are you? Do you? Why..."

"A nightmare," Gracie whispered.

Aunt Bobbie lifted the blanket. "Come on in."

Gracie slid in and lay close to Aunt Bobbie but not touching her. They both lay looking at the ceiling for a long time, glancing at the other occasionally, careful not to make eye contact, until their regular heartbeats and breathing rhythms returned to ease the last few hours till dawn.

Chapter Sixty-Two

Halfway home, Bobbie used her remaining quarters in a pay phone to tell the family that she and Gracie had slept in and were stopping at a few touristy looking places and would be home later than expected.

Kathleen listened. "I hope this means things went well, but don't tell me now, save your quarters for a candy machine. Tell us the whole story when you get home. Be safe now."

As they got back on the road, Bobbie realized Gracie was watching her more than usual and not looking away from eye contact as quickly.

"What's up, Girl Detective? Are you on a case?" she asked her.

"Who's the detective's boss?" Gracie asked.

"I don't know. Maybe a sergeant?" Bobbie was surprised by the question and didn't know the answer.

"I think I need to report to my sergeant."

Bobbie smiled, "All righty then, let's play detective, and you report in."

Gracie looked away and waited. "I'm not playing. Maybe I just need to talk to you."

Bobbie kept her eyes on the road. "Okay, kiddo, you know I'm here for you anytime, but let me ask a quick question. Do we need to stop so I'm not driving and can listen completely? Maybe a restaurant or another rest stop?"

"How about a rest stop?"

Bobbie's hands tightened on the steering wheel. "Okay, the next one I see, we'll stop."

Ten miles later, Bobbie found a truck stop and pulled off the highway. "This isn't exactly a rest stop, but we can park on the very edge of the parking lot. Will that be okay?" She had to force herself to stop her nervous talking. Wait for Gracie. This discussion was important to her or she wouldn't have asked.

Gracie nodded and stared out the front window. Her breathing was shallow. Bobbie laid her hand on the emergency brake handle, between the seats, palm up. Without looking over, Gracie slid her smaller hand into her aunt's, took a deep breath, and began speaking.

"The nightmares you asked me about? The one I had at camp and drew the picture of? I can tell you about them now, if you still want to know." She dropped her gaze to her other hand that lay in her lap.

"Yes, babe, I do." Bobbie held her breath.

"I dreamed that a monster was coming to get LeeAnn because she was sleeping on the edge of the bed while I was at camp. Or that I was gone or something, and the monster was coming to get her and Cara. But last night I dreamed the nightmare, and I saw the monster really clear and what the monster did, instead of just a bunch of colors in a big mess."

"Was that why you came and got in my bed?" Bobbie couldn't help herself from asking. Shut up and let her talk or she might just stop talking at all.

"No."

They sat in silence. A minute went by. Then two. Bobbie wondered if she should speak or ask a question, or even apologize for speaking. Best keep her damn mouth shut. Can't they sit with her pain for even a little bit?

After four or five minutes passed, Gracie looked at Bobbie. "No, I had the nightmare about what happened in the barn. I remembered it. All of it."

Tears filled Bobbie's eyes and slid soundlessly down her face. When she could speak without crying out, she spoke softly. "Oh, Gracie, I'm so sorry. I hope I didn't upset you."

"It's okay. I remembered the bad part, but I remembered trying to fight and that made me feel better." Tears glistened in Gracie's eyes. "Then I remembered the awful part, and when I felt horrible, I woke up and remembered I could come to you, and I did. Even though I couldn't tell you why, I didn't feel as horrible. I felt better. I didn't feel alone."

Bobbie couldn't speak right away. She had to put both hands over her eyes and hold her face together as it threatened to spin off into a thousand tiny pieces, a thousand tiny tears. She tried to swallow over and over and couldn't. Saliva built up in her throat, and she feared she might choke. Just when she thought she was going to come apart, she felt Gracie's hand on her shoulder.

"Aunt Bobbie, are you okay?"

Dammit, pull yourself together. You can't just fall apart and leave her out here all alone, not after what she just told you, not after how brave she's been.

She cleared her throat and swallowed convulsively. It worked. She wiped her eyes, hard. The tears receded. She looked at Gracie.

"I'm sorry, babe. I was just overwhelmed for a minute. You're always welcome with me. Anytime." Bobbie felt the pressure in her nose and eyes that the wetness was building up again. She blinked four times. "You are so brave. I mean, you don't always have to feel brave, whatever you feel is cool." Dammit, she sounded just like Dr. Langston. "I just, I mean, ah, you're always welcome to sleep with me or to come out by my desk if I'm working late or whatever..." Her voice drifted off as did her line of coherent thought.

It was enough.

"Thanks. I know that now. That's all I wanted to tell you, just that I know what the nightmares are now," Gracie said with a tiny smile.

"I'm honored you shared that with me. Do you plan on telling your mom by yourself or do you want me there with you?" Bobbie was hesitant but encouraging.

"I don't know yet."

"Okay, you don't have to know yet, but I do hope you tell her soon." She almost said, "before you forget," but caught herself before making that monumentally asinine statement. As if Gracie would ever forget.

Gracie looked out the side window. Her chest slowly expanded as she took a very deep breath, then she released it just as slowly and sank back into the curve of the seat back. "Yeah, her and Dr. L, too. I think Willie probably already knows."

Bobbie smiled. "Yeah, Willie is the first one in the house to figure most things out. Do you need a pit stop here?"

"No, I'm okay. Let's just drive."

As they headed the rest of the way back to Lawrence, Bobbie's heart danced. She felt so much freer, so much of the weight of her personal guilt released. She felt closer to Gracie, knowing that Gracie trusted her now, both with her emotional overload and her nightmares. She sang out loud, chatted with Gracie, and did everything but groove in her driver's seat. She wondered if Gracie felt the same way but hesitated to ask, not knowing the best way to do it. As they got closer to home, she realized the ride had blown her expectations away. Gracie spoke on her own initiative and always responded to Bobbie's light comments and questions. It felt as opposite from the drive down as she could imagine.

Thirty minutes from home, Bobbie couldn't stand it anymore. "Gracie, I've been trying not to ask you, but I have to ask. What happened this weekend? You're so different, and I'm so grateful. What happened inside you?"

Gracie paused. "I don't know, for sure. I mean, I cried, I cried really hard. I hurt, and I hated, but it didn't eat me up. I felt better afterward. Then you cried. I saw you felt really bad, and I knew I wasn't the only one."

Bobbie's eyes misted up, and her chest tightened. "You're right, babe. You aren't alone, and you never will be. Let me rephrase that. You can be by yourself if you want to be, but if you want someone with you, your family will always be there, I promise."

"And it was okay? Me being so mean to you? I threw rocks. I got into the car with wet pants. And then I wanted to sleep with you." Gracie bit her lower lip and pushed her hair behind her ear, in what looked like an unconscious imitation of her aunt.

Bobbie's heart melted for the three-hundredth time that afternoon. "Oh, Gracie, it was more than okay. It was honest, and real, and I was, well, I don't know how to say it exactly. It rocked my world that you trusted me with your pain, if you know what I mean."

Gracie didn't answer right away. "I think I do."

Bobbie spoke so softly Gracie couldn't hear her.

"Huh?" Gracie said.

Bobbie cleared her throat. "I said, I finally trusted someone with my pain, too, you know? I let the hurt inside slide out, all disgusting and nasty. But you didn't run away, and you didn't tell me what a horrible person I was. You forgave me. But I don't think I would have trusted anyone with that ugly stuff inside me if you hadn't trusted me first. You made me brave enough that I'll be able to try now, Gracie." She waited for a ten-year-old's absolution for her confession.

Gracie grinned. "Well, you were brave first. I was still holding a rock when you tackled me in the field."

Bobbie giggled.

Gracie waited for several beats. "Aunt Bobbie? Can I ask you a question?"

"Yes."

"When we stop for gas, can we get a pack of gum?"

Chapter Sixty-Three

Bobbie and Gracie arrived home at eight that evening and dumped their bags on the back porch without ceremony, a pair of returning heroes both weary and wiser. The two younger girls were in bed. Kathleen had taken them out to a park with Sara Jane, and they had run themselves silly.

Gracie smiled at that news. "Mom, remember how I used to make them run races so they would sleep?"

Beth, Kathleen, and Bobbie laughed. Gracie announced that she wanted to find Willie and go to bed as well. Gentle hugs were given all around, and she headed upstairs.

"Wait, Gracie." Kathleen halted her exit. "You and your aunt got some mail while you were gone."

A letter surprised Bobbie, who wasn't expecting any mail. Gracie looked surprised, but she had the hopeful expression of one who waits for mail every day.

"It's addressed to Dr. Rossi and Gracie." Kathleen handed it to Bobbie.

Bobbie opened it and scanned the first page. "It's from Angel, Gracie's Girl Scout Camp counselor. I guess I did manage to track her down after all. She remembers Gracie and her week at camp."

The adults glanced at one another. Kathleen stirred and cleared her throat. "I kind of wish I'd given the letter to Bobbie after Gracie went to bed, the way I had first planned. But it's addressed to the two of you, so I decided to give it to you together." She and Beth sat while Bobbie read the bulk of the letter.

"What does it say?" Gracie asked with more than a little dread in her voice. "Did I make her mad or something?" She scooched over to stand beside her aunt.

"No, babe." Bobbie reached up to stroke her hair. "I had written to her, asking about your nightmares. It finally got to the Girl Scout Camp, then the council, and then made its way to her. She's writing to tell me about that week."

"What does she say?" Gracie asked in an even smaller voice.

"She says you were one of her favorite girls, and one night you had a horrible dream. She got my message and wanted to write to you, if that's okay with your mother and me."

Everyone looked at Beth, who nodded.

"Then here's your part of the letter, Gracie. Would you mind reading it out loud for all of us, too?"

Gracie took the letter and began to read.

Dear Gracie,

I hope you remember me as well as I
remember you. We had such fun, and you really
got me in that water balloon fight. My real
name is Angela Washington, I live in Emporia
and go to college there. I'm studying to be a
teacher, although this is only my second year.
Your aunt wrote to me asking about the
nightmare you had. That night you came and
woke me up, and since you couldn't stop
crying, we went up to the unit house where
there were lights and we wouldn't disturb the
other girls. Bug brought us some pillows and
blankets, and we spent the whole night up
there.
Gracie, I know that dream frightened you.
It frightened me, too. I knew something that
scary meant something bad, but I didn't know
what. You were shaking so hard and crying so
loud, it was tough to understand you. I did
understand something was coming to get your
younger sisters the way it had already come to
get you.
Honey, I'm so sorry I didn't tell the camp
director about that dream. I'm not sure why I
didn't tell her. When morning came, it all
seemed so far away. After you washed your
face, I couldn't even tell it had happened.
You were quieter then, and not as outgoing as
you had been, but I didn't know what to do. I
didn't really know what happened, and in the
daylight, the monsters seemed to be gone.
Then I got your aunt's letter, and I knew
something had to be terribly wrong. I went and
talked with one of my professors. She told me
that nightmares like yours usually meant bad
things were happening at your house. She gave
me some ideas of what they might be. I called
your house and talked with your mom. She told
me what had happened and that I could write
you.
Gracie, I feel horrible about what
happened to you. You're a wonderful girl and
didn't deserve to have that happen. People can
do such terrible things to other people, and I
don't know why or how.
I told you my name is Angela, and that's
part of why I picked my camp name Angel. My
family has called me Angel for years. But
another reason I picked it is because I
believe in angels. I believe they're there
with us when we get hurt and bring us people

to take care of us. I believe they never leave us alone, even in the awful moments. When I told my mother about what had happened, she said maybe I had been an angel for you for just a little bit. It made me cry.

But she also reminded me about what your name means. Grace is something special. Grace is when something is impossible, and yet you do it through the power of love. Grace is a gift from God that lets you breathe and laugh and run, even when those things are hard to do. Grace is knowing your angels are always with you, in good times or bad. They may not take the pain away, but they're there to hold you during it.

When your mother told me what happened, I asked her how you're doing. She said you were having a tough time healing. Oh, Gracie, I wish I could do something for you. All I can do is write this letter and tell you how sorry I am and how much I hope you feel better soon. I can pray, and ask my mother's church to pray, and believe that you are called Gracie for a special reason. You are called Grace because you can reach out and take that gift and know that there's always someone with you no matter how good or how bad you feel. Take the gift, Gracie, just take that gift.

I think next semester I'm going to enroll in a class or two on being a counselor. I still want to teach, but I want to know what to do if anyone ever tells me about their nightmares again. You inspire me, Gracie. I would like it if we could be pen pals. Your mom said you used to like to write letters. If you start that again, would you write me? I'm glad we were at camp together. Take care, Gracie, and take the gift.

    Love,
    Angela "Angel" Washington

Silence held the adults captive as Gracie came to the end of the letter. She looked up with a wet face and around at the women who surrounded her always.

"Do you think it's that easy?" she whispered. "Do you think I can do impossible things? Like getting over being mad at Dad, and being afraid of people, and just being better again?"

"No, Gracie," her mother said, shocking Bobbie. "I don't think it's that easy. But I agree with Angel. If there's a gift out there and you can take it, it could make the rest much easier. You'll still have good and bad days, but at least you'll know you aren't alone. You have Angel and us, and maybe many angels with you. And remember what I told you about your name, too. Grace is a how you move beautifully in everything you do. You can walk gracefully, jump gracefully, or dance gracefully. It's just natural. I think your name means both things."

Bobbie and Kathleen stared at Beth during her long speech. Beth continued. "I do believe you can be happy and be our old Gracie again with that love and all that work. And we're around you to support you while you do it."

Gracie looked down at the letter in her hands. "I like that," she said. "I like thinking there are angels with me when I'm hurting. I bet they make me hurt not so bad."

Bobbie listened to the adults hold their collective breaths.

"But now I'm tired. I want to go to sleep and think about this some more tomorrow. Is that okay?"

Murmurs of agreement surrounded their special girl as the adults sent her off to bed. Beth, Kathleen, and Bobbie all got hugs before Gracie went upstairs. Aunt Bobbie got an extra-long hug, and Gracie whispered in her ear, "I think I can tell Dr. L about the nightmares about Dad now. At least I won't die from crying. Thank you for the trip and for not being mad when I threw rocks at you."

"Let me get a football helmet on, and you can throw rocks at me anytime," Bobbie whispered back. "Good night, babe."

Beth and Kathleen said good night before collapsing back into their chairs.

"Beth, when did this girl call, and why didn't you tell us?" Kathleen asked, and Bobbie could feel Kathleen's confusion wash over her, also.

"It was about a week and a half ago. You were both grading papers upstairs, and the girls were in bed, so I got the phone down here. Angela told me about what you'd been looking for, Bobbie, and I remembered you and Kathleen arguing about it more than once. I thought a letter would be easier for Gracie to handle than talking on the phone, and we could see what this Angela said, too. Gracie likes getting letters. I thought that if it was cool, she could keep a copy in her room."

"And what if it wasn't helpful?" Bobbie asked. "What if it upset her more?"

"Then we would take it away. But I spoke with Angela for almost a half hour, and I thought what she had to say wouldn't hurt Gracie but maybe could help her heal. I may have paid more attention to the younger two for the past few months, but I've been watching Gracie and her struggles, too."

"It was a great decision," Bobbie said.

"Not to change the subject but changing the subject, what on earth happened in St. Louis?" Beth asked.

Bobbie took a deep breath and felt her shoulders relax as she remembered. "Well, too much to tell. I think Gracie will be able to tell you herself, in time. Mostly, I think she cried herself out in safety and was able to ask some questions that I couldn't answer, and it was still okay. Then she had a nightmare and woke me up to sleep with me for comfort. Kathleen, your idea for the getaway was brilliant. I'm not Dr. Langston, but I think she turned the corner and she's going to be okay."

Beth cried and smiled at the same time as Bobbie told more about the trip. A palpable relief filled the room. Everyone else's healing could go on as well.

Beth sighed. "Well, you two, tomorrow is Thanksgiving, and no matter what else we do or don't do, the girls expect turkey, so I have to be up early to make that bird. I'm going to crash now. If I'm not careful, I may sleep ten hours just in relief. Thank you for the brilliant suggestion, Kathleen, and thank you, Bobbie, for making the journey with her."

Beth got up and headed toward the stairs. She stopped. She stood. She turned back around and stared at the two women before speaking. "Actually, thanks to both of you for making the journey with us. I don't know what we would have done without you. I guess I owe both of you a huge apology for all the horrible things I said when you came out to me. I turned you into the monsters I thought I had been, and that was nothing but fear and meanness."

She cleared her throat. "You were our family when we would have had no one else. Bobbie, you know you're half my heartbeat. And Kathleen, welcome to the Rossi family is what I guess I'm saying. You kept us going when we would have drowned."

"You would have found your way, Beth," Kathleen said. "You're a strong woman and a good mother. You would have done it."

"Well, I'm glad I didn't have to try. Good night, you two. I'll see you tomorrow." Beth went upstairs to bed.

Kathleen scooted over and put her arm along the back of Bobbie's chair. "It sounds like we have her blessing. Want to have a sleepover tonight?"

Bobbie stretched her arms up high, long and slow. "For at least the first half of the night. Maybe we can send Beth and the girls to St. Louis for a while in the summer without us. Then we could play house the whole time." She grinned at Kathleen. "Let's go, although driving half the day is so tiring, I may sleep for a long, long time."

They went to Kathleen's room, locked the door, and had their own homecoming celebration.

"Should I go back upstairs?" Bobbie yawned about two in the morning

"No, it's still early. I'll set the alarm, and you can go up later.

But I need to run to the bathroom, so keep the bed warm for me."
Kathleen jumped up and ran down the hall.

Bobbie heard her feet as she hurried back. "Ouch," she said.
"Three minutes and your toes are cold already. Keep them off me."

"Why don't you help me warm them up again?" Kathleen
whispered in the darkness.

They laughed and snuggled down together.

Bobbie woke before daylight, confused about the time. Had
the alarm gone off yet? She didn't think so. She knew what
awakened her. Kathleen was trying to push her off the bed and steal
the blanket at the same time. She rolled onto her back and looked
over at Kathleen to wake her and complain. In the low light of the
alarm clock face, she could see Kathleen's eyes, wide open with
fear. She was still on her side of the bed. The problem was Gracie,
passed out on top of the blankets between them.

"I guess she knows something now," Kathleen mouthed with a
panicked look.

Bobbie couldn't help herself. She got the giggles. She
smothered the sound with her hand, but her shoulders, then her
whole body began to shake. Kathleen got them, too. Soon the bed
was a gelatin mass of jiggles. Gracie woke up.

"Hey, you guys." Her sleepy voice stopped the giggles right
away. "Is it Thanksgiving yet?"

"Not yet, babe," Bobbie said, looking at the alarm clock above
the head of the bed. "It's only four, and you can sleep several more
hours."

"It's cold down here, I'm going back up to Willie. Aunt
Bobbie, I made you a card." Gracie handed Bobbie the card that
was slightly crumpled in her hand. She slid down to the end of the
bed and stumbled out the door and back up the stairs.

"Guess I forgot to lock the door," Kathleen said.

"That's okay, we'll figure something out. No secrets in this
family, I suppose. Maybe she'll assume that even the grown-ups
have sleepovers. Want to turn on the light so I can read my card?"

Kathleen turned on the lamp on the headboard. In its soft
glow, Bobbie looked at the brown-construction-paper card Gracie
had made her. On the front was the traditional elementary
schoolchild's turkey, drawn around one hand. On the inside, Gracie
had taped a piece of gum.

```
Dear Aunt Bobbie.

I love you. Thanks for being the gum
that makes us stick together. Eat lots of
turkey.

Love, Gracie.
```

Bobbie read and re-read the message. She laid the card on the headboard and rolled over into her lover's arms.

"I've been many things," she said. "Most recently a professor, a sister, a lover, and an aunt. But I think I like being a stick of gum the best."

"Are you ready to get up now?" Kathleen asked.

Bobbie stretched for a moment. The bed was warm with her lover and her hopes. "No, morning will come soon enough. Let's just enjoy the rest of the night."

The End

About the Author

Ona Marae is a writer in a long line of creative women. She lives in Denver, Colorado, near her beloved Rocky Mountains, where she and her fiancé spend as much time as possible. She began writing in high school, publishing in the lesbian newspapers in Denver in the 1990's, and then focusing on short stories and creative non-fiction essays. This is her first full-length novel. She tries to live every day considering Mary Oliver's question "Tell me, what is it you plan to do with this one wild and precious life?" She challenges you to do the same.

CPSIA information can be obtained
at www.ICGtesting.com
Printed in the USA
FFOW03n1820040618
47060358-49407FF